FRANCE AT THE POLLS

FRANCE AT THE POLLS
The Presidential Election of 1974

Edited by Howard R. Penniman

American Enterprise Institute for Public Policy Research
Washington, D. C.

ISBN 0-8447-3171-4

Foreign Affairs Study 22, August 1975

Library of Congress Catalog Card No. 75-15146

Printed in the United States of America

CONTENTS

PREFACE

France at the Polls: The Presidential Election of 1974 is another in the AEI series of studies of national elections in selected democratic countries. A volume covering the two 1974 British parliamentary elections has already been published. In progress are studies of the 1974 general election in Canada, the 1974 House of Councillors election in Japan, the 1975 British referendum on membership in the European Economic Community, and the parliamentary elections in Denmark, Norway and Sweden in 1973 and later.

These elections were conducted under often very different rules: in Britain a single-member-district system with plurality election of members of Parliament, in France a national majority system with a contingency runoff provision to elect the president, and various forms of proportional representation to select national legislators in the Scandinavian countries. They are being examined in this series because it is believed that the description of different election systems in action in specific elections can help readers to gain a better understanding of the operation of their own political institutions and may also usefully inform those who are responsible for writing legislation to improve their nations' electoral machinery.

The 1974 French presidential election marked only the third time in the history of modern France that the people directly elected their chief executive. A massive 88 percent of metropolitan France's registered voters participated in the second-round vote, which saw the candidate of that coalition of French parties and voters usually described as "Gaullist," Valéry Giscard d'Estaing, defeat the candidate of the Left, François Mitterrand, by the narrowest margin recorded in any of the three elections: 50.8 percent to 49.2 percent.

The record of these three presidential elections suggests that even a nation with substantial democratic traditions may encounter significant new and perhaps unanticipated problems as it changes the method of selecting a major official. In the introductory chapter of this volume, Roy Pierce notes that in 1965 and 1969 the non-Gaullist parties encountered serious difficulties in building coalitions to nominate and support a single opposition candidate for the presidency. In 1969, for example, the opposition was so fragmented that none of its potential candidates secured as much as one-fourth of the votes in the first round, and the Communists refused to support any candidate in the runoff. Meanwhile, the Gaullists, despite sharp divisions within their ranks, virtually unanimously backed Charles de Gaulle in 1965 and Georges Pompidou in 1969. The tables were turned, however, in 1974, when the Left was unified, no Center candidate appeared to divide the opposition, and the Gaullist leaders were unable to agree on one candidate. No accepted mechanism existed for settling such a disagreement within the Gaullist ranks, so three men, each claiming the Gaullist mantle, submitted their names to the voters on the first ballot. The fact that voters chose Giscard, who subsequently won election in the runoff, should not obscure the fact that the majority, like the opposition, has not yet solved the problem of candidate selection that, in J. Blondel's view, was still in 1974 "ad hoc and accidental." The prior existence of a multi-party system in France almost certainly has exacerbated the problem.

The descriptions of some election systems covered in this series include the consideration of the financing of political campaigns. French election experts agree, however, that no one can write a satisfactory description about the financing of the 1974 campaign because insufficient data are available. To be sure, the government provides candidates with free television and radio time (by contrast with British and Canadian rules, all French candidates are given exactly the same amount of air time), so an estimate of its value can easily be calculated. The difficulty lies in describing and analyzing expenses that are not covered by the state. The law does not require the candidates or the parties to report receipts and expenditures, so only those who actually handle the money have access to the necessary information. Jean and Monica Charlot, two of the authors of chapters in this volume, wrote an essay several years ago dealing with the 1969 election in which they started from known presidential campaign activities of Georges Pompidou and Alain Poher and worked back to some general estimates of campaign costs,[1] but they were the first to say that a thorough study of French campaign financing is not

---

[1] Jean and Monica Charlot, "Persuasion et Politique: Les Campagnes de Georges Pompidou et Alain Poher," *Revue Française de Science Politique*, vol. 20 (April 1970), esp. pp. 244-48.

now possible. In this respect, France differs little from many other democracies that treat the costs of campaigning as a private matter for candidates and parties.

Readers of this study may find Chapter 5 deserving of special attention because of its method of analysis as well as the substantive information it contains. The chapter presents an analysis of the voting by means of "electoral geography." Marie-Thérèse and Alain Lancelot use maps of metropolitan France not only to provide a comparison of the support for the leading candidates in the 5 May and 19 May elections, but also to show continuity and change in French regional voting patterns for presidential elections since 1965 and to compare voting tendencies in the 1973 legislative elections with those of the presidential election of 1974. Electoral geography is not unique to French political science, but French scholars have employed this analytical device longer and more frequently than has been true of scholars in other countries. It seemed desirable, therefore, to devote a chapter to this use of maps for often complex regional political analysis. Chapter 5 demonstrates both the character and the quality of the method.

Seven French and two American scholars have contributed to this book. In addition to the chapters by Pierce and by the Lancelots, J. Blondel provides an overview of the 1974 election; Jean Charlot and Serge Hurtig in separate chapters describe the selection of candidates and the campaigns of the Gaullists and the Left; Alain Lancelot discusses the opinion polls that preceded the elections; Alfred Grosser examines the role of the media in French political life with an emphasis on the 1974 election; and Monica Charlot analyzes "the language of television," comparing the style and substance of the presentations of leading candidates (Chaban-Delmas, Giscard, Mitterrand, and Royer) in their appearances on television. Richard M. Scammon provided the electoral data in the Appendix.

Howard R. Penniman

1
PRESIDENTIAL SELECTION IN FRANCE: THE HISTORICAL BACKGROUND

Roy Pierce

When Valéry Giscard d'Estaing was elected president of the French republic in May 1974, he became the twentieth person to hold the office, the fourth to be directly elected by the voters, and the third to hold the position under the Fifth Republic.

There was no French presidency until the Second Republic (1848–1852). The first French republic (1792–1804) was governed by various forms of collegial executive until Napoleon acquired pre-eminence, first as first consul, later as life consul. Eventually he destroyed the republic and became emperor of France.

The emperor's nephew, Louis Napoleon Bonaparte, became the first president of France on 10 December 1848, in an election held under an electoral system that provided for universal manhood suffrage. The magic name of Napoleon produced a landslide victory. Louis Napoleon received some 5.5 million votes against 1.5 million for Cavaignac, the right-wing republican general who had been premier since the June 1848 uprising, which he had quelled with much bloodshed. The leftists ran several candidates, but they were crushed. It was a rightist victory of colossal dimensions.

Some of the right-wing backers of Louis Napoleon, such as Adolphe Thiers, had supported him because they believed him to be a weak person who might pave the way for the restoration of the monarchy. In both estimates they were wrong. The constitution of the Second Republic prohibited the president from succeeding himself, and when Louis-Napoleon could not persuade the legislature to amend it so that he could run again, he organized a successful coup d'état on 2 December 1851 and proclaimed a revised constitution providing for a ten-year presidential term. The change was ratified by a plebiscite. One year after the coup, Louis-Napoleon proclaimed

1

himself emperor, a move which was also ratified by a plebiscite. The experience of the Second Republic left an important imprint on French republican politics. French democrats became intensely hostile to the institution of a strong and independent president, unwilling to choose executive leaders by popular election and reluctant to confer power on the young, whose support for republican institutions had not been confirmed by long experience and who might develop unacceptable personal ambitions. Louis Napoleon had been only forty years old when he was elected president of France.

The Origins of the Presidency of the Third Republic

The National Assembly, which was elected in February 1871, after the collapse of Louis Napoleon's Second Empire, contained a majority of royalists, who wanted to restore the monarchy. The royalists were divided over the claims of France's two royal families, however, and they were outmaneuvered by the republicans. The republicans succeeded in creating republican institutions, including a presidency which the royalists hoped to transform into a monarchy, but which quickly came under the control of the republicans and endured until the Third Republic collapsed in 1940.

Fourteen men served as president of France during the Third Republic (see Table 1-1), although the first, Adolphe Thiers, did not immediately assume the title "president" and never occupied the presidency under the "constitutional laws" of the Third Republic. On 17 February 1871 the National Assembly unanimously elected Thiers "Chief of the Executive Power of the French Republic." Thiers, who was seventy-three years old, had no opponents. He was France's senior statesman; during the reign of Louis Philippe (1830–1848) he had twice been premier and six times a minister. At first a supporter and later an opponent of Louis Napoleon, he also had been a deputy during the Second Empire.

The Rivet Law of 31 August 1871 conferred the title of president on the chief of the executive power and confirmed the responsibility of the president to the legislature. In that respect, Thiers governed as the premier under a parliamentary system, rather than as a president under a separation of powers system or as a figurehead president under a parliamentary system. Hard-pressed by the royalist parliamentary majority, Thiers resigned on 24 May 1873. The same day the National Assembly elected Marshal Patrice de MacMahon president by a vote of 390 to 1, with 330 members abstaining. MacMahon, who was sixty-five, was a distinguished soldier and a monarchist of little political experience.

The presidency of the Third Republic was decisively shaped during MacMahon's tenure. A law of 20 November 1873 fixed the presidential term at seven years and ended the political responsibility of the president to the Assembly. Later, in 1875, four laws (which became known as the constitutional laws) were passed, spelling out in more detail the institutional framework. The constitutional laws created a bicameral legislature, consisting of a Chamber of Deputies and a Senate, and conferred extensive powers on the presidency, which was still viewed with suspicion by many legislators as a potential source of resurgent monarchy. Among the powers conferred was the right to dissolve the Chamber of Deputies with the consent of the Senate. MacMahon employed this power on 16 May 1877, in order to try to return a majority which would support a ministry to his liking. However, the election returned a majority opposed to the president, and MacMahon had to bend to its will by appointing a ministry which the Chamber, and not he, approved.

MacMahon stayed in office for two years after this defeat, but his power had been broken, and he resigned on 1 January 1879, more than a year before the legal expiration of his term. MacMahon's use of the dissolution power had been legal, but republicans regarded both his use of the power and any subsequent use of it as a threat to the republic. No subsequent president of the Third Republic employed the dissolution power; French politicians tried to elect presidents who could be expected to abide by this unwritten rule and, generally, to remain self-effacing throughout their terms.

MacMahon's successor, Jules Grévy, was the first person to be elected president of the Third Republic under the constitutional laws of 1875. Grévy was seventy-two years old and a confirmed republican. He had been a member of Parliament during the Second Republic and had opposed the creation of a presidency. In 1871 he had been elected president of the National Assembly, and at the time of his election as president of the republic he was president of the Chamber of Deputies.

Presidential Selection during the Third Republic

Any French voter who had not been deprived of his political rights by a court and, after 1884, who was not a member of the former French ruling families was eligible for election to the presidency. This meant that virtually any male, at least twenty-one years of age, could

Table 1-1
PRESIDENTS OF THE FRENCH REPUBLIC, 1848-1974

Name	Date of Birth	Date of Election	End of Term	Position at Time of Election
		Second Republic		
Louis Napoleon Bonaparte	20 April 1808	10 December 1848	2 December 1852 (Coup d'état)	Deputy
		Third Republic		
Adolphe Thiers	18 April 1797	17 February 1871	24 May 1873 (Resigned)	Deputy
Patrice de MacMahon	13 July 1808	24 May 1873	30 January 1879 (Resigned)	Marshal
Jules Grévy	15 August 1807	30 January 1879 Reelected 28 December 1885	3 December 1887 (Resigned)	President of the Chamber of Deputies
Sadi Carnot	11 August 1837	3 December 1887	24 June 1894 (Assassinated)	Deputy
Jean Casimir-Périer	8 November 1847	27 June 1894	15 January 1895 (Resigned)	President of the Chamber of Deputies
Félix Faure	30 January 1841	17 January 1895	16 February 1899 (Died)	Minister
Emile Loubet	31 December 1838	18 February 1899	18 January 1906	President of the Senate

Name	Birth date	Term start	Term end	Previous position
Armand Fallières	6 November 1841	18 January 1906	18 January 1913	President of the Senate
Raymond Poincaré	20 August 1860	18 January 1913	17 January 1920	Premier
Paul Deschanel	13 February 1855	17 January 1920	21 September 1920 (Resigned)	President of the Chamber of Deputies
Alexandre Millerand	10 February 1859	23 September 1920	13 June 1924 (Resigned)	Premier
Gaston Doumergue	1 April 1863	13 June 1924	13 June 1931	President of the Senate
Paul Doumer	22 March 1857	13 June 1931	6 May 1932 (Assassinated)	President of the Senate
Albert Lebrun	29 August 1871	10 May 1932 Reelected 5 April 1939	10 July 1940 (Deposed)	President of the Senate
Fourth Republic				
Vincent Auriol	27 August 1884	16 January 1947	23 December 1953	President of the National Assembly
René Coty	20 March 1882	23 December 1953	8 January 1959 (Resigned)	Vice-President of the Senate
Fifth Republic				
Charles de Gaulle	22 November 1890	8 January 1959 Reelected 15 December 1965	28 April 1969 (Resigned)	Premier
Georges Pompidou	5 July 1911	15 June 1969	2 April 1974 (Died)	Deputy

Source: Adapted from *Le Monde*, 21 May 1974.

be elected. One had to be at least twenty-five years old to be elected a deputy, and at least forty to become a senator.

Presidential elections took place at a joint meeting of the Chamber of Deputies and the Senate, sitting as the National Assembly. There were neither nominating speeches nor discussion of any kind; the deputies and senators simply voted. The ballot was secret, and a majority of the valid ballots cast was required for election. It was never necessary to hold more than two ballots; of the fourteen elections, starting with the first election of Jules Grévy, ten were decided at the first ballot and only four required a second ballot.

The term of office was seven years, and there was no limit to the number of terms a president could serve. Two presidents were elected to succeed themselves: Jules Grévy in 1885 and Albert Lebrun in 1939. Half the presidents, however, did not complete their first terms of office. Again starting with Grévy, two presidents were assassinated (Sadi Carnot in 1894 and Paul Doumer in 1932); one died in office of a cerebral hemorrhage (Félix Faure); four resigned, Grévy, when his son-in-law was implicated in a scandal involving influence-peddling from the presidential palace, Paul Deschanel, who had become insane, and Jean Casimir-Périer and Alexandre Millerand, both of whom encountered the opposition of the Chamber when they sought to assert themselves politically. Lebrun was deposed by Pétain in 1940, when the Third Republic came to an end.

When a president served a full term, it was his duty to convene the National Assembly one month before the expiration of his term in order to elect his successor. If the president failed to do so, the chambers had the right to meet jointly fifteen days before the end of the term to conduct the new election. When the presidency was vacated before the expiration of the full term, the National Assembly was constitutionally required to convene and "proceed immediately to the election of a new President." As a result of this requirement, the presidency was never vacant for more than four days. On two occasions a new president was elected on the same day the incumbent resigned.

The lack of concordance in presidential and legislative terms sometimes meant that a new president was elected by a less than freshly elected Parliament. (The Chamber of Deputies was popularly elected every four years; senators were elected for nine-year terms by delegates selected by municipal councilors at elections held every three years to fill one-third of the Senate seats.) Armand Fallières was elected in January 1906 by a National Assembly which included deputies who had been elected in April and May 1902, and Raymond

Poincaré was elected in January 1913 by a National Assembly containing deputies elected in April and May 1910. Albert Lebrun was first elected by a National Assembly containing lame-duck deputies. President Doumer had been assassinated after the legislative election of May 1932, but before the new Chamber of Deputies could legally convene. The outgoing Chamber of Deputies, which had been elected in April 1928 and was further to the right in political composition than the newly elected one, met with the Senate and elected Lebrun.

By the same token, a president who was elected by one kind of majority could have difficulty if a subsequent legislative election returned a majority of a different political coloration. This is what happened to Millerand, who was elected president in 1920 after the conservatives had won a victory at the legislative election of 1919. Outspoken and assertive, Millerand openly tried to influence political affairs from the presidency, which angered the Left. In 1924, the *Cartel des gauches* (Cartel of the Left), an alliance mainly of Radicals and Socialists, won the same kind of victory that the conservative *Bloc national* had won in 1919. The new majority, rallying to the slogan *toutes les places, et tout de suite* ("all the jobs, right now"), was determined to drive Millerand from office, and succeeded in doing so by refusing to support any government while Millerand was president.

Until 1931, presidential nominations were arranged by various forms of legislative caucus.[1] There were no organized political parties

---

[1] There is no specialized study of the operation of the Third Republic's presidential nominating caucuses, but there are brief references to them in various historical and contemporary works. The comments in the text rest on the following sources: for 1879, Jacques Chastenet, *Histoire de la Troisième République*, vol. 1, *L'Enfance de la Troisième, 1870-1879* (Paris: Librairie Hachette, 1952), pp. 258-59. For 1887, Jacques Chastenet, *Histoire de la Troisième République*, vol. 2, *La République des Républicains, 1879-1893* (Paris: Librairie Hachette, 1954), p. 196; André Daniel, *L'Année politique 1887* (Paris: G. Charpentier, 1888), pp. 286-88; Adrien Dansette, *Histoire des Présidents de la République: De Louis-Napoléon Bonaparte à Vincent Auriol* (Paris: Amiot-Dumont, 1953), p. 73. For 1894, Jacques Chastenet, *Histoire de la Troisième République*, vol. 3, *La République Triomphante, 1893-1906* (Paris: Librairie Hachette, 1955), p. 62; André Daniel, *L'Année politique 1894* (Paris: G. Charpentier, 1895), p. 215; Dansette, *Histoire des Présidents*, p. 97. For 1899, André Daniel, *L'Année politique 1899* (Paris: G. Charpentier, 1900), pp. 85-88; Dansette, *Histoire des Présidents*, p. 124. For 1906, Georges Bonnefous, *Histoire politique de la Troisième République*, vol. 1, *L'Avant-Guerre (1906-1914)*, 2d ed. (Paris: Presses Universitaires de France, 1965), pp. 3-4; Dansette, *Histoire des Présidents*, p. 149. For 1913, Bonnefous, *L'Avant-Guerre*, pp. 316-21; Gordon Wright, *Raymond Poincaré and the French Presidency* (Stanford, Cal.: Stanford University Press, 1942), pp. 36-49. For January 1920, Edouard Bonnefous, *Histoire politique de la Troisième République*, vol. 3, *L'Après-Guerre (1919-1924)*, 2d ed. (Paris: Presses Universitaires de France, 1968), pp. 92-98; Jacques Chastenet, *Histoire de la Troisième République*, vol. 5, *Les Années d'Illusions, 1918-*

in France before the twentieth century, and even after their advent, only the Socialists and, later, the Communists developed close-knit national organizations which required and could command discipline among their legislative groups. The main party during the Third Republic, the Radical Socialists (officially the *Parti républicain radical et radical-socialiste*), was founded in 1901, but it remained a decentralized party based on the power and appeal of local notables. There were annual party congresses, and there was special party machinery for deciding policy during ministerial crises, but neither the Radicals nor any other party had the equivalent of a United States party's national nominating convention.[2]

There were several reasons for this. No one party ever commanded a majority in either parliamentary chamber, and a winning candidate had to be acceptable to more than one parliamentary group. Secondly, there were as many presidential elections held in emergency conditions, following upon the unexpected vacation of the office, as there were regularly scheduled presidential elections. The need for "immediate" action to fill the vacancy did not, perhaps, make partisan nominating conventions totally unfeasible, but it certainly made them inconvenient. Lastly, the members of Parliament constituted the electoral college, and no one could be elected president who was not satisfactory to a majority of them. It was at least logical, if not inevitable, that the members of Parliament should control the nomination process as well as the electoral process.

During the early years of the Third Republic, starting with the first election of Grévy, the caucuses were limited to the deputies and senators from the republican parliamentary groups. Prior to the meeting of the National Assembly (at which, it should be recalled, no discussion took place), the republican groups would determine

<hr>

1931 (Paris: Librairie Hachette, 1960), p. 62; Dansette, *Histoire des Présidents*, p. 182; François Goguel, *La Politique des partis sous la IIIe République* (Paris: Editions du Seuil, 1946), p. 218. For September 1920, Bonnefous, *L'Après-Guerre*, pp. 163-65; Dansette, *Histoire des Présidents*, p. 201. For 1924, Edouard Bonnefous, *Histoire Politique de la Troisième République*, vol. 4, *Cartel des Gauches et Union Nationale (1924-1929)* (Paris: Presses Universitaires de France, 1973), pp. 16-18; Chastenet, *Les Années d'Illusions*, p. 121; Dansette, *Histoire des Présidents*, p. 219. I found no references to caucuses in 1885 or 1895.

[2] One French political commentator thought there was a political convention in 1906. "For the first time in France there was one of those preparatory assemblies at which the American political parties customarily designate their candidates. Under the name of 'plenary meeting of the left,' a vote was taken at the Luxembourg [palace, the meeting place of the Senate] to which all the republican members of the Senate and the Chamber of Deputies were invited. A considerable majority assembled around the name of M. Fallières." Pierre de Coubertin, *La Chronique de France, 1906* (Auxerre: Albert Lanier, n.d.), p. 32. De Coubertin was incorrect on more than one count; see below.

which candidate had the most support. Then, at the election, they would concentrate their votes on their leading candidate to ensure that a monarchist, Bonapartist, or markedly proclerical candidate was not elected because of division among the republicans. Usually the republicans of the two chambers met together (as in 1879, 1887, 1894, and 1906), but once the republicans of each chamber met separately, nominating the same candidate (Emile Loubet in 1899). Sometimes there was more than one caucus, as in 1887 when the Radicals held a separate caucus before the several republican groups caucused together, and in 1894 when there was a separate Senate caucus as well as a larger republican caucus.

By 1906 the republic was secure, and the caucuses were no longer employed primarily to ensure the election of a republican. Instead, they became vehicles by which the Radicals tried to control the outcome of the elections in favor of their preferred candidates. The composition of the caucuses reflected the tactical considerations of the moment. From 1906 until 1931 (when the preelectoral caucus was abandoned), one group or another was always excluded from, or excluded itself from, participation in the preelectoral caucuses. The Socialists did not attend the preelectoral caucus in 1906, although they appear to have voted at the election for the caucus's nominee, Armand Fallières. The Radicals excluded almost 150 legislators from the preelectoral caucus they summoned in 1913 in a futile effort to elect Jules Pams, the minister of agriculture, over Raymond Poincaré, the premier. The Socialists were invited to the caucus, but they did not attend, and they ran their own candidate, Edouard Vaillant, who had been a member of the Paris Commune forty years earlier. Pams outdistanced Poincaré by fourteen votes at the third and last ballot taken by the caucus, and he lacked only one vote for an absolute majority of the votes cast. Poincaré refused to withdraw, however, and he won the election at the second ballot, thanks to the support of the conservatives and nationalists who had been excluded from the caucus. This was the first time that the candidate chosen by the republican caucus failed to win the election itself.[3] It was not the last. After the *Cartel* parties drove Millerand from the presidency in 1924, the caucus which they convened nominated Paul Painlevé, but the National Assembly elected Gaston Doumergue, the president of the Senate.

In January 1920, the Radicals employed the caucus to frustrate the presidential aspirations of Georges Clemenceau, who had been premier since November 1917. Clemenceau was too authoritative and

---

[3] Goguel, *Politique des partis*, p. 143.

forceful a political leader to be allowed the forum of the presidency. For the first time, Socialists joined the preelectoral caucus; more than thirty of them came to vote against Clemenceau. The Radicals even invited the deputies of the *Entente républicaine* to the republican caucus, even though the *Entente* was the most proclerical group in the Chamber and the Radicals did not really regard them as republicans. The Radicals, however, counted on them to vote against Clemenceau. The caucus nominated Paul Deschanel; the embittered Clemenceau withdrew from the election, and when the National Assembly ratified the caucus's choice, he resigned from the premiership and from public life.

Although there were no particular qualifications for the office, after MacMahon the president was always chosen from among the members of Parliament. Military men were sometimes put up as candidates during the nineteenth century (1879, 1887, and 1894), but none was a serious contender. Six of the presidents of the Third Republic after MacMahon were lawyers, two were engineers educated at the Ecole Polytechnique, one was a businessman, another was a bourgeois dynast, one had been a teacher of mathematics, and the last a writer on historical and colonial questions. All, however, were professional politicians. Their average age at the time of their first election to the legislature was thirty-two; their average age at the time of their first election to the presidency was sixty. Casimir-Périer was the youngest at the time of his election (forty-six), Doumer the oldest (seventy-four). Grévy was seventy-nine when he was reelected, Lebrun sixty-eight.

Carnot was a mere deputy when he was elected president, Faure was a minister in office, Poincaré and Millerand were premiers in office. Of all the presidents of the Third Republic, however, only MacMahon and Deschanel had never held ministerial office prior to their election. Deschanel had been offered ministries, but he preferred the presidency of the Chamber of Deputies, which he occupied longer than anyone else except Henri Brisson, the Radical leader who was himself an unsuccessful candidate at the four presidential elections between 1885 and 1895.

The main stepping stone to the presidency of the republic was the presidency of one of the legislative chambers.[4] Grévy, Casimir-Périer, and Deschanel were presidents of the Chamber of Deputies at the time of their election to the presidency; Loubet, Fallières, and

---

[4] There is a convenient list of the presidents of the two chambers in Yves Daudet, *La Présidence des Assemblées Parlementaires Françaises* (Paris: Presses Universitaires de France, 1965), pp. 131-39.

the last three presidents of the Third Republic—Doumergue, Doumer and Lebrun—were presidents of the Senate at the time of their election. Doumer occupied all three presidencies at one time or another (but never the fourth, the presidency of the Council of Ministers, the official title of the premier). Doumer was an unsuccessful candidate for the presidency of the Republic in 1906, when he was president of the Chamber of Deputies; he was elected twenty-five years later, when he was president of the Senate.

It may appear strange that the president of the Senate was elected to the presidency more often than the president of the Chamber of Deputies, for the Chamber was the larger body. The Senate had 300 members until 1919, when it was enlarged to 314, while the membership of the Chamber of Deputies ranged between 533 and 610. The Senate, however, had the advantage of being more politically homogeneous than the Chamber. Its dominant outlook was middle-of-the-road, and it could produce a majority in the National Assembly by allying with the moderate deputies, even when the latter were a minority in the Chamber. Although the secrecy of the ballot makes it impossible to attribute votes to particular groups, it seems almost certain that the senators allied with the conservative deputies to elect Doumergue over Painlevé in 1924 and Doumer over Briand in 1931. By 1932 there appeared to be a growing tradition that the president of the Senate would become the president of the republic.

Presidential Selection during the Fourth Republic

The method of electing the president employed during the Fourth Republic (1947–1958) was virtually a carbon copy of the system used during the Third Republic. The president was elected by the members of Parliament. (The popularly elected chamber, formerly called the Chamber of Deputies, was now called the National Assembly; the old Senate was now called the Council of the Republic, but by 1948 the name "Senate" had returned to common usage.) The constitution set the term at seven years; an incumbent was eligible for a second term only; and members of the former reigning families were ineligible for the office. The constitution makers were unable to resolve the questions of whether the balloting should be open or secret and what kind of a majority would be required for election, so they left the constitution silent on those matters, with the tacit understanding that the election of the first president of the Fourth Republic would be by secret ballot.[5]

---

[5] Philip Williams, *Politics in Post-War France: Parties and the Constitution in the Fourth Republic* (London: Longmans, Green and Co., 1958), p. 171.

Both issues were politically important. In the past, it had often been argued that the secret ballot encouraged the election of mediocrities, but now it was believed that the secret ballot would operate to the advantage of Charles de Gaulle if he were to become a candidate for the presidency. Leftist admirers of the general might violate party discipline if the voting were secret, while they would not do so if their votes were made public. The Left parties also preferred requiring that election be by a large, qualified majority, again presumably because the requirement of only a bare majority would be to de Gaulle's advantage. When, in January 1947, the two houses of Parliament met to elect the first president of the Fourth Republic, they followed the same rules used during the Third Republic. Balloting was secret; a majority of the valid ballots cast was required to elect; and there could be no voting by proxy. Shortly before the second (and last) presidential election of the Fourth Republic, in December 1953, those rules were enacted into law, and they were followed in the election. On neither occasion could the rules have had the disputed effect, since de Gaulle was not a candidate for the presidency either in 1947 or 1953.

In the 1947 election, Vincent Auriol was elected on the first ballot, by a narrow majority over three other candidates.[6] Auriol, the first Socialist to become president of the republic, had as strong a claim to the office as anyone after de Gaulle. Born in 1884, Auriol became a deputy at thirty, was minister of finance in the popular-front government of Léon Blum, and was one of the eighty members of Parliament who voted against establishing the Vichy regime in July 1940. Active in the Resistance, Auriol was imprisoned, escaped, and joined de Gaulle in London in 1943. He was a member of the Consultative Assembly established at Algiers, and throughout the late war and early postwar years he was probably de Gaulle's chief adviser on partisan questions. He was president of both constituent assemblies, and worked tirelessly at promoting agreement among the contending forces. He was not only virtually the father of the constitution of the Fourth Republic, but also carried out functions similar to those of the president well in advance of his election.

Auriol became president of the republic during the period of tripartism, when France was governed by the three large parties of the early post-World War II period, the Communists, the Socialists, and the *Mouvement républicain populaire* (MRP). At the time of his election, Auriol was president of the National Assembly, a post he

---

[6] For Auriol's election, see Roger A. Priouret, *La République des partis* (Paris: Les Editions de l'Elan, 1947), pp. 9-29.

had occupied for the brief period in 1946 after the election of the Assembly in November, and to which he had been reelected just a few days before his election to the presidency of the republic.

Shortly after the legislative election of November 1946, the Communists tried to persuade the other parties to accept the principle of the "interdependence of presidencies," by which they meant that the presidency of the republic, the presidency of the National Assembly, the presidency of the Council of the Republic, and the presidency of the Council of Ministers (premiership) would be allocated to the parties according to an agreed plan. The Socialists refused to accept the principle, and when Auriol was first elected president of the National Assembly in December 1946, the Communists ran a candidate against him.[7]

The next day the Communist party nominated its leader, Maurice Thorez, for the premiership. The Socialists, who were convinced that Thorez had no chance of winning, decided to vote for him in the hope that the Communists would later support a Socialist for the presidency of the republic.[8] Thorez failed, as predicted, in his bid to become premier, but the Communists supported Auriol at his election as president of the National Assembly on 14 January 1947 and at his election to the presidency of the republic on 16 January 1947.[9] The balloting for president was secret, and it is therefore impossible to know exactly who voted for each candidate, but if all the Communist and Socialist legislators who participated voted for Auriol, he still drew some forty votes from other quarters.

Auriol served as president with distinction, but he had made enemies during his seven-year term, and he decided not to run for reelection in December 1953. By that date, the parliamentary situation had changed drastically from what it had been in 1947. The Communists, who had left the government in May 1947, were in the opposition, and there were over 100 Gaullist deputies in the National Assembly, most of them in opposition to the constitutional system. The MRP was much weaker than it had been in the early postwar period, and the Radicals and conservatives were now more numerous. Intense conflict over such issues as decolonization and the European Defense Community (EDC) Treaty widened the gaps between parties and leaders. The Council of the Republic, now generally referred to as the Senate, was a more conservative chamber relative to the

---

[7] *L'Année politique 1946* (Paris: Editions du Grand Siècle, 1947), pp. 280-81.
[8] François Goguel, *France under the Republic* (Ithaca, N. Y.: Cornell University Press, 1952), p. 18.
[9] All the Socialist deputies did not vote for Thorez, but even if they had done so he would not have received enough votes to become premier.

Assembly than it had been in 1947. The first Council of the Republic had been selected in a way that made it more or less the image of the Assembly; a new electoral law adopted in 1948 operated to the advantage of the conservative and middle-of-the-road groups. Like the Senate of the Third Republic, the Council of the Republic after 1948 was both more politically homogeneous and more conservative than the popularly elected chamber.[10]

The 1953 presidential election was a lengthy and difficult process. It took seven days and an unprecedented thirteen ballots to elect the president.[11] No fewer than eleven candidates entered the competition at one phase or another of the balloting, nine of them seriously.[12] After the first ballot, the Communists withdrew the candidacy of their elder statesman, eighty-four-year-old Marcel Cachin, and threw their support to the Socialist candidate, Marcel-Edmond Naegelen, a deputy and former governor-general of Algeria, who was the leader of the anti-EDC forces in the Socialist party. The Gaullists also withdrew their first-round candidate, Paul-Jacques Kalb, an Alsatian who was one of the vice-presidents of the Council of the Republic, and threw their support to Joseph Laniel, the conservative premier, who was a major contender. The MRP kept their leader, Georges Bidault, in the race for one more round, but after that he also withdrew and the MRP legislators announced their support for Laniel.

From the third through the eighth ballots, the competition was essentially a test between the obstinacy of Laniel and the ingenuity of the Radicals, who employed a succession of strategies to prevent Laniel from being elected.[13] On the eighth ballot, Laniel came close

10 Deputies still outnumbered senators. In 1947, there were 617 deputies and 315 councilors of the republic; in 1953, the numbers were 627 and 319.

11 Unprecedented for France, but not Italy. The method of electing the president of the Italian republic is essentially the same as the French system during the Third and Fourth republics. The electoral college consists of the two houses of Parliament plus a small number of delegates from each region. The ballot is secret and it requires a two-thirds majority to elect during the first three ballots, after which an absolute majority suffices. The first two presidents elected under this system, Luigi Einaudi in 1948 and Giovanni Gronchi in 1955, were chosen on the fourth ballot. Antonio Segni was chosen on the ninth ballot in 1962, Giuseppe Saragat on the twenty-first in 1964, and Giovanni Leone on the twenty-third in 1971.

12 The account of the 1953 election which follows draws mainly from Constantin Melnik and Nathan Leites, The House without Windows: France Selects a President (Evanston, Ill.: Row Peterson and Co., 1958). See also L'Année politique 1953 (Paris: Presses Universitaires de France, 1954), pp. 83-89.

13 For the first three ballots they ran Yvon Delbos; on the fourth ballot they divided their votes among three different Radicals, none of whom was an announced candidate. On the fifth, sixth, and seventh ballots they ran Jean Médecin, and on the eighth ballot they voted for Naegelen, the Socialist, and some miscellaneous, unannounced candidates.

to the required majority, and his opponents among his own conservative group (on whose behalf the Radicals had been operating) openly joined the stop-Laniel movement. Pierre Montel, a conservative deputy, entered the race for the ninth and tenth ballots, and Laniel's doom was sealed. Montel did not draw as many votes as the anti-Laniel Radicals had done earlier, but they were enough to make it clear that Laniel could not win. Laniel withdraw after the tenth ballot, and the conservatives ran Louis Jacquinot in his place on the eleventh. Jacquinot did not do as well as Naegelen, probably because of opposition to him by the MRP, and the conservatives switched to René Coty at the twelfth ballot. He did well, and on the thirteenth ballot he went over the top. President Auriol's successor had been chosen.[14]

President Coty was in the tradition of presidents of the Third Republic. He was virtually unknown to the public outside his department, but he was seventy-one years old, the senior vice-president of the Council of the Republic,[15] well liked by his parliamentary colleagues, and unscarred by participation in the sharp political conflicts of the period. In point of fact, he was to play an active role in bringing de Gaulle to power during the military revolt of May 1958, exceeding his constitutional powers in doing so. He threatened to resign if de Gaulle were not accepted as premier by the Assembly. If Coty resigned, Socialist André Le Troquer, the president of the National Assembly, would have become acting president. The president's threat of resignation, therefore, confronted the deputies with a choice between a conservative president and a Gaullist government, on the one hand, and a Socialist president and an unknown government—perhaps even a popular front—on the other.[16] The deputies chose de Gaulle, and with him a new regime.

Presidential Selection during the Fifth Republic

Charles de Gaulle had been a bitter opponent of the Fourth Republic even before it was formally launched in 1947. In January 1946 he

---

[14] Naegelen, the Socialist candidate, stayed in the race to the end, consistently drawing the support of Communists, Socialists, and some fifty others, probably radical deputies. The Socialists thought of trying to reelect Auriol midway through the lengthy balloting, but they received no encouragement from the other groups.

[15] In June 1955, Yvon Delbos, the unsuccessful Radical candidate for the presidency, exchanged his seat in the Assembly for one in the Senate, now restored as a source of presidents.

[16] Philip Williams, *Crisis and Compromise: Politics in the Fourth Republic* (London: Longmans, 1964), pp. 202-03.

resigned as president of the Provisional Government, in large part because of his displeasure with the kind of decisions being made by the First Constituent Assembly concerning a new constitution.[17] The Second Constituent Assembly had barely convened before de Gaulle made a major pronouncement on constitutional questions in a speech at Bayeux on 16 June 1946. In many respects, the Bayeux speech was a blueprint of the constitution of the Fifth Republic, which was drafted during the summer of 1958. The method of electing the president prescribed by the constitution of 1958 was a faithful reflection of the model that de Gaulle had sketched at Bayeux, when he said that the chief of state should be elected "by a college which includes Parliament; but [which is] much broader. . . ."[18]

The Original Method of Presidential Election. The presidential electoral college originally provided for in the constitution of the Fifth Republic consisted of more than 80,000 people. The college included the members of Parliament, the more than 3,000 members (*conseillers généraux*) of the departmental councils (*conseils généraux*), the members of the assemblies of France's overseas territories, and representatives of France's 38,000 communes according to a sliding scale ranging from the mayor alone for the more than 30,000 communes having fewer than 1,000 inhabitants to all the municipal councilors for the towns and cities with more than 9,000 inhabitants. In addition, the municipal councils of cities with more than 30,000 inhabitants could designate one additional delegate to the electoral college for every 1,000 persons of the population exceeding 30,000. Arrangements were also made for the participation of delegates from the former French colonies which had not yet become independent, referred to as Member States of the Community, as well as for additional delegates from the overseas territories.

The members of the electoral college met in their various departmental and other territorial capitals for the actual election. Two ballots were provided for by the constitution. To be elected on the first ballot, a candidate had to win an absolute majority of the valid ballots cast. If no candidate won such a majority, the candidate

---

[17] A constitutional draft adopted by a Communist-Socialist majority in the First Constituent Assembly, but rejected by the voters at a referendum in May 1946, would have had the president elected by roll-call vote of the members of a single, popularly elected legislative chamber. A majority consisting of two-thirds of the members would have been required for election. If no such majority were achieved during three ballots, the voting would have been adjourned until the next day, from which point on a three-fifths majority would have sufficed to elect.

[18] The text of the Bayeux speech appears in *L'Année politique 1946*, pp. 534-39.

winning a plurality on the second ballot, one week later, would be declared elected. The organic law governing the detailed electoral procedure provided that no new candidate could enter the race between the two ballots, unless two candidates on the first ballot agreed to let a single new candidate run in their place.

Only one presidential election was held under these original constitutional provisions. That was the election of 21 December 1958, in which, to no one's surprise, Charles de Gaulle was elected the first president of the Fifth Republic. De Gaulle had only token opposition. Despite the fact that candidacy required only the endorsement of fifty members of the electoral college holding elective office, there were only three candidates: de Gaulle, Georges Marrane, a Communist elder statesman with experience in both chambers, and Albert Chatelet, the honorary dean of the Faculty of Sciences of Paris, who was presented by a small non-Communist leftist group, the *Union des forces démocratiques* (UFD).[19] The UFD, whose leaders included François Mitterrand, who was to run as a popular-front candidate against de Gaulle in 1965, nominated Chatelet as a gesture "against the dangerous simplification which tends to present French politics as a conflict between two blocs."[20] All the major parties except the Communists supported de Gaulle, however, and the general won the election handily (see Table 1-2).

The Referendum of October 1962. The year 1962 was a major turning point in the history of the Fifth Republic; indeed, there is a sense in which it represented the end of an interregnum and the real beginning of the Fifth Republic, much as the Third Republic, which historians normally date from 1870, did not take on its permanent characteristics until 1875 or even later. In 1962 the Algerian war was ended and Algeria achieved independence; Michel Debré, who had headed the government during the first years of the Fifth Republic, was replaced as premier by Georges Pompidou; the first signs of a popular-front alliance between Communists and Socialists developed during the legislative elections of November that year; a new group of conservatives, called the Independent Republicans and led by Valéry Giscard d'Estaing, was formed in alliance with but separate from the main Gaullist party, the Union for the New

---

[19] De Gaulle, born in 1890, was the youngest candidate; Marrane was born in 1888 and Chatelet in 1883. Marrane had been the unsuccessful Communist candidate for the presidency of the Council of the Republic after its launching in 1946.

[20] *L'Année politique 1958* (Paris: Presses Universitaires de France, 1959), p. 155.

Table 1-2

RESULTS OF THE PRESIDENTIAL ELECTION
OF 21 DECEMBER 1958

	Regis-tered Voters	Valid Ballots	Votes by Candidate		
			Charles de Gaulle	Georges Marrane	Albert Chatelet
Metropolitan France	76,359	74,391	57,649	10,125	6,617
Overseas departments	1,262	1,151	937	176	38
Algeria	66	65	65	0	0
Sahara	220	219	214	2	3
Overseas territories	214	208	204	0	4
Member-states of the community	3,643	3,436	3,325	52	59
Total	81,764	79,470	62,394	10,355	6,721
Percent of total			78.6	13.0	8.4

Source: *Recueil des Décisions du Conseil Constitutionnel et de la Commission Constitutionnelle Provisoire, 1958-1959* (Publié sous le haut patronage du Conseil constitutionnel, Imprimerie Nationale), p. 49.

Republic (UNR); and the constitution was amended by referendum to provide for the direct popular election of the president.

The method of presidential election provided for originally in the constitution of 1958 had been criticized from the start, because the electoral college consisted of a disproportionately large number of electors from the small towns, as opposed to the cities, thereby violating the principle of equal representation.[21] By 1962, the Gaullists had additional cause to be concerned about the structure of the presidential electoral college. The overwhelming majority of its members consisted of municipal councilors and delegates elected by them, but the Gaullists had not been successful in winning local elections. The presidential electoral college was similar in many respects to the senatorial electoral college, and the Gaullists had

[21] Maurice Duverger calculated that without even taking into account the members of Parliament and the departmental councilors, a majority of the delegates to the electoral college came from towns of fewer than 1,500 inhabitants, representing only 33 percent of the metropolitan French population. Maurice Duverger, *Institutions politiques et Droit constitutionnel*, 9th ed. (Paris: Presses Universitaires de France, 1966), p. 502.

always done less well in electing senators than they had in electing deputies. It was extremely doubtful that any Gaullist, even de Gaulle himself, would be elected to the presidency again under the existing system. De Gaulle had been elected in very special circumstances in 1958. There was war in Algeria, the possibility of a military coup d'état had not yet been dispelled, and de Gaulle was supported by almost all the parties. By 1962 opposition to de Gaulle, his policies, and the regime he had established had grown greatly, and there was no possibility of de Gaulle, and even less of another Gaullist, repeating his 1958 triumph in the electoral college.

In the fall of 1962 de Gaulle announced his intention to amend the constitution, by popular referendum, in order to provide for the direct popular election of the president. The proposal was instantly attacked by all the parties except the Gaullists, both because popular election of the president was outside the traditions of French democratic institutions and because de Gaulle was proposing to establish it by means which violated the terms of the constitution on which he had insisted in 1958. The constitution contained a provision for constitutional amendment that required any proposed amendment to be adopted first by the National Assembly and the Senate and then ratified either by a referendum or by a three-fifths majority of the two houses of Parliament sitting jointly. There was little chance that the Assembly and none that the Senate would vote in favor of direct election of the president, so de Gaulle chose another route for amending the constitution. Another provision empowered the president, on the initiative of the government, to hold a referendum on measures affecting the organization of the public authorities. Two referendums, both concerned with the status of Algeria, had already been held under that provision, in January 1961 and April 1962. There is little doubt that that particular provision of the constitution was not intended by the framers of the constitution to be used for amending it, but that is the instrument which de Gaulle chose. The government cooperated by taking the formal initiative, even though the initiative was in fact de Gaulle's, and the National Assembly adopted a motion of censure against the government for the first time during the Fifth Republic. De Gaulle promptly dissolved the National Assembly, and at the subsequent legislative election in November the Gaullists were returned in greater numbers than they had had in the previous Assembly. However, in October, before the election, the referendum was held on de Gaulle's proposal for the direct popular election of the president. Despite the opposition of all the parties except the Gaullists, de Gaulle's proposed constitutional amendment was approved by more than 60 percent of the persons who voted.[22]

The new constitutional provisions governing the election of the president stated that "the President of the Republic is elected for seven years by direct universal suffrage." [23] Provision is made for two ballots. A candidate receiving an absolute majority of the valid ballots in the first round of voting is declared elected. If no candidate receives such a majority, a second ballot is held on the second following Sunday. Only two candidates may run on the second ballot. Those two candidates must have run on the first ballot, and they must be the two candidates who received the most votes at the first ballot among those candidates who do not choose to withdraw from the competition. In other words, if neither the candidate who won the most votes at the first ballot nor the candidate who won the second most votes chooses to withdraw from the race, they are the only candidates eligible for running on the second ballot. However, if the candidate who won, say, the second most votes at the first ballot decided for some reason to withdraw, the candidate who won the most votes and the candidate who won the third most votes at the first ballot would be the only candidates allowed to compete at the second ballot.[24]

---

[22] Six and a half million registered voters abstained; more than 13 million voted "yes"; almost 8 million voted "no."

[23] In the fall of 1973, President Pompidou followed the formal procedure for amending the constitution, in order to change the length of the presidential term from seven to five years, beginning with the scheduled presidential election of 1976. The bill of amendment passed both houses of Parliament separately, but did not carry by three-fifths of the combined membership of the two chambers. Pompidou neither had the two houses convened jointly to ratify the amendment nor called for a referendum on the issue. There is no time limit on the completion of the amendment process once it has begun, so presumably the proposed change in the presidential term could be taken up again at the stage to which it was carried.

The seemingly innocuous proposal aroused considerable controversy. Some opponents of the change argued that it would add excessive strength to the presidency. Some Gaullist fundamentalists regarded it as a violation of de Gaulle's basic constitutional philosophy. Neither Michel Debré nor Maurice Couve de Murville voted for the change. Two of de Gaulle's premiers were therefore opposed to the third. Communists and Socialists favor a five-year term, but they also voted against the change, because it was not accompanied by other changes they desire to weaken the position of the president.

[24] The constitution of the German Weimar Republic (1919-1933) also provided for the direct popular election of the president, under a two-ballot system that required for election a majority of all the votes cast at the first ballot or a plurality at the second ballot. The German system set no limit to the number of candidates who could run on the second ballot, however, and even new candidates could enter the race. When Field Marshal Paul von Hindenburg was first elected president of Germany in 1925, it was on the second ballot, and he had not been a candidate on the first ballot.

When a president is in office, a new presidential election must be held at least twenty days and not more than thirty-five days before the expiration of his term. If the presidency is vacated for any reason (except force majeure), an election must be held within a similar twenty to thirty-five day period following the vacancy. In the latter case, the president of the Senate becomes acting president with restricted powers.

At the same time as the 1962 referendum ratified the amendment of two articles of the constitution governing the presidential electoral system, it also ratified amendments to the basic ordinance governing the nomination of candidates. Under the new ordinance, candidates had to be nominated by at least 100 citizens who were either members of Parliament, members of the Economic and Social Council (a constitutional advisory body for economic affairs), departmental councilors (of whom there are some 3,000), or elected mayors (of whom there are almost 38,000), and those 100 sponsors had to include elected officials from at least ten departments or overseas territories.[25] In order to prevent candidates from exploiting the names or positions of their sponsors for campaign purposes, the names of the people who sponsor the various candidates were not made public.

The ordinance also provides that candidates who do not receive at least 5 percent of the valid ballots forfeit both the deposit which is required of each candidate and the small sum for campaign expenditures which is allocated on an equal basis to all candidates. A decree of 14 March 1964 set the size of the deposit at 10,000 francs (about $2,000 at the time) and the amount of state-provided campaign funds at 100,000 francs per candidate.

The Presidential Election of December 1965. Presidential nominating politics for the election of 1965 took place within the framework of a multiparty system into which de Gaulle and the Gaullists had made substantial inroads since 1958.[26] De Gaulle had not only

---

[25] There are ninety-five departments for metropolitan France, four overseas departments, and six overseas territories.

After 1958 members of France's former ruling families were no longer ineligible for the presidency.

[26] For brief accounts of the 1965 presidential election, see Elijah Ben-Zion Kaminsky, "The Selection of French Presidents," in Donald R. Matthews, ed., *Perspectives on Presidential Selection* (Washington, D. C.: The Brookings Institution, 1973), pp. 93–106, and Philip M. Williams, *French Politicians and Elections 1951-1969* (Cambridge: Cambridge University Press, 1970), pp. 186–203. More detailed accounts appear in *L'Election présidentielle des 5 et 19 décembre 1965* (Paris: Armand Colin, Cahier de la fondation nationale des sciences politiques 169, 1970), and Roger-Gérard Schwartzenberg, *La Campagne Prési-*

won substantial majorities at several successive referendums, including the referendum of October 1962 amending the constitutional provisions governing the election of the president, but the Gaullists had also won more than 30 percent of the votes at the legislative election of November 1962.[27] For the Gaullists, the first (and as it turned out the only) question was whether de Gaulle would run for a second term. For the left-wing parties, the problem was whether and what kind of a coalition of voters could be created to outdistance the Gaullist candidate. For the Center and anti-Gaullist conservatives, nomination politics had two aims: defeat the Gaullist candidate if de Gaulle did not run; hold their voters if he did.

Uncertainty over whether de Gaulle would be a candidate in 1965 rested on two considerations. First, at the time of the referendum to provide for the direct election of the president, de Gaulle always suggested that he was thinking of his successor's need for a firm base of popular support; at no time did he indicate that he would be a candidate under the proposed new electoral system if it were adopted. Indeed, he proposed the new method of presidential election shortly after the closest escape he had yet had from several attempts to assassinate him. Secondly, de Gaulle chose deliberately to conceal his intentions with regard to running for reelection until close to the last minute. De Gaulle was the last of the major candidates to announce his candidacy. The deadline for filing was 16 November; de Gaulle announced his candidacy on 4 November.

The first major political leader to make known his presidential aspirations was Gaston Defferre, the mayor of Marseilles and leader of the Socialist group in the National Assembly. Defferre announced his candidacy in December 1963, but he could neither win the wholehearted support of his own party, nor build the kind of partisan coalition which he believed to be necessary if he were to have a chance of winning the election.

Defferre refused to seek the support of the Communist party. Instead, he tried to build a centrist coalition which would include the Socialists, the Radicals, and the MRP. The voters of those three

dentielle de 1965 (Paris: Presses Universitaires de France, 1967). See also L'Année politique 1965 (Paris: Presses Universitaires de France, 1966), pp. 89-115.
[27] The constitution of 1958 was ratified by almost 80 percent of the voters; a referendum in January 1961, to ratify the policy of self-determination for Algeria, carried by 75 percent of the voters; and a referendum in April 1962, ratifying the Evian Accords (by which Algeria became independent), carried by over 90 percent. De Gaulle's position on those questions was always supported by some or most of the non-Gaullist parties. His most impressive referendum victory was in October 1962, over the constitutional amendment, when his position was opposed by all the non-Gaullist parties.

parties, he seems to have reasoned, would be numerous enough to ensure his eligibility for the second ballot, at which Communist voters would support him as the only left-wing candidate. Defferre's efforts to build such a centrist coalition failed, largely because a substantial group within the Socialist party, including Guy Mollet, its secretary-general, preferred to keep open the possibility of an alliance with the Communists. Moreover, there was no groundswell of enthusiasm for Defferre's candidacy, which might have strengthened his hand in his efforts to placate both the left-leaning wing of his own party and the party furthest to the right in the alliance he hoped to create, the MRP. In June 1965 Defferre withdrew his candidacy.

Defferre's withdrawal left the way open for another left-wing candidate and another political strategy. François Mitterrand, who had been among the first politicians to support Defferre for the presidency, made known his availability as a popular-front candidate. Mitterrand's anti-Gaullist credentials were impeccable: he had voted against de Gaulle when the general returned to power in June 1958 (so had Defferre) and he had urged a "no" vote at the referendum on the constitution of 1958. (Defferre had supported "yes.") He was a member of a virtually nonexistent party called the *Union démocratique et socialiste de la Résistance* (UDSR) which resembled the Radical party in the middle-of-the road quality of its few central figures. Mitterrand's lack of a solid partisan base was a valuable asset for him. His candidacy could not advance the fortunes of any party at the expense of either of the two main parties of the Left, the Communists and the Socialists. Furthermore, the availability of an appropriate candidate who was neither a Communist nor a Socialist facilitated the creation of a popular front when it is doubtful that either the Communists or the Socialists would have accepted a standard-bearer from the other party.

Mitterrand won the backing of the Communists and the Socialists surprisingly easily. The Communists made no demands on him, and the Socialists made it clear that it was much more important to them to defeat the Gaullists than it was to elect a Socialist to the presidency. The small *Parti socialiste unifié* (PSU) was more grudging in its support, but it nevertheless gave it. The Radicals, as usual, split over the question, but most of them decided both to endorse Mitterrand and to join with the Socialists in an umbrella organization called the Federation of the Democratic and Socialist Left, which played no role during the presidential election, but which was to tighten the links among the parties on the Left at the legislative elections of 1967.

The preferred candidate of the cluster of parties and politicians usually referred to, somewhat erroneously, as the centrists, and consisting of the MRP, the anti-Gaullist conservatives, and those Radicals who refused to support Mitterrand because of his alliance with the Communists, was Antoine Pinay. Pinay, one year younger than de Gaulle, had been the only premier during the Fourth Republic— except for Pierre Mendès-France—to arouse any kind of genuine popular enthusiasm. Pinay also was minister of finance from June 1958, when de Gaulle returned to power, until January 1960, when he was dismissed because of his objections to virtually all of de Gaulle's policies. Pinay might have made a strong showing against any Gaullist other than de Gaulle himself, and he might have run if de Gaulle had withdrawn, but he did not want to run against de Gaulle. The centrists canvassed several other possibilities, and eventually decided on Jean Lecanuet, a young (forty-five years old) senator who was president of the MRP, a post which he resigned when he became a presidential candidate.

De Gaulle, Mitterrand, and Lecanuet were the main, but not the only, candidates. The very first candidate to announce was Jean-Louis Tixier-Vignancour, a right-wing extremist who rallied the support of the oldest and newest—and most implacable—of de Gaulle's enemies, the Vichyites and the last-ditch defenders of French control over Algeria. Another candidate was Pierre Marcilhacy, an obscure senator from western France, whose candidacy served no useful purpose after Lecanuet entered the race. At the last moment, a sixth candidate filed: Marcel Barbu. Barbu had served for several months as a deputy in the First Constituent Assembly, but the eccentricity of his candidacy underscored the liberality of the regulations regarding eligibility for candidacy for the presidency.[28]

The results of the first ballot surely disappointed, and probably also surprised, the Gaullists. De Gaulle, who had displayed his overconfidence by not using all his allotted radio and television time during the early part of the campaign, did not win a majority of the votes. He won only 44 percent of the votes, against 32 percent for Mitterrand and 16 percent for Lecanuet, and was faced with a runoff against Mitterrand two weeks later.

---

[28] Others had announced their candidacy but withdrew: André Cornu, a senator from Brittany who had received some votes on the fourth ballot of the marathon presidential election of 1953, withdrew after he was injured in a fall from a horse; Paul Antier, a Poujadist-style peasant leader, withdrew in favor of Lecanuet when the latter became a candidate. General Boyer de la Tour, former resident general in Tunisia and in Morocco, announced that he was thinking of becoming a candidate, but did not do so.

Preelection polls conducted by two major public opinion survey organizations, IFOP and SOFRES, indicate clearly that it was Lecanuet's voters who prevented de Gaulle from winning a first-ballot victory. Figure 1-1 shows the evolution of vote intentions of those people who expressed them to IFOP and SOFRES interviewers prior to the first ballot on 5 December. It appears that Mitterrand's supporters did not vary much in total numbers from the start of the campaign until the actual balloting; he mobilized most of his support quickly. De Gaulle, on the other hand, started out with an enormous lead that melted away as the campaign proceeded. Lecanuet began the campaign in October with minimal popular backing, but his strength grew as the campaign continued. It was the flow of votes away from de Gaulle and towards Lecanuet that meant the difference between a first-ballot victory for de Gaulle and the necessity for a runoff.

De Gaulle won the runoff against Mitterrand comfortably, although it was hardly a landslide victory. De Gaulle won 54 percent of the vote in metropolitan France, an average performance by comparison with recent United States experience in two-candidate presidential elections.

None of the candidates who were required to withdraw from the runoff tried to throw their support to de Gaulle. Tixier-Vignancour, who had received 1.25 million votes (and had run best in those areas where there were large concentrations of people who had migrated from Algeria after it became independent), asked his first-ballot voters to switch their support to Mitterrand; so did Barbu. Marcilhacy made no recommendation to his voters; after lengthy hesitation, Lecanuet asked his supporters not to vote for de Gaulle, but did not ask them to vote for Mitterrand. It is not possible to state with precision how closely Tixier-Vignancour's and Lecanuet's recommendations were followed by their supporters; IFOP's pre-runoff polls, however, suggest that at least 60 percent of Tixier-Vignancour's voters switched to Mitterrand and that at least 45 percent of Lecanuet's voters switched to de Gaulle.[29]

The electorate's vote intentions for the second ballot, as recorded in surveys conducted by IFOP and SOFRES, correspond remarkably with its actual behavior at the second ballot. De Gaulle mobilized the support of right-wing voters to an impressive degree, and Mitterrand mobilized the support of left-wing voters almost equally fully. Centrist sympathizers divided almost three to one in favor of de Gaulle, and the nonpolitical also favored de Gaulle, although his

---

[29] *Sondages*, no. 4 (1965), p. 38.

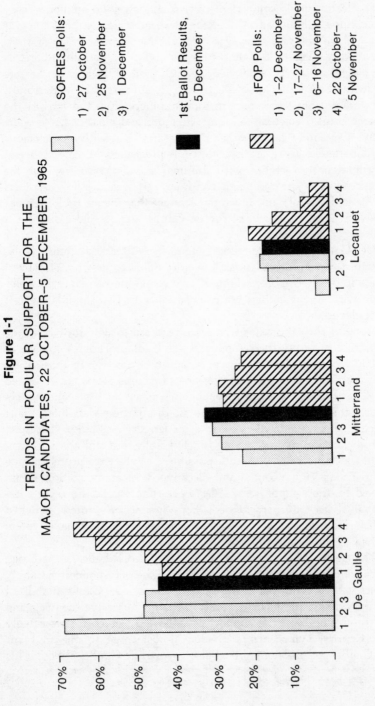

Figure 1-1

TRENDS IN POPULAR SUPPORT FOR THE
MAJOR CANDIDATES, 22 OCTOBER–5 DECEMBER 1965

SOFRES Polls:
1) 27 October
2) 25 November
3) 1 December

1st Ballot Results,
5 December

IFOP Polls:
1) 1–2 December
2) 17–27 November
3) 6–16 November
4) 22 October–
5 November

Source: Emeric Deutsch, Denis Lindon and Pierre Weill, *Les Familles politiques, Aujourd'hui en France* (Paris: Les Editions de Minuit, 1966), p. 56, and *Sondages*, no. 4 (1965), p. 15.

margin varies with the measurement instruments employed by the two polling organizations.

IFOP reported the breakdown of presidential vote intentions for the second ballot by three clusters of partisan preferences (expressed in terms of the party that the respondent would vote for in the case of a legislative election), as well as a category including those people who expressed no partisan preference. The three clusters of parties each included the main parties that supported one of the three major candidates at the first ballot. One cluster included people who preferred the Communists, the Socialists, or the Radicals, who officially supported Mitterrand; another included those preferring the MRP or the National Center of Independents (the anti-Gaullist conservatives), who supported Lecanuet; and the third included the people who preferred the Gaullist UNR or Giscard d'Estaing's Independent Republicans.[30]

In an important book dealing with the bases of French political attitudes, Eméric Deutsch, Denis Lindon, and Pierre Weill reported the breakdown of a SOFRES survey of second-ballot vote intentions by the voters' self-placement within five categories ranging along a Left-Right scale from the extreme Left through the Center to the extreme Right, as well as by a category they call the *marais*, which includes those people who could not classify themselves in Left-Right terms or who classified themselves as centrists but had no interest in politics.[31]

The two types of classification of political location, IFOP's use of discrete party preference and SOFRES's use of Left-Right self-placement, produce different, but related categories. The Communists, Socialists, and Radicals are perceived as the parties of the Left, and the UNR and the Independent Republicans are regarded as parties of the Right. The MRP and the anti-Gaullist conservatives, who joined together in the *Centre démocrate* in 1966, tried to present themselves as centrists, and the *Centre démocrate* was generally perceived as centrist or moderately right of Center. We would, therefore, expect the voters in the corresponding categories of the two modes of measurement to behave similarly politically.[32]

---

[30] Ibid.

[31] Eméric Deutsch, Denis Lindon and Pierre Weill, *Les Familles politiques, Aujourd'hui en France* (Paris: Les Editions de Minuit, 1966).

[32] For popular perceptions of the Left-Right location of the French parties, see Deutsch, Lindon and Weill, *Les Familles politiques*, p. 45, and Samuel H. Barnes and Roy Pierce, "Public Opinion and Political Preferences in France and Italy," *Midwest Journal of Political Science*, vol. 15 (November 1971), p. 647.

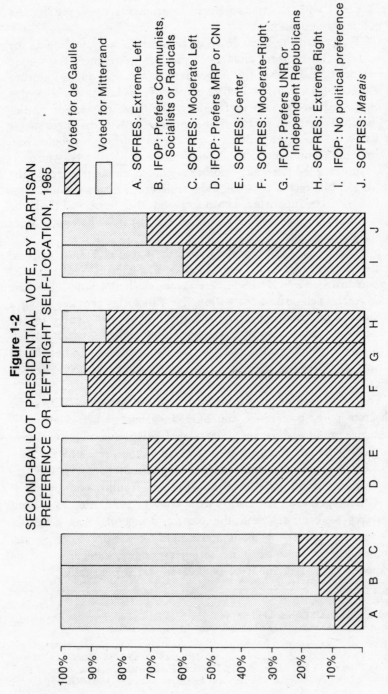

Figure 1-2

SECOND-BALLOT PRESIDENTIAL VOTE, BY PARTISAN
PREFERENCE OR LEFT-RIGHT SELF-LOCATION, 1965

Voted for de Gaulle

Voted for Mitterrand

A. SOFRES: Extreme Left

B. IFOP: Prefers Communists,
    Socialists or Radicals

C. SOFRES: Moderate Left

D. IFOP: Prefers MRP or CNI

E. SOFRES: Center

F. SOFRES: Moderate-Right

G. IFOP: Prefers UNR or
    Independent Republicans

H. SOFRES: Extreme Right

I. IFOP: No political preference

J. SOFRES: *Marais*

Source: Emeric Deutsch, Denis Lindon and Pierre Weill, *Les Familles politiques, Aujourd'hui en France* (Paris: Les Editions de Minuit, 1966), p. 76, and *Sondages*, no. 4 (1965), p. 38.

Figure 1-2 shows that that was indeed the case at the second ballot of the presidential election of 1965.[33] De Gaulle mobilized almost as fully as possible the voters who preferred the right-wing parties or who believed themselves to be on the Right or the extreme Right; Mitterrand rallied almost as large a proportion of the voters who preferred the leftist parties or who regarded themselves as leftists or extreme leftists. The people who preferred the parties that presented themselves as centrist or who were themselves centrists divided about three to one in favor of de Gaulle. So, approximately, did the nonpolitical: those people who did not express a partisan preference or whom Deutsch, Lindon, and Weill classified among the *marais*. De Gaulle and Mitterrand produced a sharp polarization of Left and Right, but the Center and the nonpolitical opted for, and gave the victory to, de Gaulle.

The Presidential Election of June 1969. The major political events which occurred between the presidential election of 1965 and the presidential election of 1969 were, in order of occurrence, the legislative election of 1967, the popular upheaval of May-June 1968, the Russian and other Eastern European Communist countries' invasion of Czechoslovakia in August 1968, and de Gaulle's defeat at the referendum of April 1969, which provoked his resignation from the presidency, thereby requiring a new presidential election in June.

The background. The legislative election of 1967 was a replay of the presidential election of 1965 with regard to the main political forces which were in competition, although the outcome was considerably different. Three main groups competed for seats in the National Assembly in 1967: a Gaullist bloc, a leftist bloc, and a centrist bloc. The two Gaullist parties, the UNR and Valéry Giscard d'Estaing's Independent Republicans, agreed to present only a single candidate in each electoral district. The Federation of the Democratic and Socialist Left, which had been formed shortly before the 1965 election and consisted of the Socialists, the leftist Radicals, and a new group which Mitterrand had encouraged, called the Convention for Republican Institutions (CIR), also decided to run only one candidate in each district it contested. In addition, the Communist party and the small PSU made an agreement with the federation to support on the second ballot the leftist candidate who was best placed to win

---

[33] The same comparison for the first ballot does not show such strikingly concordant results.

29

the seat in each district.[34] Shortly after the 1965 election, the parties that had supported Lecanuet—the MRP and the anti-Gaullist conservatives of the CNI—formed the *Centre démocrate*, and they too shared candidacies so that they would not compete with each other at the legislative election. Inasmuch as Mitterrand was president of the federation and Lecanuet was president of the *Centre démocrate*, and both men played an active role during the election campaign, there was a strong similarity between the earlier presidential and the later legislative elections.

At the first ballot of the legislative election of 1967, the leftist parties amassed more votes than Mitterrand had on the first ballot of 1965, but the Gaullist parties did not do as well as de Gaulle had done alone on the same ballot and the centrist parties did not do as well as Lecanuet. On the second ballot the left-wing alliance held up remarkably well, with the result that the Communists and the parties of the federation gained about sixty seats and the Gaullists lost about forty. The Gaullists failed to win a majority of the seats in metropolitan France, and they held a small majority over all other groups in the Assembly only because they won most of the seventeen seats from the overseas departments and territories.

The Gaullists were in serious difficulty after the legislative election of 1967, not only because the narrowness of their majority meant that they could be defeated on particular issues if the opposing groups remained united and there were defections among their own ranks, but also because there was a severe contest for power among the Gaullists themselves, between the orthodox Gaullists of the old UNR (now called Union of Democrats for the Fifth Republic, abbreviated as UD-V⁰) and the Independent Republicans. At the same time, the parties of the Left were consolidating the alliance that had shown considerable strength at the presidential election of 1965 and even more at the legislative election of 1967. The federation and the

---

[34] The electoral system for the National Assembly is similar to, but not identical with, the system for the election of the president. France is divided into single-member districts. If a candidate wins a majority of the votes in his or her district, including at least 25 percent of the registered voters, that candidate wins the seat. If no candidate wins such a majority, there is a runoff ballot one week later. A second ballot is normally required in the great majority of electoral districts. There is no fixed limit to the number of candidates who may run on the second ballot, but only candidates who won the votes of at least 10 percent of the registered voters on the first ballot may compete on the second ballot (as long as that rule leaves at least two candidates eligible in the district—if not, the rule is relaxed to ensure a contest). The candidate who wins a plurality on the second ballot is elected.

Electoral alliances among parties may be formed on the second ballot by the deliberate withdrawal of some candidates in favor of other candidates.

Communist party reached agreement on a "common declaration" of policy in February 1968. This common declaration pointed out the differences between the two left-wing groups, particularly over foreign policy, as well as their points of agreement, but it represented a further stage in the development of a new popular front by beginning to give policy content to what had been only an electoral alliance in 1965 and 1967.

Given the difficulties of the Gaullists, both in the face of an increasingly united opposition and among themselves, it is doubtful whether the legislature elected in 1967 would have run its normal term. As it turned out, the legislature lasted barely over a year, but the reason for its curtailment was not the difficulty of the parliamentary situation. It was, instead, the greatest social upheaval that has ever taken place in a modern society.

This is not the place to enter a discussion of the revolt of May-June 1968, an event which shook the Fifth Republic, although it did not topple it. From the perspective of French presidential politics, however, it produced two important results. It weakened support for de Gaulle among the Gaullist political leadership and strengthened the position of the premier, Georges Pompidou. It also shattered, albeit temporarily, the unity that had so far been achieved by the left-wing parties.

De Gaulle appears at first to have underestimated the seriousness of the crisis, and when he decided to act, he proposed holding a national referendum on a vaguely formulated plan for increasing popular participation in educational, social, and economic affairs. De Gaulle's call for a referendum produced no positive response among the public and disappointed his followers among the political leadership; indeed, the national strike wave continued and it would have been literally impossible to conduct a referendum. De Gaulle appeared, for a while, to be helpless, and cabinet ministers became almost invisible men. The only clear sign of energy and confidence on the part of the Gaullists came from Premier Pompidou, and it was apparently he who persuaded de Gaulle to drop the idea of a referendum and, instead, to dissolve the National Assembly and hold new elections. By the time de Gaulle announced the dissolution of the National Assembly he had regained his tone of authority, but he was now in the position of backing his premier rather than describing the course that his premier should follow.

At the same time, cracks developed in the leftist bloc. Mitterrand made public statements without consulting the Communists, and the latter regarded these as contrary to the requirements of the left-wing alliance. The parties of the federation feared that the Communists would be blamed for the strikes and disorders, and that the blame would carry over to them because of their alliance with the Communist party. The electoral alliance between the federation and the Communists (as well as the PSU) was retained for the 1968 legislative election, but relations among the left-wing parties had cooled considerably, and mutual recriminations followed the smashing electoral victory which the Gaullists won in June 1968. The Gaullists upped their proportion of the first-ballot vote to 44 percent, while all the parties of the Center and the Left lost votes. The results in terms of seats were even more striking. The orthodox Gaullists (now called the Union of Democrats for the Republic, UDR) gained almost 100 seats and held a majority by themselves; this was the first time in French history that a single party had held a majority in the popularly elected chamber. Giscard d'Estaing's Independent Republicans also gained seats, while the Center lost 20 percent and the Left lost more than half of the seats it had held before the election.[35] The left-wing alliance failed in June 1968, and it was shattered completely (although not, of course, permanently) when Russia and other Eastern European Communist countries invaded Czechoslovakia in August. For the first time in its history, the French Communist party expressed disapproval of a Russian foreign-policy move, but that was not enough to persuade the non-Communist Left to maintain links with the Communists. The federation was allowed to wither away as well, with the result that by 1969 what had been a remarkably united Left now consisted of three separate parties, two of which—the Socialists and the Radicals—were divided within themselves as to the strategy and tactics that might best enable them to recoup their losses.

De Gaulle's motives in calling a national referendum in April 1969 are far from clear. In part, he may have felt compelled to carry out the referendum he had announced during May, but which was frustrated by events. In part, he may have wanted to make additional institutional changes along lines that he had sketched at Bayeux in 1946, thereby placing his stamp on the constitutional structure even more clearly than he had done already. Whatever the reasons, de Gaulle staked his continuation as president upon the outcome of a single referendum on two complicated questions: the establishment of regional councils and the reorganization of the Senate. If it had passed, the bill of referendum would have amended almost twenty

---

[35] Less than magnanimous in their hour of victory, the Gaullists of the UDR promptly removed Giscard d'Estaing from the chairmanship of the Finance Committee, which he had held since 1966 and wanted to retain.

articles of the constitution by the same unconstitutional method by which the constitution had been amended in 1962 to provide for direct popular election of the president. This time, however, the changes proposed by de Gaulle were neither simple nor popular. The changes would have weakened the Senate, and that produced opposition among the local councilors who populate the senatorial electoral colleges and who view the Senate as the defender of local interests. Few of the Gaullist leaders could generate much enthusiasm for the proposals, and Giscard d'Estaing even advocated a "no" vote. Pompidou, whom de Gaulle had removed from the premiership right after he had organized the greatest partisan electoral victory ever won in France, dutifully campaigned in favor of a "yes" vote, but refused to stake his political career on the outcome. The result was a defeat for de Gaulle: 53 percent of the voters voted "no," and only 47 percent voted "yes." De Gaulle immediately resigned as president.

The candidates and the election. Georges Pompidou had declared himself a candidate for the presidency before there was a vacancy in the office.[36] In January 1969, after de Gaulle had become committed to holding the referendum on regionalism and the Senate, Pompidou made a statement while abroad, in Rome, indicating that he would run for president after de Gaulle left the office. It was widely believed that Pompidou's announcement of his candidacy cost de Gaulle favorable votes at the referendum (an opinion that de Gaulle appears to have shared).[37] De Gaulle's announcement that he would resign if the referendum did not carry lost some of whatever force it might have had in view of the fact that Pompidou, who had been de Gaulle's premier for six years, had already offered himself as de Gaulle's successor.

Whatever the impact of Pompidou's early statement that he would be a candidate for the presidency may have been on the outcome of the referendum, he officially announced his candidacy 29 April, the day after de Gaulle resigned. On the same day, he

---

[36] Brief discussions of the 1969 presidential election appear in Kaminsky, "The Selection of French Presidents," pp. 106-11, and Williams, *French Parties and Elections*, pp. 282-87. A fuller account appears in Roger-Gérard Schwartzenberg, *La Guerre de succession: Les élections présidentielles de 1969* (Paris: Presses Universitaires de France, 1969). See also *L'Année politique 1969* (Paris: Presses Universitaires de France, 1970), pp. 34-53.

[37] Expressed to Pompidou in a letter of 30 April 1969 in which de Gaulle said, "Undoubtedly it would have been better if you had not announced [your candidacy] several weeks in advance. That caused certain 'Yes' votes to be lost. . . ." Raymond Tournoux, *Le Tourment de la fatalité (1958-1974)* (Paris: Plon, 1974), cited in *Le Monde*, 12 April 1974.

received the support, first, of the political bureau of the UDR's parliamentary group in the National Assembly, then of the UDR parliamentary group itself, and, lastly, of the executive office of the UDR's party organization. The following day, he also received the endorsement of the Independent Republicans' parliamentary group in the National Assembly.[38] Later he picked up the support of almost a third of the centrist deputies.

Pompidou's principal opponent was Alain Poher, the sixty-year-old president of the Senate. Poher, a centrist from the MRP, had served in the first Council of the Republic from 1946 to 1948; he was elected to the Senate in 1952 and had been regularly reelected ever since. He briefly held a few junior ministerial posts during the Fourth Republic, but his main activity was in the field of European affairs. A disciple of Robert Schuman, Poher held a variety of posts in European agencies and had been president of the European Parliament from 1966 through 1968.

Poher had been elected president of the Senate in 1968, according to one newspaper account, because of his "qualities as a diplomat and thoughtful negotiator, for his care in never scandalizing his opponents, and his flair for coming up with middle-of-the-road solutions."[39] The description sounds very much like that of the characteristic president of the Third Republic, but the analogy would not be wholly accurate. Poher was surely not well known to the public, but as president of the Senate, he had taken a very active role in campaigning against de Gaulle at the referendum, and in that sense had as good a claim as anyone to having been the leader of the victorious "no" forces. Moreover, when de Gaulle resigned from the presidency, Poher became acting president, and that role gave him additional opportunities to increase his visibility to the electorate.[40] Poher postponed a final decision about running until almost the last moment and did not formally announce his candidacy until 12 May, the day before the deadline for filing. By the time he announced, however, he had secured the support of a variety of groups including the Radical party, most of the centrists, the extreme Right, and certain departmental federations of the Socialist party.[41]

In the 1969 presidential election, the Gaullists had their candidate in Georges Pompidou and the centrists had Alain Poher as their

---

[38] Schwartzenberg, *La Guerre de succession*, pp. 36–37, 41.

[39] Maurice Denuzière in *Le Monde*, 14 May 1969.

[40] During the referendum campaign, Poher said that if he became acting president and then also decided to become a candidate for a regular term, he would step down as acting president; however, he did not resign the interim presidency.

[41] Schwartenzenberg, *La Guerre de succession*, pp. 92–97.

standard-bearer, but there was no single candidate on the Left, as there had been in 1965. François Mitterrand did all he could to enhance his visibility, and the Communist party probably would have supported him as they had before, but Mitterrand's standing had dropped sharply as a result of the Left's defeat in the 1968 legislative election, and neither the Radicals nor most of the Socialists wanted an alliance with the Communists so soon after the invasion of Czechoslovakia. In fact, most of the non-Communist leftist leaders believed that no left-wing candidate could win against Pompidou at the second ballot in 1969, as centrist voters would throw their support to Pompidou. Accordingly, their strategy was to back an anti-Gaullist centrist, and Poher's candidacy was to satisfy them on that score.

Gaston Defferre, the Socialist who had failed in 1965 in his attempt to build a coalition of Socialists, Radicals, and the MRP in support of his candidacy, made another bid for the office in 1969. He received the formal endorsement of his party's congress on 4 May, but many of the Socialist delegates who supported his candidacy seem only to have wanted a multiplicity of left-wing candidates in order to ensure that the centrist candidate would place second on the first ballot and, therefore, be eligible to run on the second ballot.[42]

When it was clear that there would be no single left-wing candidate, the Communist party presented one of their long-time leaders, Jacques Duclos. Duclos, who was seventy-three at the time, was a senator (he had also served many years as a deputy) and member of the political bureau of his party. The PSU nominated their thirty-eight-year-old secretary-general, Michel Rocard, and a Trotskyite group called the Communist League presented the even younger Alain Krivine (twenty-seven), who ran as a supporter of the revolutionary currents of May–June 1968. While there had been one leftist candidate for the presidency in 1965, there were four in 1969.

In addition to Pompidou, Poher, and the four leftist candidates, a millionaire businessman named Louis Ducatel also ran. Like Marcel Barbu, Ducatel had had some genuine political experience, but his candidacy served no useful purpose.[43]

---

[42] The Socialists took no risks on that score. The same congress that endorsed Defferre's candidacy also adopted a motion which would have provided a basis for Defferre's withdrawal from the second ballot, in favor of a centrist, in the event that Defferre came in second on the first ballot. See ibid., p. 74.

[43] A number of bills have been introduced that would tighten up the requirements for nomination, and in December 1973 the Senate passed a bill that would, if enacted, require candidates to be endorsed by at least 500 elected office-holders from at least thirty departments, including at least fifty departmental

On the first ballot, Pompidou ran first, as expected, with about the same proportion of the vote as de Gaulle had won on the first ballot in 1965. Poher came in second, but he won less than a quarter of the votes, confirming a downward trend in his support that had been recorded by the polls. Poher had been surprisingly strong early in May, but he lost about a third of his support as the campaign proceeded. Duclos proved to be an effective vote-getter. He ran third, very close to Poher, and he won more votes than his party had in the legislative election of 1968 and almost as many as it had won in 1967. Defferre, on the other hand, did poorly, with barely more than 5 percent of the votes.

For the second ballot, Defferre recommended that his supporters switch to Poher (so did Ducatel), the Communist party recommended that its followers abstain, and the two small leftist groups that had sponsored candidates at the first ballot, the PSU and the Communist League, recommended that their supporters either abstain or cast blank ballots.[44] The most interesting (and important) recommendation was the Communist position in favor of abstention. The Communist party rarely abstains on any question, but this decision appears to have been made before the first ballot, as Duclos emphasized during his campaign that there was no difference between Pompidou and Poher. Communist abstentions at the second ballot would work to the advantage of Pompidou, helping to ensure the continued existence of the heavily right-wing Assembly that had been elected in 1968. If Poher were to be elected president, sooner or later he would either have to dissolve the Assembly or allow the presidency to become the predominantly honorific post it had been during the Third and Fourth republics. But the Communists could not be sure of guaranteeing a victory for Poher; if they supported him and he lost, they would have compromised their leftist purity for nothing. And even if Poher won and dissolved, the Communists might well be isolated alongside two contending blocs, the Gaullists on the one hand, and the Socialists, Radicals, and centrists on the other. In 1969, the Communists appeared to be firmly committed to a policy of promoting the kind of leftist alliance that had been formed for the presidential election of 1965 and the legislative elections of 1967 and 1968. Poher's failure (and Duclos's comparative

councilors and twenty-five members of Parliament. The government endorsed the Senate measure during the summer of 1974, as well as a proposal to require the publication of the names of the sponsors of the various candidates. But the National Assembly did not act on the proposal.

[44] Tixier-Vignancour, the extreme right-winger, supported Poher on the first ballot but shifted to Pompidou on the second.

success) strengthened the Communists' hand in that regard, as subsequent events were to demonstrate.

Pompidou won the second ballot easily, with fewer votes—but a larger proportion of the votes cast—than de Gaulle had received at the second ballot in 1965. Proportionally, there were more abstentions and invalid ballots, taken together, than at any national election or referendum since World War II (although the abstention rate alone was only the third highest since the war). About two-thirds of Duclos's first-ballot supporters abstained at the second ballot, an impressive demonstration of the discipline of the Communist electorate.[45] The non-Communist Left's centrist strategy lay in ruins. Within a month, the Socialist party started to look leftward toward the Communists once again, and the chief architect of the centrist strategy, Guy Mollet, was eased out as secretary-general, a post he had held since 1946, and replaced by Alain Savary, who had unsuccessfully sought the endorsement of the Socialist party as a presidential candidate who would try to unite all the parties of the Left. Within a year, Savary was replaced as head of the party by François Mitterrand, who proceeded to put back together, for the legislative election of 1973 and the presidential election of 1974, the left-wing alliance of which he had been the symbol since 1965.

Historical Perspectives on French Presidential Selection

If we leave aside the early and ill-fated experiment with popular election of the president in 1848 and begin our overview with 1870, the pattern of historical development in presidential *election* in France is obviously one of enlargement of the number of participants. There was, first, a long period when the only participants in the electoral process were the parliamentary elites; that system operated from 1870 until 1958 (with an interruption during the Vichy regime). Then, with the launching of the Fifth Republic, there was what turned out to be an interim system under which the presidential electoral college was enlarged to include some 80,000 persons, all of whom may be classed among the political elites, although most were active only at the local level. Finally, de Gaulle's constitutional amendment of 1962 opened up presidential elections to all men and women twenty-one years of age. In July 1974 the age of majority was lowered to

---

[45] For survey analyses of the 1969 election, see Alain Lancelot and Pierre Weill, "L'évolution politique des électeurs français, de février à juin 1969," *Revue Française de Science Politique*, vol. 20 (April 1970), pp. 249-81, and *Sondages*, no. 3 (1969).

eighteen. In one sense, therefore, the democratization of the presidential electoral system took at least twice as long in France as in the United States.[46]

It is difficult to be categorical about developments in the *nomination* of presidential candidates over the same time span. From the start of the Third Republic throughout the entire period discussed in this chapter, presidential nominations were decided by relatively small groups of political elites. Throughout the Third Republic, the nomination of the major candidates was exclusively in the domain of the parliamentary groups that also elected the president. During the Fourth Republic, however, there was some enlargement of the circles of participation, in that various nonparliamentary party agencies also participated in the preparation of electoral strategies and the actual nomination of candidates, although the degree to which that was so varied across parties and elections.

The slight widening of the elite involved in presidential nominations during the Fourth Republic was due to the growth of parties and not to any change in the mechanisms of presidential election. There is no indication that the parties have developed new nominating procedures as a result of the new method of electing the president. Of course, there were very special circumstances surrounding the presidential election of 1958, which made it much like the United States presidential election of 1789 with regard to the amount of competition involved. But the situation had changed considerably by 1965 for all the parties except the Gaullists, and to the author's knowledge, no party adopted a special procedure for nominating or endorsing a presidential candidate. Both in 1965 and 1969, the endorsements of presidential candidates were made by a variety of party groups, sometimes including party congresses, but more often only involving party executive committees, somewhat larger party councils, and/or the parliamentary groups. The Socialist party was the only party to endorse presidential candidates both in 1965 and 1969 at full party congresses, although the candidate they endorsed in 1965 (Defferre) withdrew before the election and lesser party bodies, the *comité directeur* and the *conseil national*, then made the crucial decision to support Mitterrand. In all those respects, the parties' behavior reflected their traditional organizational characteristics rather than any new, common set of imperatives imposed by

---

[46] Depending on how one counts. From 1789 to 1832 in the United States and from 1879 to 1965 in France is 1:2. But American presidential democracy may reasonably be dated from 1824, and the start of the dominant modern French system may be set at 1871.

the new method of presidential election or even by the enhanced powers of the presidency.

One characteristic of French presidential nominating politics, therefore, is the diversity of decision-making groups and processes. Another central characteristic is that presidential nominating politics is a form of coalition politics within the framework of a multiparty system. Presidential candidates can win more than the fractional shares of the vote that normally go to their parties at legislative elections only if they represent coalitions of parties; they can normally expect to place first or even second at the first ballot only if they are assured of coalition support. In that respect, presidential nominating politics during the Fifth Republic bears some resemblance to the efforts to solve ministerial crises during the Fourth Republic, although the process is less orderly and more complex, as the parties must consider electoral responses at two popular ballots and not simply the reactions of parliamentary groups. The process is fluid, in that various alternatives are explored or tested before firm decisions are made. What one party will do is conditioned by what is done by others, and while some candidates may see advantages in announcing their availability early (Defferre in 1965 and 1969, Pompidou in 1969), others may prefer to hold their counsel until the last minute (de Gaulle in 1965, Poher in 1969).

In the period of the Fifth Republic discussed in this chapter—the period up through the election of 1969—the parties of the Left obviously had a more difficult time in arriving at a settled strategy than did the Gaullists. The constant problem that faces the French Left is whether to try to build a coalition that includes the Communists and excludes the Center, or a coalition that includes the Center but excludes the Communists. In 1965, the Left chose the former; in 1969, it chose the latter. In the circumstances of those years, when the Communists were committed to trying to build a left-wing coalition, the Socialists occupied the pivotal position, swinging one way at one time and another way at another.

The Gaullists had an easier time of it. No Gaullist dared risk a contest with de Gaulle for the nomination in 1965. Similarly, in 1969, while a contest for the nomination among Gaullists was by no means excluded, Pompidou's successful management of the 1968 legislative election had earned him a preeminence that his rivals among the orthodox Gaullists of the UDR and the Independent Republicans did not care to challenge in an open struggle. There was no reason to think, however, that the comparative harmony within Gaullist ranks would continue indefinitely.

The UDR was rife with factional conflicts and personal rivalries, and it was a party peculiarly inexperienced in settling leadership contests. The UNR had been formed to support a heroic leader who despised parties and never attended a formal session of any of its deliberative agencies. Second-level Gaullist leaders challenged his policies but never his place, and the road to power and influence ran through the government which de Gaulle controlled rather than through the party which he inspired. When de Gaulle appointed Georges Pompidou as premier in May 1962, Pompidou was resented as much by the UNR for not being a party man as he was by the other parties for not being a member of Parliament. Most (but far from all) Gaullists came to accept Pompidou's leadership, especially after June 1968, but the fact remained that neither he nor de Gaulle, if for different reasons, had been selected by the Gaullist party in an intraparty competition. There was no way of knowing whether the UDR could manage the internal conflicts that future presidential politics might produce.

Moreover, the Gaullists were divided into two parties, the UDR and the Independent Republicans, with different leaders, different parliamentary groups, and competing claims for policy, power, and place. The leftist parties had been divided in 1969, both one from another and—particularly in the case of the Socialists—among themselves, while the Gaullist parties had been remarkably united. It required no great effort of the imagination to conceive of the possibility that one day the situation might be reversed: with the Left united and the Gaullists torn asunder.

2

THE RISE OF
A NEW-STYLE PRESIDENT

J. Blondel

Nineteen seventy-four will perhaps be remembered as the most eventful year of the decade for European politics. It will almost certainly be regarded as a watershed year in French politics. Within three months, the leaders of the three major Western European countries left the scene, Edward Heath through electoral defeat, Georges Pompidou through death, and Willy Brandt mostly through disillusionment. The oil crisis was creating major economic difficulties everywhere. The Franco-British rapprochement of the early seventies was replaced by a revival of the Franco-German alliance of the early sixties. But internal political change was, for a time at least, more dramatic, and at least as important.

The political upset was particularly marked in France. Brandt's replacement by Schmidt was rapid; Heath's replacement by Wilson resulted, temporarily, in a minority government for Britain. The replacement of Pompidou by Giscard d'Estaing was a momentous affair, with far-reaching consequences, not all of which can be clearly detected. On the surface, a Gaullist conservative president has been replaced by a near-Gaullist conservative president. But this is not the real story. After an election campaign which showed the enthusiasm of the French for the selection of their president by universal suffrage, the result was the closest that the country has ever witnessed, the margin between the two candidates on the second ballot being little more than 1 percent. The result also showed that one man, with little organization, but considerable will power and intellectual prestige, could succeed in a period of a few weeks in profoundly undermining—perhaps even destroying—the party basis of the Fifth Republic under de Gaulle and Pompidou, while at the same time edging above a candidate supported from the start by nearly all the forces of the Left and almost all organized forces of the working class. Giscard d'Estaing's feat ranks at least alongside that of John F. Kennedy in 1960. It is one of the most surprising results in French electoral history, and it is ripe with profound consequences for French political life in the coming decade.

Pompidou's Last Months

The last months of the Pompidou presidency were sad. Indeed, from the time the French people returned a reduced Gaullist majority to the National Assembly in the general election of March 1973, everything seemed to go wrong for the French president. France seemed in crisis, economically, socially, and politically. Though the regime itself was not really in question, signs of disaffection were numerous among the political elite, business and trade-union groups, and even the population at large.

The Problems of the Economy. The oil crisis at the end of 1973 revealed some of the weaknesses of the French economy. During his five years as president, Pompidou had been a staunch supporter of rapid economic growth. But modern French industrialization remained somewhat fragile, partly because of the speed at which it was conducted, partly because of the narrow capital base of French business, and partly because of an overemphasis on extremely advanced technology at the expense of some much needed machine tools and heavy equipment. Developments took place mostly in electronics, aviation, and the nuclear field—all largely financed by the state—and in consumer goods, not, in contrast with Germany, in less spectacular capital goods. Consequently, the balance of foreign trade was only in very slight surplus in the early 1970s, and it fell into appreciable deficit after the oil crisis. By the mid-1970s, France, unlike Germany, Sweden, and the Netherlands, still did not have a healthy and diversified range of exports.

Social Tensions. Rapid industrialization created social tensions. In May 1968, France was at an almost complete standstill, and had been for some weeks. The aims of the strikers were varied and somewhat unclear. Some wanted more money; others, particularly among the young, wanted a different life, better working conditions, more "participation" and less authoritarianism in the workplace and in local, regional, and national government. Pompidou endeavored to avoid a repetition of such events by skillful manipulation, but in the

1970s tensions were still there, under the surface. Every spring brought some, though limited, unrest. Wildcat strikes occurred, particularly among lower-paid workers, the *ouvriers spécialisés*, and in factories employing large groups of women and immigrants. Unlike the strikes of previous years, these were often long and bitter, though frequently not supported by the largest trade union, the Communist-inclined *Confédération Générale du Travail* (CGT). Various firms became household symbols of the fight against capitalism, *Rhodiaceta* and the *Joint Français* in particular.[1] In 1973, for almost a year, the workers of the largest French watch factory, *Lip*, refused to accept the bankruptcy of the firm and occupied the plant to prevent the breakup of the company and the dismissal of much of the work force.[2] In the end, they succeeded almost entirely. Meanwhile, university students, who had been the source of the 1968 troubles, and high school students were involved in demonstrations on behalf of various causes. The government seemed able to retain control only through careful manipulation. It appeared to be tottering on the edge of a precipice. By the early spring of 1974 a new wave of small strikes seemed to forecast further difficulties for the president and his team.

Political Problems. Despite unrest and economic difficulties, the majority of the electorate was not willing to give the Left a chance, as was shown by the results of the 1973 general election.[3] The Gaullist party, the *Union des Démocrates pour la République* (UDR), was again returned as the largest party in the National Assembly by far, though not with the unprecedented majority which it had obtained in the aftermath of, and as a backlash from, the 1968 troubles. The UDR had 180 deputies; together with its allies, the Independent Republican party of Giscard d'Estaing and the Center for Democracy and Progress of Jacques Duhamel, the Gaullists could muster a

---

[1] Strikes in these and other companies in the provinces were mainly organized by the Catholic trade union, *Confédération Française Démocratique du Travail* (CFDT).

[2] Prime Minister Pierre Messmer's government procrastinated for months before coming to a solution acceptable to the workers. In the end, it agreed to allow the company to be reconstructed under a well-known (Socialist) business leader.

[3]

	Second-ballot votes	Seats
Gaullists (UDR and others)	46.3%	262
Center	6.1	32
Socialists and Left Radicals	26.4	104
Communists	20.6	73
Other	0.6	19

majority of about thirty to forty seats in the 490-member National Assembly. But the majority coalition remained somewhat demoralized, partly because of scandals, and partly because of a leadership crisis affecting the prime minister, Pierre Messmer, and the president himself.

Beginning in 1972, the once "moralistic" UDR had been undermined by a series of shady property deals and other unseemly affairs. Pompidou even had to dismiss Messmer's predecessor as prime minister, Jacques Chaban-Delmas, because his personal position, though not strictly irregular, smacked of tax dodging. Other affairs had led to court cases and one deputy had had to resign. Also, irregularities in public works contracts were alleged. The moral fabric of the government seemed to be shattered, and the permanent linkage between the Gaullist party and the state administration was questioned more and more openly.

Neither the president nor the prime minister seemed able to restore confidence. Messmer had been appointed in 1972 to help present a better image of the Gaullist party to the electorate. And a year later the Gaullists did win. But, while Messmer was generally considered to be morally above reproach, he remained politically weak. Despite many efforts, he did not put across an image of dynamic change. Consistently rated very low in the opinion polls, the premier just did not match the increasingly strong challenge of François Mitterrand, who, after many years of work, had rejuvenated the old Socialist party and allied Communists and Socialists around a common government program. The 1973 electoral victory seemed but an episode, as if the Gaullists had only won a reprieve.

Leadership had to come entirely from the skillful Pompidou, but his health had been the subject of periodic rumors since 1972. Repeated denials as well as the courageous—almost superhuman— efforts of the Gaullist leader did stall the waves of questioning. But the denials failed to dispel uncertainty, while making impossible any open discussion of the succession. Pompidou's illness probably also undermined his ability to look at the future with calmness and foresight. Politics seemed more chaotic and, as had been the case in de Gaulle's very last years, policy seemed more unrealistic.

The Increasingly Bitter Twist of Foreign Policy. As if to counterbalance their domestic difficulties, French leaders were once more engaging in a foreign policy of prestige operations and isolationism. Pompidou began his presidency in 1969 by improving relations with the United States and by giving a new impetus to European unity.

By the end of 1972, perhaps because of the relative failure of the Paris European summit, perhaps because of the lack of cordial relations between the French president and the German chancellor, French policy was once more presented rigidly and arrogantly, as if it were axiomatic that France was the guardian of the European soul. Hence, there were misunderstandings, animosities, and ostracism, which, in turn, appeared to justify the suspicions of the French. The appointment of Michel Jobert as foreign minister seemed to mark a return to the most nationalistic period of the de Gaulle era. To what extent this new twist to French policy was a consequence of the physical and mental strain under which Pompidou was operating during his long illness remains a mystery. But the combination of an uncompromising nationalistic posture, social and economic difficulties at home exacerbated by the oil crisis and rather difficult political prospects suggested that perhaps a real crisis would come in the near future. The Fifth Republic was in its sixteenth year, and no modern French regime except the Third Republic had lasted even two decades.

The Death of Pompidou and the Selection of the Presidential Candidates

The Absence of a Regular Selection Process. Perhaps because the illness of Pompidou had been discussed and denied for so long, the death of the president took the French and the French political parties by surprise. There had been occasional speculation about a possible resignation, but such rumors had always been stopped before a serious discussion of possible candidates could occur and, of course, before candidates could declare themselves. On the evening of 2 April, when France learned by a radio and television flash that the president had suddenly died, the succession process had not even begun, at least as far as the Gaullist party and the ruling majority were concerned.

Nor was there any real guidance as to how the candidates were to be selected. Of course, there are some minimal legal requirements. The candidates must be backed by at least 100 elected mayors from at least ten departments (a rather modest requirement since there are about 38,000 mayors in France).[4] But these legal points provide little effective guidance—as little as the U.S. Constitution provides for the

[4] The law also requires that candidates put up a deposit of 10,000 francs (about $2,000), which is lost by candidates who do not obtain at least 5 percent of the votes.

selection of American presidential candidates. However, unlike the American, the French political system still had not developed customary arrangements for candidate selection by 1974. The tradition of popular presidential election was too short, and both previous elections under the Fifth Republic had been exceptional.[5] Up to 1958, the French president, like the West German or Italian presidents, was appointed by a parliamentary college. There was no election campaign; the selection took place in party caucuses on the spot, and compromise candidates were produced as they seemed to be required. Even in 1958 de Gaulle was elected president not by universal suffrage, but by an electoral college of about 80,000 locally elected officials. Only since the constitutional reform of 1962 was the election of the president by universal suffrage, and the first such election took place in 1965.

But the 1965 presidential election was no ordinary election. No candidate selection was needed among Gaullists, and among the opposition parties—since no one expected de Gaulle to lose—the question of how candidates would be selected was not given top priority, even on the Left. Moreover, in 1965 the Fifth Republic still seemed provisional. It was widely believed that the system would not survive de Gaulle. The idea of holding conventions on the American model was therefore never seriously considered.

Thus, the first popular presidential election of the Fifth Republic did not help to develop a real nomination process; nor did the second. This was in part because the second election did not take place in 1972 as expected, but in 1969 after de Gaulle's resignation when his proposal for regionalism and reform of the Senate was defeated by popular referendum. Had de Gaulle remained in office until the end of his regular presidential term, candidates might have slowly emerged, and perhaps a real nominating campaign would have been fought, as in the United States. But de Gaulle resigned in 1969, the day after the referendum was held. According to the presidential electoral law, a new election had to take place within thirty-five days. The candidates had, therefore, to be selected in a matter of days.

Hence the rush to choose the Gaullist candidate in 1969; hence, too, the disarray of the opposition parties. The UDR turned to Pompidou, whom de Gaulle himself, somewhat cryptically, had once designated as someone "promised to high destiny" and who had been the only really successful prime minister among the three who

---

[5] The constitution of 1848 provided for the election of the president by universal suffrage. Napoleon's nephew was elected, and he subsequently turned himself into an emperor under the title Napolean III. Hence the traditional resistance of liberals and democrats to the popular election of the president.

had served the Fifth Republic. Center and Left parties were so divided that they presented no less than four major candidates, each of whom lacked prestige and broad popular appeal. Pompidou benefited from these divisions. He won on the second ballot by a fairly large margin—but amidst considerable abstention—over Alain Poher, the Center party candidate and president of the Senate, who, as such, was acting president of the republic.[6]

Thus, on 2 April 1974 there was still no tradition for the selection of presidential candidates by the political parties. And once more the president had not served his whole term and candidates would have to be selected in a hurry almost from scratch.

The Common Candidate of the Left, François Mitterrand.

This time, however, one side was ready. The Left had made such a poor showing in the 1969 presidential election owing to its lack of unity that it had been forced to reappraise its strategy. Two points seemed clear: first, no Communist candidate would ever be elected, given that the Communist party, though supported by about 20 percent of the voters, alienates or profoundly frightens the rest of the French electorate. Even in parliamentary elections, Communist candidates find it difficult to attract Socialist voters in districts where Socialist candidates have withdrawn, and they attract only a small fraction of the vital floating voters of the Center and Center-Left. Second, it is not enough that a candidate of the Left be a Socialist and not a Communist. He has also to demonstrate real popular appeal. The Socialist presidential candidate in the 1969 election obtained a bare 5 percent of the votes, and even the Center candidate polled only 23 percent.

The Left was ready for a change in 1969, but that the change was so successful was due to the energy and skill of François

[6] The results of the presidential elections of 1965 and 1969 were as follows:

	1965			1969	
	First ballot	Second ballot		First ballot	Second ballot
De Gaulle (UDR)	43.7%	54.5%	Pompidou (UDR)	44.5%	58.2%
Mitterrand (Socialist)	32.2	45.5	Poher (Center)	23.3	41.8
Lecanuet (Center)	15.9	—	Duclos (Communist)	21.3	—
Tixier-Vignancour (extreme Right)	5.3	—	Defferre (Socialist)	5.0	—
			Rocard (independent socialist)	3.6	—
Marcilhacy (conservative)	1.7	—	Ducatel (independent conservative)	1.3	—
Barbu (independent)	1.3	—	Krivine (extreme Left)	1.0	—

47

Mitterrand. Once a deputy identified with a small Center group, he had become the "united" candidate of the Left against de Gaulle in 1965, because Communists and Socialists were unable to agree on a more prominent name and because it was assumed that the fight against de Gaulle would be a token show. Mitterrand seemed ready to fight the battle in which no one else wished to be the sacrificial lamb. Forecasts were somewhat upset when de Gaulle was not elected on the first ballot (thanks to the presence of a Center candidate, Jean Lecanuet, who obtained 15 percent of the votes) and the candidate of the Left mustered 45 percent of the votes on the second ballot. Yet Mitterrand was discarded in 1969. Only because the results of the Left—in particular the Socialist party—were so poor in that election was Mitterrand able to force a reconstruction of the Socialist party, oust the old guard, and become party leader. In the 1973 parliamentary election, the Socialist party's substantial gains in votes confirmed Mitterrand's strength. By April 1974 his claim to be the sole candidate of the Left was unchallenged. He was not Communist and he was popular; he seemed therefore to meet the main requirements. He was selected without opposition by the Socialist party, the Communist party, the Left Radicals (or liberals) and the small United Socialist party. For 1974 at least, the problem was solved on the Left, but it was solved ad hoc; the need for a selection process that would be viable in the long term remained.

The Difficulties on the Gaullist Side and the Choice of Chaban-Delmas. On the Gaullist side and among the Center groups, the situation was quite different. In 1969 Pompidou was the heir apparent to de Gaulle; in 1974 there was no heir apparent to Pompidou. Various names were mentioned, but none had the support of all tendencies within the party. Jacques Chaban-Delmas was the most talked about among the Gaullists. As prime minister between 1969 and 1972, he had shown imagination and dynamism, but his image had been marred by his tax problems and by the various scandals of the Gaullist party. Hence, there was some limited support for Prime Minister Messmer, but his image was low and his leadership weak. Perhaps Pompidou had been hoping to build him up as his successor, but he had not had time. Few believed that Messmer could win against Mitterrand. The situation was fluid. Only the opinion polls seemed to provide guidance, and they pointed to Chaban-Delmas as the only Gaullist candidate likely to beat Mitterrand.

Pompidou had declared himself a candidate a few days after de Gaulle's resignation in 1969. Chaban-Delmas probably thought that the best tactic was to follow the same course, but the situation was complicated for reasons of protocol. The shock and official mourning following Pompidou's death were bound to be obstacles in the ex-prime minister's path. Yet he did win the first round. The UDR Council, with almost surprising ease and probably in order to show the appearance of unity deemed to ensure success, endorsed him as a candidate even before the official memorial service for Pompidou had taken place.

The Hopes of the Center Parties and Giscard's Decision to Stand. At the best of times—1968, with Charles de Gaulle running—the Gaullist party only obtained 45 percent of the votes on the first ballot, 55 percent on the second ballot. Under the less auspicious circumstances of 1974, Chaban-Delmas would have had a difficult fight. There was a strong candidate on the Left, and the Center was unquestionably about to put up a strong fight.

The Center had been the great casualty of the Fifth Republic. It had dominated the Third Republic; it had managed to make a comeback after the liberation in 1945. But de Gaulle's 1958 return to power and the streamlining of the party system after the 1962 election had condemned the Center to a much weaker position. Gaullists governed, while Socialists and Communists, forced to work more closely together, were gradually becoming "the" opposition. The various Center groups seemed reduced to becoming satellites. The *Mouvement Républicain Populaire* (MRP, the French Christian democrats), once prominent in Fourth Republic politics, had even had to be disbanded. "Independent conservatives," who, unlike Giscard d'Estaing, did not follow the Gaullist lead in 1962, were routed at the polls. And the once dominant Radical party was reduced to a small band of deputies torn between support for the government and ties with the opposition.

The presidential election of 1965 had produced a glimmer of hope, however. Jean Lecanuet, previously an MRP deputy and since then unceasing in his efforts to unite centrist groups, had obtained 15 percent of the votes, largely because of widespread unease about de Gaulle's nationalism and anti-Common Market posture. The 1969 retirement of de Gaulle had raised greater hopes and provided some satisfaction: the Center candidate, Alain Poher, president of the Senate and an ex-MRP politician, obtained a quarter of the votes and was the challenger at the second ballot. Since that election, efforts had been made to bring some of the Radicals, under the leadership of Jean-Jacques Servan-Schreiber, founder of the weekly magazine *Express*, and a somewhat unpredictable, but very active "modern" politician, closer to the followers of Jean Lecanuet. And, while the 1973 election was a disappointment for the Center because the Gaullist coalition remained basically solid and the real advance was made by the Socialists, the death of Pompidou seemed to give the Center its first real opportunity to make a comeback.

The first blow to Chaban-Delmas was therefore struck by the president of the National Assembly, Edgar Faure, a politician of the Center from the Fourth Republic who had rallied to de Gaulle in the more recent period and had become minister of education in 1968 with a brief to reform university structures. Although not really popular, and over sixty, Faure seemed to have at least a hope of mobilizing a fraction of the electorate. He was driving a wedge into the governmental majority; Chaban-Delmas's nomination would not rally the support of all the "non-Left" forces. Others were still on the fence, in particular Giscard d'Estaing, who stated that it was unseemly to become a candidate before a reasonable period had elapsed after Pompidou's death.

Valéry Giscard d'Estaing had always been uneasily associated with the Gaullist majority. He was too young to have been involved in the Fourth Republic (he was only thirty-two in 1958), but one of his grandparents had been a deputy of the traditional Right. From very early on, he trod a difficult path at the border of Gaullism. Refusing to associate himself with efforts made in 1962 by Center party leaders to unseat de Gaulle's government and enforce parliamentary control, he started a faction of "Gaullist conservatives." He was rewarded late in 1962 by being appointed minister of finance in Pompidou's government. He strengthened the franc and introduced balanced budgets, though at the expense of economic growth. But his stabilization plan of 1963 came to be considered the cause of the social troubles of subsequent years, and he lost his ministerial post in 1966. Perhaps in revenge, he turned against de Gaulle during the fateful referendum of 1969, but he quickly supported Pompidou for the presidency and was duly rewarded by being given the Finance Ministry in the government led by Chaban-Delmas.

Giscard d'Estaing's popularity increased—an uncommon achievement for a finance minister. Renowned for his intellectual brilliance (his ability to speak about the state of the economy and to quote figures without notes became proverbial), he also showed distaste for scandals and prosecuted tax dodgers. He disassociated himself, often through his lieutenants, from some of the more nationalistic postures of the regime, and he was careful to build a small party organization—the Independent Republicans—who were associated with, but distinguishable from the Gaullist UDR.

In a somewhat melodramatic fashion, Giscard threw down the gauntlet to the UDR and declared himself a candidate on Monday, 8 April. He gambled on the Center party's not fielding a candidate if he stood, and the gamble paid off: Faure soon withdrew from the race, showing that his candidacy was perhaps tactical. The battle on the Right and Center was therefore to be confined almost entirely to Giscard d'Estaing and Chaban-Delmas, although the situation seemed more complicated for a while when the minister of posts and telecommunications, Jean Royer, decided to run. Royer was well known for his moralistic stands, and popular in the city of Tours, on the Loire, of which he had been mayor. But after an initial impact, Royer proved unable to mobilize real support among his natural followers, the shopkeepers, who had voted for Poujade in the 1950s.[7]

On nomination day, after a period in which it was suggested that up to thirty or forty candidates might stand, twelve persons (eleven men and one woman) stood officially. The three main candidates were Jacques Chaban-Delmas (UDR), François Mitterrand (Socialist, with Communist support), and Valéry Giscard d'Estaing ("independent Gaullist," with Center support). Jean Royer could be classified as "independent conservative," and he had the support of small shopkeepers. Emile Muller, an ex-Socialist, expected to gather some Center votes, but only some. There were two candidates of the extreme Left, Alain Krivine, who had stood in 1969 and who might be labelled as a "traditional" extreme-Left candidate of the Trotskyite variety; Arlette Laguiller, who had become known as a radical trade unionist in a recent bank strike, represented a more "modern" form of the extreme Left. The demographer and sociologist René Dumont stood as a supporter of "ecology." The extreme Right was represented by an unknown royalist, Bertrand Renouvin, and a much better known veteran of the French Algeria movement, Jean-Marie Le Pen. The last two candidates were complete unknowns.

---

[7] Pierre Poujade launched an organization for the defense of shopkeepers and artisans (UDCA) in the last years of the Fourth Republic. The candidates of the organization obtained 12 percent of the votes in the 1956 parliamentary election and this result contributed further to the instability of the regime. "Poujadism" disappeared as a force—though not as a word—with the return of de Gaulle to power in 1958.

One, Jean-Claude Sébag, was a "federalist"; the other, Guy Héraud, was an "independent." [8]

The presidential election of 1974 still did not provide the Fifth Republic with a regular nominating process. The selection was ad hoc and accidental. The Left was united by the will power of one man, Mitterrand, not because permanent procedures and arrangements had been established. The Gaullists had found a candidate quickly, but perhaps not wisely. Self-selected candidates with strong personalities still had a field day. The UDR repeated the scenario which had proved successful in 1969, but its candidate lacked general appeal. Giscard, almost alone, basing his candidacy on sheer personal strength and an underlying mood for change, had decided to step in. He did not seem likely to win, though he seemed able to help Mitterrand's victory by dividing the Right and Center vote. Could France be a country in which millions of electors would mobilize behind a candidate without party support? Could this be done in a month? What kind of presidential campaign would emerge from a selection process in which candidates decided personally to stand in hopes of attracting mass appeal?

The First Phase of the Campaign and the Results of the First Ballot

Georges Pompidou died on the evening of 2 April. A week later the three main candidates were already chosen (or had selected themselves) and had begun their campaigns. A last effort by Prime Minister Messmer to avoid the battle between Chaban-Delmas and Giscard d'Estaing was of no avail. Giscard said that he would withdraw if Chaban also withdrew, but Chaban refused to do so. The maverick president of the Radical party, Jean-Jacques Servan-Schreiber, wavered for another week, then decided not to stand. [9] By 10 April, and despite an Easter lull in mid-April, the election campaign had started in earnest. The candidates had less than four weeks to go; the first vote was to be held on 5 May.

---

[8] For the results of the first ballot, see p. 57.

[9] Jean-Jacques Servan-Schreiber, president of the Radical party, had been a supporter of Mendès-France in the 1950s and founder of the successful magazine, *Express*, which he modelled on *Time*. He had acquired a considerable, but very controversial reputation for some of his views (in particular regionalism), but he also attracted considerable attention among the political class. He was to be made minister for reforms by Giscard after the presidential election, only to be dismissed after a few days for having openly attacked the president's decision to carry on with nuclear testing in the Pacific.

Mitterrand's Strategy. The strategies of the three main candidates seemed fairly clear at the outset. Mitterrand seemed certain to win the most votes on the first ballot, since he could count on at least 40 percent of the votes from the combined Socialist and Communist forces, while the split between Giscard and Chaban ensured that neither would obtain more than a third of the votes. The question was not whether Mitterrand would come in first, but how near he would come to the 50 percent required for election. His goal was to collect at least 45 percent on the first ballot, an objective that seemed within reach, given the results of the 1973 election. But the first opinion polls gave him little encouragement. They showed Mitterrand drawing only about 40 percent of the electorate.

Mitterrand had, therefore, to attract a fraction of the uncommitted voters. To do this, he had to surmount three hurdles. First, the alliance between Communists and Socialists was a subject of worry for uncommitted voters. There was concern because of the inevitable presence of Communists in the government in the event of a victory of the Left. Mitterrand stressed that he, as president, would be the man in charge. While the Left had typically attacked the constitution of the Fifth Republic on principle, and had attacked even more de Gaulle's "presidential" interpretation of that constitution, Mitterrand's strength depended, paradoxically, on presidential strength. He said that *he* would choose the government. He stated that the prime minister would not be a Communist, and implied that Communists would not be appointed to the sensitive posts of defense, interior, and foreign affairs.[10] The tactic was therefore to enhance Mitterrand's personal role in a Left-based executive.

Second, there was the problem of the majority in Parliament. The National Assembly had a Gaullist-centrist majority. How could a leftist-inclined government, appointed by the president, survive in the Chamber of Deputies? Would Mitterrand's election not entail a dissolution and thus a further two months of electioneering during which economic troubles would become more pressing? On this point Mitterrand remained vague. He was clearly counting on the various technical tricks of the constitution (though these tricks, too, had been attacked by the Left). For instance, a government can survive as long as an *absolute* (not a relative) majority does not pronounce against it.[11] Faced with a popularly elected president, the Assembly might not openly challenge the president's right to choose

---

[10] On 17 April.

[11] Article 49 of the constitution states that a motion of censure is only deemed to be passed if an *absolute* majority of the deputies cast their votes for such a motion. The government does not have to resign unless such a motion is passed.

the government as long as controversial legislation was not being introduced.

But this raised Mitterrand's third problem. The Communist-Socialist alliance was based on a "common program of the Left," which had been adopted for the parliamentary election of 1973. Though a compromise between the two left-wing parties, and not as radical as Communists would have wanted, it was far-reaching enough to frighten uncommitted voters. Efforts had been made to patch up differences between Communists and Socialists where they were truly irreconcilable, particularly in the field of foreign affairs. The Socialist party had always been pro-European, pro-Atlantic, and a defender of individual liberties. The Communist party was traditionally anti-European, pro-Russian, and authoritarian. Mitterrand had to try to allay the fears of the non-Communist electorate. He emphasized his strong commitment to individual liberties and to Europe, and he stressed that France would remain associated with the West in the same loose way it had under de Gaulle and Pompidou.

Mitterrand's main problem was, perhaps, the many nationalizations in banking, aviation, and the technological fields called for in the common program of the Left. Though the program specified the scope of nationalization in a carefully hedged about fashion, the plan was an electoral handicap, and its implementation seemed fraught with the prospect of long political upheavals, which would complicate what was already a difficult situation. Without a majority in the Chamber, a Left-based government would find it hard to succeed.

Thus Mitterrand had to counterattack. He did so in two ways: He emphasized the need for a "better deal" for the underprivileged, especially for the workers who had created the extra wealth during the previous decade. He stressed that freedom was not just political, but also entailed being relieved of the boredom and dirt of factory life, which was often coupled with a small income.[12] He also tried to reassure the uncommitted by claiming financial orthodoxy: the budget would be balanced, taxes would meet extra expenditures, the franc would return to the European "snake," and its value would be maintained.[13] He claimed that he was proposing less extra expenditure than his main opponents and that he, not Chaban or Giscard, was the real defender of the public purse.

Mitterrand was clever, though some serious problems did remain in the dark. He was pungent and active, and was greeted with

---

[12] In particular in a dialogue with Giscard d'Estaing on 26 April.
[13] On 19 April, in particular.

enthusiasm by large crowds in the various parts of France. He was banking on a general desire for change, and he had, seemingly, a long head start.

The Plight of Chaban-Delmas and the Rise of Giscard d'Estaing.

The tasks of Chaban-Delmas and of Giscard d'Estaing were more difficult. At first, Chaban tried to model his campaign on that of Pompidou. He was the official candidate of the UDR. He could assume—and could act as if he assumed—that he was the only candidate with a real chance to beat Mitterrand on the second ballot. Yet there was a "mood for change" in the electorate, which forced Chaban-Delmas to defend the accomplishments of the government during the previous fifteen years—while suggesting that he also wanted change. He could and did stress that as prime minister (between 1969 and 1972) he had promoted a "new society." And it was true that his "contracts of progress," by which trade unions and employers negotiated agreements to enable workers to benefit fully from economic growth, had indeed been a significant step in the direction of change.

But this path was narrow, and Giscard d'Estaing could more credibly claim that he, not Chaban, was likely to bring about change. He was not a member of the Gaullist party. He had been associated with government policy in the previous five years, but as a supporter of Pompidou rather than of the UDR. He could therefore assert that he would bring about change in fields ranging from ecology to pensions and social security, and from foreign affairs and defense to radio and television.[14] He was the youngest of the three candidates—by more than a decade—and he stressed that, if elected, he would indeed be the youngest president of France for generations. He could help to create a new majority of the Center—that very majority which Poher had failed to create in 1969 in his contest with Pompidou.[15] He was preoccupied with the future, not with the past, and the future was to be a society based on economic development and financial stability, and with more social equality and fewer scandals (various innuendoes were made by Giscard supporters all through the campaign).

Yet the path was narrow for Giscard as well as for Chaban. Giscard's electoral credibility seemed somewhat in doubt at the beginning of the campaign. Early opinion polls indicated that Chaban

---

[14] On 23 April.

[15] This was one of his main themes when he declared himself a candidate on 8 April.

was better placed to beat Mitterrand on the second ballot; Giscard's candidacy might not benefit Giscard at all. It might merely hurt Chaban by helping Mitterrand. If this view proved correct, Giscard would lose all his cards, and might disappear for a long time from the political map.

Two events helped Giscard. First, contrary to expectations, opinion polls swung in his favor, at first very slowly, then increasingly fast.[16] Perhaps he can be said to have won already on 9 April when an opinion poll gave him a margin of one percentage point over Chaban (27 percent to 26 percent). For the first time in French politics, opinion polls made, rather than recorded, history, as, for the "political class" at least, reading the opinion polls became both a daily pastime and a basis for future action.

The 9 April poll seems to have triggered the second event. A sizeable group of UDR deputies, led by Jacques Chirac (who was to become Giscard's first prime minister, and who held at the time the key position of minister of the interior) came out openly against Chaban and in favor of Giscard.[17] The role of the "group of 43," as Chirac's group came to be known, seems to have been decisive; it demoralized somewhat the Chaban-Delmas camp by dividing the UDR.

The last two weeks of the campaign saw the steady rise of Giscard d'Estaing. While Mitterrand's rating in the opinion polls moved very slowly upwards but remained below 45 percent, Chaban-Delmas's support declined from a quarter of the respondents to less than a fifth. Giscard's campaign was stressing dynamism, youth, and the emergence of a great new majority. (Much money was spent to drive the candidate across France and to show his youthful image, and much energy was spent by numbers of teenagers, led by Giscard's own children, with the slogan *Giscard à la barre*—"Giscard to the helm"—printed on their tee shirts, riding bicycles in a climate of joyful comradeship.) Chaban was meanwhile forced to retreat to the position of "middle of the road candidate," as if he had become the candidate of the Center warning the French of the dangers coming from the Right and the Left.[18] Chaban claimed to be more progressive than the "conservative" Giscard, reversing their roles. Chaban be-

---

[16] Opinion polls recorded between 25 percent and 27 percent for Giscard up to 25 April and 30 percent or more afterwards. The support recorded for Chaban was about 25 percent up to 16 April, and it fell gradually to 20 percent by 20 April, and to 17 percent by 26 April.

[17] On 15 April.

[18] In particular on 27 April.

came the Lecanuet of the 1974 campaign while Giscard had become its Pompidou, if not its de Gaulle.

The Result of the First Ballot. There was little surprise on the evening of 5 May when, a few minutes after the polls closed, radio and television computer predictions announced that Mitterrand was first, Giscard second, and Chaban third—and therefore eliminated from the second ballot and the presidency. But if the placing of the top three was no longer a surprise (though it would have been a great surprise only four weeks earlier), the percentages did produce some shock. Giscard had done better than expected, while Mitterrand and Chaban (as well as Royer) proved to have done somewhat worse.[19] Giscard had almost a third of the votes. He had been credited with only 30 percent at an opinion poll published two days earlier. Chaban had less than 15 percent of the votes (as against slightly more in the latest opinion poll), a far cry from the 26 percent of four weeks earlier and of the 40 to 45 percent of the two previous UDR presidential candidates, de Gaulle and Pompidou. Giscard had taken the Center vote, and he had taken also the majority of the traditional Gaullist vote. Only in the Southwest, near Bordeaux (of which he is mayor), did Chaban-Delmas do reasonably well, but even there he won only a little more than a third of the votes. In every other region Giscard was the clear winner of second place. A page had been turned: Gaullism was dead; a new Right was in the making.

The outlook for Mitterrand was reasonable but not really good. He had obtained 43.4 percent of the votes, less than the Left had won in the 1973 parliamentary elections. He was short of the 45 percent target which seemed necessary if the Left was to win. Yet the reason for this minor setback was uncertain. One of the two candidates of the extreme Left had received 2 percent of the votes, which was a much better showing than had been expected, and the candidate who had campaigned for "ecology" had obtained over 1 percent of the

---

[19] The results of the first ballot were (including overseas territories):

Mitterrand (Socialist)	43.4%
Giscard d'Estaing (independent conservative and Center)	32.8
Chaban-Delmas (UDR)	14.8
Royer (independent conservative)	3.2
Laguiller (extreme Left)	2.3
Dumont ("ecologist")	1.3
Le Pen (extreme Right)	0.7
Muller (independent Center)	0.7
Krivine (extreme Left)	0.4
Three others	0.4

votes, more than had been forecast. Including these votes, Mitterrand could count on about 47 percent of the electorate on the second ballot. But this was not enough. He seemed to have missed everywhere votes which had almost been forthcoming in 1973. The second ballot would be an uphill fight. Though it would be difficult for Giscard to rally around his name nearly all of the Chaban and Royer voters, theoretically he could draw on a potential 53 percent of the votes. Would the new man of the Center succeed in mobilizing this potential? Had he become truly credible, not just as a candidate, but as a president?

The Final Phase of the Campaign and the Result

Mitterrand, Giscard, and the Question of UDR Support. On the evening of 5 May, and for the following two weeks, Mitterrand and Giscard d'Estaing were at last face to face, unemcumbered by splinter candidates and the important figure of Chaban-Delmas. Mitterrand still had many advantages. First, he had come out on top of the first ballot. This had never before happened to a candidate of the Left, and it gave Mitterrand a definite edge. One can always expect a first round winner in any contest to win extra votes in the second round simply because he *seems* to be a winner. Indeed, this was what had been predicted on the assumption that Mitterrand obtained 45 percent of the votes on the first ballot.

Even with only 43.4 percent of the votes, Mitterrand still seemed in a good position to win, because the behavior of the electors of Chaban-Delmas remained uncertain. Many were likely to feel bitter because their candidate had been eliminated. The blame would obviously be put on Giscard and his supporters. Indeed, Chaban-Delmas's first declaration when he conceded defeat on the evening of the poll seemed to help Mitterrand: Chaban would not help the candidate of the Left, but he refrained from positively stating that he would support Giscard d'Estaing. Would he abstain, and might he also ask his supporters to abstain?

The personal fate of Chaban-Delmas was not the only matter at stake. The fate of the whole UDR, of the Gaullist movement, and of the governing groups of the previous fifteen years hung in the balance. The UDR appeared broken. Would it not be better healed by allowing the victory of a natural opponent—Mitterrand—rather than that of a near ally, of a minister whose ambitions had wrecked the basis of the Fifth Republic? Perhaps the party would benefit from some serious opposition and become once more the pole of attraction for an electorate disillusioned by its experience with the Left.

The UDR had therefore a reason to recommend abstention on the second ballot. Yet there were also risks. If it were followed by only a fraction of its electorate, would not the UDR appear even more of a rump? If Mitterrand were then elected and quickly introduced controversial policies, would the UDR recover from the odium which it would have attracted. Given pressures within the party, pressures stemming from the forty-three deputies who had pressed for Giscard all along and who were gathering support, given the fact that the party associated for so long with the government could still hope to retain its preeminence in a Giscard regime, and given the serious dangers of the common program of the Left, the UDR did decide, without real opposition and almost immediately, to support Giscard openly on the second ballot.

Giscard's Serious Hurdles. Yet this boost did not solve Giscard's problems. Though the leaders of the UDR might openly and officially favor Giscard, Mitterrand might still benefit from much latent discontent. Giscard needed an extra 17 percent of the votes, and only 20 percent were available. If Mitterrand could convince a fifth of these electors to vote for him, or a third to abstain, or some combination of both, he would win the election.

This seemed possible, even likely. The supporters of Chaban had positive reasons for not supporting Giscard. Would he really bring about change? At least Chaban-Delmas, as prime minister, had proposed a "new society." Giscard's conversion to change seemed very recent. He appeared to be *"grand bourgeois,"* a member of the upper middle class, a true conservative, and a spokesman for the employers (polls showed that managers supported Giscard more than Chaban-Delmas). Gaullism always had a popular, almost populist, appeal. It had proclaimed the need for cooperation between capital and labor; it had nationalized a number of basic industries in 1945; and in 1958 de Gaulle had drawn away from the Communist party about 5 percent of the electorate who might be expected to be Gaullists, but not conservatives.[20]

Mitterrand's "Gaullist Strategy." Mitterrand and his supporters made the most of the Gaullist line, claiming that real Gaullists, at least progressive Gaullists, should support the candidate of the Left

[20] From 1946 to 1956 the Communist vote declined slightly from 28 percent to 26 percent. In the 1958 election, it fell to 20 percent and has remained approximately at this level ever since.

and not the mouthpiece of management. Some fringe Gaullist elements even came out openly in Mitterrand's favor, while leader after
leader of the Left coalition—including Communists—praised the
"popular" virtues of the Gaullist heritage while stressing the rightness
of the "nationalistic line" which had often brought Communists into
sympathy with the attitudes of the Fifth Republic's founder.[21] The
Left seemed to be in a position to beat Giscard d'Estaing because it
was confronting a true man of the Right. They might mobilize in
their favor a fraction of the "populist" Gaullists, and thus win the
crucial 3 or 4 percent needed for victory.

Giscard's Trump Cards. Giscard's position was difficult. He had to
win on two counts. First he had to convince enough electors that
he would bring about *real* change, not just gimmicks. He had to
present a credible program, not merely in terms of financial arithmetic (a field on which he was bound to win with uncommitted electors,
always suspicious of the "spending sprees" of left-wing governments),
but in terms of a real attack on social problems. He had to say and
convince voters that he, too, would raise the minimum wage, that he,
too, would increase pensions, and that he, too, was concerned with
full employment and the quality of life. To make this convincing, he
presented himself as a young man not completely tied to the errors of
the past and unencumbered by the internecine battles of the various
parties. He would be able to act quickly and decisively for social
justice.

On this score, he seemed to gradually win support throughout
the campaign, especially between the first and second ballots. Surprisingly enough, the impression that he was a *grand bourgeois*
representing management lessened markedly as the days went by.
Mitterrand and the Left made the point, but the attack became less
convincing. The "populist" campaign that Giscard ran succeeded.
He did come across as the candidate of the young, although the
young voted more for Mitterrand than they did for Giscard.[22] Giscard
succeeded in presenting Mitterrand as a prisoner of the past, while
he was the man of the future. He was not fighting the battles of the

---

[21] The secretary-general of the Communist party, Georges Marchais, did appeal
to Gaullists as early as 8 May.

[22] Lowering the voting age to eighteen had not been implemented, though it
had been promised, under Pompidou. Opinion polls had suggested that the age
groups below twenty-one split roughly 5 to 4 in favor of Mitterrand, and many
argued later that the Socialist candidate could have been elected if the voting
age had been lowered. Under Giscard's initiation, however, the reform was
passed by Parliament before the summer recess, less than two months after the
presidential election.

1930s and 1940s; he was concerned with the 1980s and 1990s. His case for social justice did not rest on what had happened to workers in an earlier phase of capitalism. It rested on the need for more equality in the "post-industrial" society of tomorrow. Thus he could truly claim that he would be the "President of all the French." [23]

In order to convince the necessary fraction of the electorate, however, Giscard needed also to win on a second count. He needed to convince electors that he, more than Mitterrand, was of presidential calibre. Mitterrand had come a long way in the previous ten years. Originally a relatively unknown politician with an honorable, but somewhat undistinguished, record as a Fourth Republic minister, he had earned a reputation for his hostility to de Gaulle since 1958. He had been selected to run in 1965 in order to be a "victim" and because the leaders of the Left could not agree on anyone more prominent. He had become a skillful manipulator in the early 1970s, and had reconstructed the Socialist party and given it new energy. But he was not known to be particularly expert in economics nor truly well versed in the management of a modern society. He was always viewed as, first and foremost, a politician, not perhaps a politician of the old style, but as one who did place more emphasis on eloquence and party maneuvering than on a really popular style.

Giscard could hurt Mitterrand on this point. Giscard might appear too much of a "technocrat," devoid of charismatic popular appeal, but his behavior all through the campaign showed that he had devised a style Kennedy-like in some respects—perhaps more intellectual, but equally strong and self-assured—which proved to be more effective than Mitterrand's more traditional leftist discourse. Somehow, Mitterrand appeared older, while Giscard seemed more brilliant, more modern, and more in touch with the real problems of society. When opinion polls asked samples of electors about the qualities of the two leaders, Giscard emerged as more "intelligent" and more "relevant," although Mitterrand might be more "concerned." [24] It is arguable that the French are more sensitive to sheer brilliance and intellectual superiority than any other nation. However that may be, Giscard did seem to profit from his intellectual style, while the *bonhomie* which Mitterrand displayed worked against him.

But if Giscard was to prove both his intellectual superiority and his genuine concern for change, he needed time and the means to

[23] Giscard's "official" election slogan.

[24] These images were reflected in particular by the opinion poll that took place after the radio and television confrontation between the two candidates on 10 May.

present his image. He was helped in this by two factors: the constitutional provision that two weeks had to elapse between the two ballots, and the mass media, television in particular. The gap between the two ballots gave time for the wounds of the Gaullist voters to heal. As the days went by, the first ballot receded into the past, and Chaban-Delmas was forgotten. The delay was long enough for the first ballot to evolve into a "primary," rather than the first ballot of the same election.

Meanwhile, the personal confrontations organized by the radio and television stations helped the candidates to be better known, but they also showed Giscard's great debating qualities. The most crucial confrontation of all was the "face-to-face" television debate which took place on 10 May. It was presented by the mass media as the climax of the campaign, and was followed by a very large proportion of the electorate. During an hour and a half, the two candidates talked to each other (and not, as in the Kennedy-Nixon debates, to journalists asking questions in turn to the two men). All aspects of governmental policy were discussed. Unquestionably, Giscard won, though the electoral effect of this face-to-face is still unknown. Political correspondents and a voter sample surveyed immediately after the program confirmed the impression that Giscard was the winner, and it is at least arguable that enough electors may have been converted to give him a majority.[25]

The Very Close Result. Still, until 19 May the result seemed uncertain. Opinion polls occasionally recorded a tiny majority for Giscard, but more commonly reported a fifty-fifty split. Thus voters went to the polls in what seemed the most open election of French modern history. From the very early morning, however, one indication seemed to point to a Giscard victory: the turnout was proving to be the highest of the postwar period. If the poll was heavy, Mitterrand could not count on Gaullist passive discontent, and somehow electors were going to the polls out of fear of a leftist experiment. Yet, in the evening, after the polls closed, the computers were unable to make a firm prediction for a few tantalizing minutes, and when they did declare that Giscard was winning, it was only by a little over 1 percent of the votes.[26]

---

[25] The poll was conducted on the basis of telephone interviews, and its scientific validity was held to be somewhat questionable.

[26] The result of the second ballot for metropolitan France was: Giscard d'Estaing 50.7 percent, Mitterrand 49.3 percent. There was a gap of 350,000 votes between the two candidates in a turnout of 87.9 percent of the electors.

Giscard had achieved the impossible. He had collected an over-whelming majority of the Chaban and Royer supporters, though a small fraction did vote for Mitterrand, while some abstained. Giscard had made gains in a new electorate—3 percent more of the electors voted than on the first ballot, for a record of 88 percent turnout—while Mitterrand had remained unable to capture all the Left votes on which he had counted. In a dramatic upset, Giscard d'Estaing, by sheer will power and intellectual skill, had broken the UDR without letting the candidate of the Left take the presidency. For the first time in French politics a leader had been elected by basing his whole strategy on popular appeal. A new era of French political life seemed to have begun. What style, structures, and institutions would come to mark this era?

The 1974 Presidential Election and the Future of French Politics

The Popularity of the Election. Because of the almost unpredictable character of the result, the French presidential election of 1974 poses a number of questions alongside those which it solves. On the credit side, the result demonstrated the importance of the popular election of the president, while probably giving a new lease on life to a seemingly ailing regime. In proposing the election of the president by universal suffrage in 1962, de Gaulle made a gamble. He had gambled that the election would be a truly national occasion which would attract the interest of the electorate. The bulk of traditional politicians opposed the idea at the time, partly because they genuinely feared that some new Bonaparte (de Gaulle himself?) would seize the opportunity to give the country a plebiscitary system and impose a dictatorship, and partly because they regretted the loss of power at the parliamentary level. It was precisely in order to end political manipulation that de Gaulle wanted the reform. The Fourth Republic was too distant from the people, it was a house, as Leites and Melnik said, "without windows." [27] But the move would only succeed if men could be found who would make the campaign a serious debate. The country did not need a new Bonaparte, it needed the Roosevelts or Kennedys who would appeal to the electorate. If the campaigns were lifeless, the old procedure might be reintroduced. Yet the conditions of the 1965 and even 1969 elections had been exceptional, not precedents from which to forecast the climate of a future contest.

[27] Nathan Leites and C. Melnik, *The House without Windows* (Evanston, Ill.: 1958).

France was lucky that Giscard d'Estaing was keen to fight the election. The people showed interest in the campaign. They followed radio and television debates because something was going on. They voted to an unprecedented extent, because the result seemed to be on a knife-edge and every vote counted, and counted equally; the man who had most votes would be president. The institution of popular selection of the president was strengthened by the 1974 election, making any future attempt to return to the maneuvers of the parliamentary game more difficult.

Yet the 1974 election remained exceptional. It occurred after the sudden death of the incumbent, and therefore left no room for real preparations. Once more, the election of a French president was a makeshift arrangement. Only when the political leadership—particularly in the parties—come to view the nomination process as one of the main elements of the life of the country will the popular election of the president be truly entrenched. As long as conventions do not select candidates, at least in the main parties, the risk does remain that the presidency is not a full partner in the decision-making process; it might be reduced in strength by the party machines and the parliamentary groups.

The Revitalization of the Regime

Giscard's election also provided solutions to some of the difficulties of the Fifth Republic. During Pompidou's last months the government seemed unable to lead. Observers noted at the time that the British, French, and German executives appeared in disarray. But France's disarray was specifically linked to the role of the president, while being also more than in part tied to the long period of power enjoyed by the UDR. A change was needed. Since the uncertainties and, perhaps, dangers of a leftist coalition—which might bring about another Chile—seemed unacceptable to a majority in 1973, only a change within the majority could overcome some of the problematic and possibly lethal aspects of the Fifth Republic.

Because Giscard's was a personal victory, because it was based on personal appeal without being tainted by the exaggerations of radical populism, the new president has been able to give a new style to the presidency and to form a government which is basically different, in ministers and in approach, from that of the Gaullist-led administrations which preceded it. The prime minister, Jacques Chirac, comes from the UDR, though from the faction of the UDR that supported Giscard from the start. But UDR ministers are in a minority, while members of the Center parties, Lecanuet in particular, give the government a more liberal air, and "technocrats," especially in the Foreign Affairs and Finance ministries, vouch for expertise. In his first few weeks, Giscard introduced or proposed reforms in etiquette at the Elysée Palace, parliamentary procedure, telephone tapping, police records, mass media, and voting age, which brought a breath of fresh air to a country whose leaders have always seemed to fear freedom. In foreign affairs there is better understanding of the need for good relations and compromise. In economic matters, more stress is placed on stability than on grandiose programs. In social matters, a genuine effort is being made to equalize taxes and help the lower-paid. Giscard's government truly has a new style. If the French did want change, they have not been betrayed, as it is not the same men with the same ideas who are in power, though broadly the same "majority" supports the government.

Structural Problems: The Need for a Large "Conservative" Party.
Yet this election poses major structural questions for the long-term future of the Fifth Republic. Of course, politics is the art of the possible, and politicians can only be expected to solve the problems of today. But the election of an outsider, however brilliant, raises the question of the future of institutions which seem to rely permanently on brilliance for their very existence. By successively knocking the UDR and the Left out of action Giscard created two problems. First, he raised long-term questions about the Gaullist party and the party structures which would hold together the Right and Center of the electorate. Up until the Fifth Republic, one of the major French political problems had been the absence of solid party structures on the Right and Center. From 1946 to 1958, every election saw the rise and fall of a party of the Right, first Christian, then Gaullist, then "Poujadist," and then Gaullist once more. This volatile Right was also divided in numerous factions which often were no more than cliques of deputies clustered around a chieftain. For the first time in French history a large right-wing party—the UDR—emerged in 1962, with many varying strands, but flexible and yet solid enough to remain united and to gather the votes of two-fifths or more of the electorate. If Giscard has inflicted a mortal wound on that party, if the UDR is to become a rump, and if it is not quickly replaced by a new conservative party, incorporating the men who have formed, for over a decade, the fabric of the Right, politics on the Right and Center may become marred once more by infighting and manipulation. Soon after Giscard's election, the closest adviser of the president and min-

ister of the interior in the new government, Michel Poniatowski, stated that he was looking for a new large party which would group together all the forces which were not of the Left. This has to be done, for chaos on the Right and Center might undo very quickly the political streamlining and clarification that has been one of the main benefits of the Fifth Republic.

The Problem of the Unity of the Left. If the Right and Center were to break up again, divisions would quickly reemerge on the Left, where attempts at unity still only paper over the cracks between two generations. The French Left has not really adjusted to modern society, as Giscard pointed out while attacking Mitterrand for being mainly concerned with problems of the past. But the Socialists cannot adjust to reality as long as the Communists are a major force, since the competition between the two is always present. Only through the powers of the presidency can the Communist party be forced to recognize that it has no future unless it accepts the leadership of the Socialist party. Yet divisions are so deep that only with great skill can the uneasy alliance be expected to survive. Mitterrand had this skill, but after his defeat and because of his age (sixty) he may not be a candidate in the next presidential election, and the search for a new leader of the Left will raise major problems.

Had Mitterrand been elected, a spate of other problems might have been solved. The Left has been opposed to the basic framework of the Fifth Republic from the start. The Left's traditions of parliamentary government and its dislike for a strong executive lead it in the direction of the governmental system of the Fourth Republic. But if Mitterrand had had to use the presidential powers, both to force Communist ministers to toe the line and to retain control of a restive assembly, a process would have begun by which the French Left would have been reconciled to the necessity of strong executive leadership. But this did not happen. More time in opposition is unlikely to encourage a more moderate approach to the "common program" of the Left, while it might exacerbate their opposition to the constitution and their latent desires for direct action.

The Need for Social Reforms. In the last analysis, however, much will depend on the ability of the new president to solve and be seen to solve the major social and economic problems that the country faces. Giscard needs to build a strong, cohesive party on the Right, unless the UDR is to be allowed to constitute, in a slightly modified form, the backbone of the new Right. Mitterrand needs to be able to push his party further in the direction of responsible government, both by increasing the numerical strength of Socialists in relation to Communists and by convincing Communists, once and for all, that they have no hope of governing unless in a secondary, perhaps minor role. But this will not happen unless the new president can convince electors that change has taken place, that Giscard and Giscard's men are worthy of support, and that revolution—or even radical reform— is not a solution, even in desperation. France needs more than minor adjustments to the income tax system, social security, and the minimum wage. Structural reforms are overdue and need implementing.

These reforms center around questions of hierarchy and inequality, which France has been less able to solve than other Western nations in the almost two centuries since the revolution. The legacy of the Napoleonic state has been coupled with perpetual anxiety which derives from the fact that no French government since the *Ancien Régime* has seemed strong enough to fully accept the tenets of liberalism and democracy. The result has been an almost unparalleled control of local authorities by the administration, an almost equally unparalleled tutelage of universities and schools by the education ministry, and the constant fear that without prodding, firms would not expand or improve their machinery and techniques—in short, enlightened despotism rather than liberalism. It is counterbalanced by the "anarchism," that is, irresponsibility, of nearly all businessmen and farmers, who count on the state to rescue them, of mayors and local councilors, who ask for subsidies or hide behind "prefectoral edicts," of trade unions more anxious to make demands than seriously discuss improvements, and of students and left-wing intellectuals waiting for miraculous changes rather than working patiently towards reforms. From this situation, too, arises the widespread belief that, in the meantime, one should see to one's own salvation, escape taxes, and get as much as one can. Short-term social Darwinism comes to be combined with the dream of a cooperative commonwealth, whose realization is pushed off even further into the future by the attitudes and behavior of all.

It is because Giscard d'Estaing, more than any other figure, has the political power to bring about some degree of change that his election might, indeed, constitute a real watershed, not just in French politics, but in French society. In their different ways, the Fourth and Fifth republics have made the change possible, brought it within reach. Economic growth made the country richer. Attitudes have drastically altered. All during the Fifth Republic, new attitudes to society have emerged. Pressure groups have grown; regionalism has developed; educational reform has come to seem a necessity. Thus the country is ripe for reforms, and it can afford them. Under the Gaullist leadership, however, there were too many "hangovers" from the past, one being the passionate desire to ensure the "greatness of France," a point which might have been meaningful after the defeats of the Fourth Republic but which makes little or no sense now that France has become the fourth industrial power and third trading nation of the non-Communist world, with prospects for growth second only to those of Japan among industrial nations. Under leftist-inclined leadership, too many battles rooted in the past would have to be fought. Too much time and effort would be devoted to debates over ideology, nationalization, and the myth of the working class— at a time when unskilled industrial workers are decreasing as a percentage of the work force and the differences between workers and nonworkers are becoming much less apparent. The problems of the day concern money, to be sure, but also the quality of life, the role of the provinces, and the value of education. On all these matters Giscard, and Giscard alone among those who ran for the presidency in 1974, can be expected to act, unencumbered by myths or friends, on the basis of his sheer personal prestige and popular appeal. Furthermore, he is young enough to see that life in the 1990s will be for him as well as his children. Here lies the opportunity of steering France firmly onto a new course not just for the twentieth century, but for the twenty-first.

Will Giscard do it? This fundamental question has to remain unanswered. Too many leaders have begun in a blaze of personal popularity and enthusiasm in their first "hundred days," only to find themselves entangled in the less lofty problems of the mystifying real world. He has clearly won, not just the election, but the confident support of most of the French, with his early decisions. On the evening of 19 May, the trade unions seemed bitter and there was much speculation about the troubles that the government would face. Partly because it was too late in the spring, partly because common sense did prevail, but partly also because Giscard's first decisions, the structure of the new government, and even the "austerity" program seemed to be the elements of a "new deal," the social climate remained good, and the nation—the whole nation— appeared ready to wait for and expect new and hopeful developments from their president. To a very large extent, the keys of the future are in the hands of the gods (or sheikhs). If world prices continue to fall, if inflation is reduced, if the overseas balance really starts to improve, then relative tension might decrease sufficiently to give

Giscard a breathing space for the basic reforms that are clearly required. If the situation is less rosy, even if short of catastrophe, and international economic problems become more pressing, the opportunity for change may disappear. Serious difficulties on the Right and on the Left may once more pollute the political ambience. Giscard needs luck if he is to bring about the change which he convinced a majority of the French he would bring about. But luck is a commodity which he has had in abundance in his brilliant career.

3
THE END OF GAULLISM?

Jean Charlot

We must be wary of the "laissez-faire" enthusiasts who tend to advocate, in fact, "laissez everything." They play the role of the dashing officers in our passive, egotistical society. In the name of liberalism and modernism, they solve society's problems without taking into account the hardships their solutions impose on the individual.[1]

Excessive elegance, would-be liberalism, ignorance of the hardships of life in today's world, passivity going hand-in-hand with a desire to let things rip—all these charges were aimed at Valéry Giscard d'Estaing during the 1974 presidential election campaign, twelve days before the first ballot. His rival completed the portrait in a television broadcast viewed by millions of electors: "Mr. Giscard d'Estaing is quite simply in the process of resuscitating the Right . . . the eternal Right, harsh to the weak. General de Gaulle had absorbed this Right, or perhaps we should say he had neutralized it."[2]

All French politicians seek to avoid association with the Right at all costs, for in France the Right is synonymous with reactionary policies, with immobilism, inequality, and social injustice. This attack would, therefore, be dangerous for Giscard if the public believed the insinuations. Giscard's rival had planned his attack with care, ridiculing the pullover sweater that the brilliant young finance minister wore in public (in order to appear on the same level as the people he was addressing) and scornfully dismissing Giscard's desire to ride the Paris subway or play the accordion in a local festival in Auvergne. The attack on Valéry Giscard d'Estaing's political views was even

---

[1] Jacques Chaban-Delmas, speech, Nancy, Wednesday, 24 April, as quoted in *Le Monde*, 26 April 1974.

[2] Jacques Chaban-Delmas, interviewed by Georges Suffert on television, Friday, 26 April 1974.

more pointed when it came to foreign affairs: ". . . after his pact with Mr. Lecanuet he now declares himself in favor of the policies carried out by Mr. Jobert. I wonder on which occasion he is misleading himself . . . or us." [3]

There is of course nothing unusual in competing political candidates hitting below the belt during an election campaign. But the violence of this attack is the more striking when one learns that it was launched not by François Mitterrand, the candidate of the Left, but by Jacques Chaban-Delmas, the Gaullist candidate, a member of the same majority coalition as Valéry Giscard d'Estaing. Chaban was prime minister under Georges Pompidou from 1969 to 1972, and his finance minister during those three years was Valéry Giscard d'Estaing.

At the beginning of the campaign Chaban had declared that he was determined—just as was Giscard—to attack only François Mitterrand and his Socialist-Communist coalition. "I do not intend to attack Mr. Giscard d'Estaing," he announced over the air on 11 April.[4] And on the following day he wisely remarked, "One must not pick the wrong enemy." [5]

On the whole, he did follow the strategy he had planned, as long as the opinion polls remained favorable to him—or rather as long as they remained not too unfavorable—in other words, roughly until 22 April. Once his percentage in the opinion polls dropped, Chaban tried—in vain, for it was too late—to adapt his strategy, to change his image, while Giscard d'Estaing, with the wind behind him, glided forward, keeping to his original course of nonaggression towards his principal rival within the majority.

The Collapse of Chaban

As the campaign opened, Chaban had the tranquil assurance of a winner. Indeed, he had no reason to lack confidence. On 9 April, before the list of candidates for nomination was closed but after the official announcements of Mitterrand and Giscard, the French Insti-

---

[3] Jacques Chaban-Delmas, speech, Lyons, Monday, 22 April, as quoted in Le Monde, 24 April 1974. Jean Lecanuet, president of the Centre Démocrate, former president of the Mouvement Républicain Populaire (Christian democrats), centrist candidate against General de Gaulle in the 1965 presidential election, is seen as a pro-European, pro-Atlantic centrist, in opposition to Michel Jobert, the late Georges Pompidou's minister of foreign affairs.

[4] Jacques Chaban-Delmas, interview on radio France-Inter, Thursday, 11 April 1974.

[5] Jacques Chaban-Delmas on Radio-Télé Luxembourg (RTL), Friday, 12 April 1974.

tute of Public Opinion (IFOP) showed the former prime minister five percentage points ahead of his one-time minister of finance—with 28 percent as against 23 percent—should Faure remain a candidate, and two percentage points ahead—29 percent to 27 percent—should Faure withdraw. The SOFRES polling organization, which at this time showed Giscard one percentage point ahead of Chaban, also indicated that 39 percent of the electors thought Chaban would win the first ballot, as against 21 percent who believed Giscard would be the winner, while 30 percent saw Mitterrand winning. The same poll indicated that 71 percent of Chaban's electors believed he would finally become president, as against only 57 percent of Giscard's electors. The withdrawal of Faure, and the candidacy of the outsider Jean Royer, former minister of shopkeepers and artisans and a moralistic partisan of the fight against the permissive society, certainly seemed to be to Chaban's disadvantage rather than Giscard's, for as the campaign opened on 16 April Giscard was two percentage points ahead of his Gaullist rival. But nothing was settled as yet, and Chaban, whom the opinion polls still showed as the better candidate to represent the majority on the second ballot against Mitterrand, remained convinced that the election campaign would be to his advantage and would enable him to draw level with and then decisively beat the minister of finance—especially at a time of galloping inflation.

Chaban. A minister on several occasions, president of the National Assembly for eleven years (1958–1969), prime minister for three years (1969–1972), mayor of Bordeaux, the fifth largest city in France, for the last twenty-seven years, Jacques Chaban-Delmas, as he confided to millions of electors in the first television broadcast of the campaign, was a happy man. He has a wealth of experience behind him, and is still young, physically very fit (he has played rugby for France and is a brilliant tennis player), and full of energy and enthusiasm. However, his campaign consultants advised him not to rush up stairs four at a time nor come running into his meetings with flocks of photographers at his heels. He must, they said, project a more serious, solemn image, the image of a future president of the republic. This advice succeeded only in destroying the image Chaban already had and in making him seem rigid and unnatural—at least until he decided, fairly late in the campaign, to throw the counsel of his advisers to the winds.

Chaban has always been a Gaullist. In 1940 he joined the Resistance in occupied France, was ultimately promoted to the rank of general, and, in 1944 at the age of twenty-nine, was nominated national military delegate for occupied France by General de Gaulle. On 24 August 1944 he joined forces with General Leclerc at Arpajon and entered Paris, which had been liberated by the Resistance, in his company. He has played a part in all the Gaullist movements: *Rassemblement du Peuple Français* (RPF), the first Gaullist party created by de Gaulle in 1947, *Républicains Sociaux* in 1954, when de Gaulle himself had abandoned the Gaullists, and the *Union pour la Nouvelle République* in 1958, when de Gaulle returned to power. Minister of national defense in the last government of the Fourth Republic, he played a part in bringing General de Gaulle back to power. He is one of the Gaullist "barons," along with Michel Debré, Roger Frey, and Olivier Guichard. But he is also, by his political origins and temperament, a Radical-Socialist. It was as a Radical-Socialist from Gironde that he was first elected to Parliament on 10 November 1946. He only left the old Republican Radical and Radical-Socialist parties in 1950 when the party obliged its members to leave other political parties if they wished to remain Radicals. Chaban left the Radicals and remained in the RPF. His career in government began in June 1954, under the Fourth Republic, in Pierre Mendès-France's government. He was minister of public works, transport and tourism. He later belonged to governments more typical of the Fourth Republic—those of the Socialist Guy Mollet and the Radical Félix Gaillard—which earned him criticism from Michel Debré and other orthodox Gaullists, and some disfavor from de Gaulle himself. During the eleven years from 1958 to 1969 de Gaulle gave him no post in his successive governments. "The general was fond of you," Madame de Gaulle told him when de Gaulle died. But if de Gaulle appreciated Chaban's energy and personal loyalty, he reproached him for having a certain unorthodox mixture of ideas and too great a capacity for adaptation. And Chaban is, indeed, at home with radical socialism, with its taste for nuance, for political flexibility, and for improvisation.

From 1969 to 1972, thanks to Georges Pompidou, he was prime minister, and able to exercise his talents to the full. Surrounded by a team composed to a large extent of former partisans of Mendès-France—in particular Simon Nora and Jacques Delors—he outlined at the National Assembly on 16 September 1969 his "new society," which was to free French society from the fragility of its economy, the bureaucracy and inefficiency of its state system, and the conservatism of its social structure. The cornerstones of this new society were increased economic expansion and full employment, a more rapid increase in low salaries than in salaries as a whole, a doubling of the old-age pension, creation of a system of continuous adult education, and a policy of systematic consultation with the unions with a view to concluding "contracts of progress," which would eliminate strikes. The prime minister was soon almost as popular as the president of the republic, who was not over-pleased at this. The team surrounding Chaban, his policies of discussion with the unions and of liberalizing state radio and television, and his lack of diplomacy towards his political friends and allies soon alienated him from the most conservative elements among the Gaullist deputies in the National Assembly. On 5 July 1972, taking advantage of a drop in Chaban's popularity (linked to the attacks on his supposed non-payment of taxes), Georges Pompidou unjustly attributed to him the semi-failure of the April referendum on the entry of Great Britain into the Common Market (36 percent "yes," 17 percent "no," a victory, but with an extraordinarily low turnout) and replaced him as head of the government with Pierre Messmer.

Chaban was certainly not spared personal attacks during this period. The publication of his tax forms by the left-wing satirical paper *Canard Enchaîné* kept an anti-Chaban campaign alive throughout 1972. It was all the stronger because it took place in an atmosphere of political and financial scandal concerning certain backbenchers within the majority. In fact, Chaban was merely benefiting from a provision of the tax law that permits corporate shareholders to deduct from their normal taxes credits that result from over-taxation of their shares.

Chaban's private life was also attacked. Already married twice—divorced once and a widower after the death of his second wife in a car accident—Chaban married for the third time in September 1971. His bride, Micheline, had also been divorced. This was the starting point of a vast campaign of gossip, insinuation, and calumny, which was to last all through the presidential campaign. The faithful right-hand man of Giscard, Michel Poniatowski, did not hesitate to take advantage of this campaign, speaking publicly of the "frailty" of the Gaullist.

When he first stepped into the race for the Elysée, Chaban was full of confidence. But he immediately came up against a lack of enthusiasm—in truth, a poorly disguised hostility—in the ranks of his own party, the UDR.

The UDR Divided. When Pompidou ran for president in April 1969, he immediately received the unreserved support of the Gaullist party, the UDR, that of Giscard d'Estaing and the Independent Republicans, and that of the opposition Center faction that, under Jacques Duhamel, Joseph Fontanet, and René Pleven, had formed a new party, the *Centre Démocratie et Progrès* (CDP). In April 1974 the situation was far less favorable to the Gaullist candidate. Outside the majority he had no support; the *Centre National des Indépendants et Paysans* (CNI) had hesitated and then refused its support. Inside the majority he was opposed by the Independent Republicans. In theory he could count on the UDR on the one hand and the CDP on the other. The CDP's support was immediate and virtually unreserved, at the instigation, in particular, of Jacques Duhamel and of the minister of education, Joseph Fontanet, who supported Chaban's social policies. However, within the UDR Chaban came up against the opposition of Jacques Chirac, the young, impetuous minister of the interior, the hesitation of Prime Minister Messmer, and the fears of those backbenchers whom Chirac had convinced that Chaban had no earthly hope of winning against Giscard and that the only solution was another candidate and the withdrawal of both Chaban and Giscard. It was suggested that this candidate might be Messmer; Gaullism and the majority would thus be saved. Messmer wavered, torn between the belief that it was his duty to run and the fear that his unpopularity—which a long sequence of opinion polls had faithfully recorded—would benefit Mitterrand. The day after Pompidou's death, Chirac almost managed to convince Messmer to run. But Messmer dithered and lost the support of some of the Gaullist ministers who had been ready to stand by him. Then there was a rumor that Chirac's friends—in particular Marie-France Garaud, who was a member of Pompidou's personal team—were pressing Faure to run so that the sheer number of majority candidates would necessitate some form of selection procedure enabling Messmer to come into his own. The most obvious result of all this was to convince Chaban that he must declare his intention of running earlier than he had originally planned. He did so on 4 April, the day Pompidou was buried, in the hope of putting an end to the scheming:

> It would have been . . . natural to wait until, say, the beginning of the following week. . . . That seemed obvious to me. But very quickly, indeed, on the following morning, while I was under the sway of grief and emotion, I realized that the political schemers were already at work. So that on the day after, the day of reflection and prayer . . . the day on which Georges Pompidou was buried, at a time when his tomb had scarcely been sealed, I learned that if I did not act immediately, I ran the risk—not as far as my career is concerned, but as far as the idea that I have of my duty is

concerned, the duty I have to be a candidate in this election—I ran the risk of not being able to fulfill this duty. . . .
I preferred to be thought of as too precipitate rather than
too cowardly.[6]

But Chaban's enemies did not lay down their arms. Giscard saw
Messmer and told him that he would only stand down if the prime
minister were to become the candidate of a united majority. Faure,
who had announced his intention of running, now declared that his
decision would depend on what Chaban and Giscard did. At the
Hotel Matignon the partisans of a Messmer candidacy—Chirac,
Hubert Germain, Jean Taittinger, and Pierre Juillet—and those of
Chaban—Guichard, Debré, a former prime minister, Alexandre
Sanguinetti, general secretary of the UDR, and Claude Labbé, president of the UDR parliamentary party—together with Chaban and
Messmer themselves, were unable to reach any agreement. Chaban's
enemies insisted on his vulnerability because of the personal attacks
that would be launched against him. Messmer's adversaries insisted
on the low level of his popularity throughout the country. On the
evening of Pompidou's funeral everything seemed settled: Chaban
and Giscard would run, and Messmer, while regretting that the majority was not united behind a single candidate, would step down.

On the following evening, 5 April, the UDR executive bureau
unanimously declared itself in favor of supporting Chaban, and on
7 April the Central Committee and the parliamentary groups of the
UDR ratified this decision "by acclamation" in a joint meeting held
in Paris. Chirac expressed his regret that the divisions within the
majority would hamper the struggle against the Socialist-Communist
candidate of the Left. Messmer insisted that it was his duty to try
and prevent a multiplicity of candidacies which might well doom the
majority, but it was clear that his remarks were aimed at dissuading
Faure, who was still a candidate, and Christian Fouchet, who had
declared that he alone defended the political legacy of General
de Gaulle. So with Messmer bringing his support to Chaban, and
Couve de Murville—de Gaulle's last prime minister—urging that if
the unity of the majority could not be preserved, at least that of the
UDR must remain intact, Sanguinetti was confident in the outcome:
"We are what we have been—as everyone knows—for the last
thirty-four years; we shall not falter . . . , we are the most numerous,
the best organized, the strongest."[7]

---

[6] Jacques Chaban-Delmas, interview on RTL, Friday, 12 April 1974.
[7] Alexandre Sanguinetti, press conference after the UDR executive committee
meeting, Sunday, 7 April, as quoted in Le Monde, 9 April 1974.

But two days later it was clear that nothing had been settled after all. Shortly after eleven in the morning, Messmer published a declaration announcing the conditions on which he would run. All he asked was that the other candidates of the majority should stand down. Faure did so immediately, no doubt relieved to find a way of exiting gracefully. Fouchet announced that he would not drop out of the race, and Chaban presented his reply to Messmer in person, in an interview which lasted less than five minutes. He categorically refused to withdraw. The CDP had already reasserted its support of Chaban. Later that same evening, Messmer announced that, since his conditions had not been met, he had decided irrevocably not to run for president. Giscard had not had to intervene. He had simply reminded Messmer, the press, and the public, by the intermediary of a note from his brain-trust, that he had told Messmer from the outset that he would withdraw if Messmer were a candidate. Chaban was thus discreetly accused of being the sole person responsible for the divisions within the majority.

Coming as it did two days after the "unanimous" support of the UDR for Chaban, six days after Chaban's first declaration, and on the day after Giscard's public declaration of candidacy, Messmer's initiative was bound to fail. It could but weaken the majority and, more surely still, the position of the official candidate of the UDR, Chaban-Delmas. A curious sequence of events, as one newspaper noted: "All the stranger, this maneuver, as it has in the end done harm to at least two people: Pierre Messmer himself, who ought to have been more clairvoyant, and Jacques Chaban-Delmas, for no one can go on believing that he has the total approbation of the UDR." [8] Four days later, on 13 April, another blow was aimed at Chaban and the unity of the UDR. On Chirac's initiative, a manifesto was published bearing forty-three signatures, those of four ministers (Chirac, Jean-Philippe Lecat, Olivier Stirn, and Taittinger), thirty-three UDR back-benchers (out of 182), three centrist back-benchers, two Independent Republicans, and one "reformer." Once again drawing the attention of the candidates of the majority to the risks of fragmentation, and giving Messmer credit for having tried to obtain a single candidate, the forty-three declared that they intended to join forces and figure out the best way to ensure the defense of the essential principles of the Fifth Republic and the defeat of the Socialist-

[8] André Guerin, leader in *Aurore*, a right-wing newspaper, 10 April 1974. The press on the whole treated the events with scorn: "ridiculous" (*Liberation*, ultra-Left); "the battle of the clans" (*Parisien libéré*, favorable to the majority); "personal rivalries" (*Combat*, favorable to the Left); "grandeur, a thing of the past" (*Humanité*, Communist).

Communist candidate. Vague, cautious, the text spoke of the Fifth Republic and not of Gaullism, and it recognized the danger from the Left, but did not refer to the risks of conservatism. In fact it left its signatories completely free to designate the candidate they thought would best defend their aims. Chirac was convinced that Giscard would outdistance Chaban, and he wanted to ensure from the outset the reconciliation of the UDR with its victor and the reunification of the majority. Was Chirac clairvoyant or was this merely a political choice? Did the persistence with which the minister of the interior pursued Chaban contribute to the success of Giscard?

Giscard, for his part, had no doubts. He declared on radio France-Inter: "I understand the appeal of the forty-three and I approve of it, even though I played no part in it." [9] Fouchet had no doubts, either, as to the purpose of the forty-three, and accordingly withdrew in favor of Chaban: "faced with betrayals, with half-betrayals, with quarter-betrayals, in the parliamentary lobbies and in the party headquarters, one wonders whether the reeds of the dead will not flower again." [10]

A meeting of the UDR parliamentary party was called on 17 April to reiterate the party's support of Chaban. This showed clearly, if indirectly, that confirmation was necessary. The meeting took place in an atmosphere of doubt and ambiguity, but it did confirm support, which is not surprising considering that the group of forty-three—reduced for the moment to thirty-six active members—had met and decided on a free vote, and that Chirac had emphasized that the forty-three represented a body which would distinguish the UDR from Chaban should Giscard outdistance him.[11]

Thus, well before the official campaign opened after the nomination of candidates on 16 April, the UDR Gaullists had for some ten days publicly displayed their internal divisions. During these ten days Chaban's score in the public opinion polls had fallen from 29 percent to 25 percent, while that of Giscard had remained at a steady 27 percent. Things did not augur well for the Gaullist.

[9] Valéry Giscard d'Estaing, interview on radio France-Inter, Tuesday, 16 April 1974.

[10] Christian Fouchet, statement, Monday, 15 April 1974.

[11] On 21 April, in Metz, while still theoretically a supporter of Chaban-Delmas, the official candidate of the UDR, Pierre Messmer, the prime minister, in fact adopted Jacques Chirac's tactics and his close friend Hubert Germain let it be known that the prime minister would only really commit himself after the first ballot was over. On 24 April the forty-three, at a subsequent meeting, received a dozen new signatories, including three ministers.

Strategy in Question. To understand Chaban's strategy, one must go back to the beginning of the campaign, when Chaban was certain he would win. His analysis of the French political situation led him to separate himself as much as possible, if not from Gaullism —though his references to it are sparse, save in the field of foreign affairs—at least from the UDR. He believed that the image of the UDR was too conservative, too authoritarian, too unpopular for it to be identified with social reform, with the "new society" he wished to create and which he believed corresponded to the expectations of the people, eager for real change and greater justice. He was thus brought to refute both the bureaucratic, authoritarian, even totalitarian social-ism that Mitterrand, through his alliance with the Communists, stood for, and the modern version of capitalism represented by Valéry Giscard d'Estaing. From the practical point of view, this attempt to create a middle way between capitalism and socialism implied the creation of a third force capable of finding an electorate in the Center or slightly to the left of Center—the enduring ambition of French radicals:

> I am convinced that in addressing not only . . . the electors of the presidential majority of yesterday or of tomorrow, but also all Frenchmen, that is all those who up to now have voted for left-wing parties because they were dissatisfied, because they were anxious, because they were unhappy and saw no other way out for themselves. . . . I believe that in addressing myself to all the French people, and in particular to the afore-mentioned, I shall be heard; and that in conse-quence, . . . I should be capable of winning.[12]

Contrary to General de Gaulle, who always saw foreign affairs (that is, the grandeur and independence of France) as the essence of politics, Chaban was interested almost exclusively in domestic policy and social change. While de Gaulle spoke continually in terms of the "sacred union" of all the French people, whatever their views or social identities, for the greater glory of France, Chaban reasoned in terms of Left and Right:

> Mr. Giscard d'Estaing represents a tendency which is gen-erally qualified as liberal, but which, given his alliance with Mr. Lecanuet, is clearly a conservative element. . . . I per-sonally represent a current somewhere between what I call a Communist party that hides its head, and a right-wing that is rearing its head once again.[13]

[12] Jacques Chaban-Delmas, interview on radio France-Inter, Thursday, 11 April 1974.

[13] Jacques Chaban-Delmas, interview on RTL, Friday, 12 April 1974.

Not only were such statements not Gaullist, they were not realistic. Chaban did not have at his disposal an electorate corresponding to his strategy and he had no chance of finding one. By explicitly rejecting the moderate Right and the Center (Jean Lecanuet), by visibly neglecting the UDR electorate in order to fish in the waters of the Left, Chaban left the field free for Giscard, who speedily took advantage of it. The illusion that Chaban could create a great left-of-center movement grew out of an underestimation of the strength of the Socialist party and its candidate, Mitterrand, who, while joining forces with the Communist party, had sufficiently distinguished himself from it for the traditional Socialist electorate not to default. Chaban chose to ignore the bipolarization of contemporary French politics—attested by opinion polls and previous elections—and he was to pay for this error in judgment.[14]

An analysis of Chaban's potential electorate, confirmed by the opinion polls published before Giscard outdistanced him—in other words, prior to 29 April—shows clearly that the electorate he was seeking was not that which was willing to vote for him. When the campaign opened, his electorate included a higher proportion of women than the electorate of the majority ever had under the Fifth Republic, sixty women for every forty men, instead of fifty-seven women for forty-three men in favor of de Gaulle on the eve of the first ballot of the presidential election of 1965, fifty-eight women for forty-two men favorable to the majority in 1967, fifty-four to forty-six in 1968, and fifty-seven to forty-three in 1973. The electorate that favored Chaban and his new society at the outset of the campaign also included proportionally more retired electors than any previous electorate of the majority: thirty out of every hundred, compared to twenty-eight out of every hundred for de Gaulle in 1965, twenty-four in 1967, nineteen in 1968, and twenty-seven in 1973. Contrary to Chaban's hopes, the lower classes were not particularly responsive to his appeal. Twenty-eight out of every hundred electors voting for de Gaulle in 1965 came from working-class families; at the beginning of the 1974 campaign Chaban had only twenty-six electors of working-class origin out of every hundred supporters.[15]

---

[14] See, for example, the study of the general election of 4-11 March 1973 edited by Jean Charlot, *Quand la gauche peut gagner* (Paris: Alain Moreau, 1973), p. 216. Forty-seven percent of the centrist electors voted for the majority on the second ballot in 1967, 60 percent on the second ballot in 1968, and 65 percent on the second ballot in 1970; each time the choice was between majority and non-Communist Left candidates.

[15] Source: IFOP surveys.

It is not surprising that Giscard—more traditional than Chaban and consequently less disquieting for the electorates of the majority and the Center—should have gotten the better of his rivals. On 22 April, six days after the opening of the campaign, Giscard was only three percentage points ahead of the Gaullist. Three days later, four days after the opening of the official television campaign, an IFOP opinion poll published by *Point* showed that Giscard had pulled further ahead of Chaban. The gap between the two candidates had risen from three to thirteen percentage points, 31 percent for Giscard, 18 percent for Chaban. The die was cast; the gap would not lessen before 5 May.

A comparison between Chaban's potential electorate at the beginning and at the end of the campaign confirms this analysis of Chaban's faulty strategy (see Table 3-1). The disenchantment of the voters is particularly noticeable in those social categories traditionally most attached to the majority (rural commune residents, women electors, the retired, and the over sixty-five), in which Chaban had, at the beginning of the campaign, managed to outdistance Giscard. These electors are on the whole more concerned about security than with reform, and in the end were to find themselves better represented by Giscard than by Chaban-Delmas, even though they had consistently voted first for de Gaulle and Pompidou. Within the traditional electorate of the Center, Chaban was clearly outdistanced by his rival from the beginning of the campaign. Only among the over sixty-five was Chaban's handicap slight, and it was precisely among these electors that he was to lose ground toward the end of the campaign. Of those electors who had voted for the majority in 1973 and who preferred Chaban (44 percent) to Giscard (41 percent) at the beginning of the presidential campaign, Chaban lost, in particular, a good number of women and old people and in the end lost his advantage. Of 100 women favorably inclined toward the majority at the outset of the campaign, forty-seven were inclined toward Chaban and forty toward Giscard. By the end of the campaign thirty-five remained supporters of Chaban, and fifty-three voted for Giscard. Among the older voters (sixty-five and over), the percentage of Chaban's supporters fell from fifty-five to forty-two, while Giscard's rose from thirty-seven to forty-six.[16]

Chaban, by presenting himself as the builder of a new society and loosening his links with Gaullism, alienated his strongest supporters without gaining any kind of new support. A poll conducted

[16] Source: IFOP surveys of 16, 18, and 22 April for the beginning of the campaign, 24-25, 29 April, and 3-4 May for the end of the campaign.

Table 3-1

EVOLUTION OF VOTING INTENTIONS IN FAVOR OF GISGARD AND CHABAN, FIRST BALLOT

	Beginning of Campaign[a]		End of Campaign[b]		Difference (percentage points)	
Social Categories	Giscard	Chaban	Giscard	Chaban	Giscard	Chaban
Electorate as a whole	27%	24%	30%	17%	+3	−7
Sex						
Men	25	19	27	15	+2	−4
Women	29	28	33	19	+4	−9
Age						
21-34	24	20	27	14	+3	−6
35-49	28	21	32	15	+4	−6
50-64	29	25	30	19	+1	−6
65 and over	27	32	33	24	+6	−8
Profession of head of household						
Executives, liberal professions	45	21	50	15	+5	−6
Industrial and commercial employers	30	21	35	17	+5	−4
Employees	31	18	35	15	+4	−3
Industrial workers	15	19	17	13	+2	−6
Retired	28	32	33	23	+5	−9
Peasants	34	32	36	25	+2	−7
Residence						
Rural districts	28	31	32	21	+4	−10
Urban districts of less than 20,000	23	25	27	20	+4	−5
20,000 to 100,000	28	22	30	16	+2	−6
over 100,000	30	20	32	16	+2	−4
Paris and district	25	18	29	12	+4	−6
Political preferences, first ballot, 1973						
Communist	3	3	3	3	0	0
Non-Communist Left	8	5	8	5	0	0
Reformers	48	22	54	14	+6	−8
Majority	41	44	51	35	+10	−9

[a] Three surveys, 16, 18, 22 April 1974, IFOP.

[b] Three surveys, 24-25, 29 April, 2-3 May 1974, IFOP.

by SOFRES on 20-22 April 1974, before Giscard widened the gap between himself and Chaban, showed that among the motivations for voting for Chaban, the fact of seeing the candidate as "a real Gaullist" was more decisive than any vision of a new society. Moreover, Chaban's and Giscard's potential electors saw the competence and personality of the candidates as more important than their programs. In this they were fundamentally different from Mitterrand's supporters. The left-wing electorate was by and large firmly attached to Mitterrand; the centrist and right-wing electorate remained fluid, but was not attracted to the Left. Thus the major error a candidate could make was to mistake his target.

A poll conducted for *Figaro* by COFREMCA at the very beginning of the presidential campaign concerning the hopes and fears of the French with regard to the future and the links they established between the candidates and their expectations enables us to study even more closely the reasons why Chaban failed (Table 3-2). The electorate willing to support Chaban when the campaign opened proved to be both more strongly Gaullist and less ready to accept change than any other part of the electorate. Chaban centered his campaign on the need for radical change and played down his Gaullism. The Gaullism of Chaban's potential electorate in the first phase of the campaign was characterized by a certain type of nationalism (for instance, a nationalism that included the desire to see French industry the strongest in Europe [item 1.3]), a lower level of rejection than any other electorate of the idea of a substantial increase in the population of France (item 1.9), and a relative wariness towards Europe, whether it be the development of European institutions (item 1.7), the power of Europe as opposed to that of France (item 1.8), or the free circulation and work of the French in Europe (item 3.5). The conservatism of Chaban's electorate was clear on all counts. The former prime minister's supporters boasted the most women and the least enthusiasm for "women's lib." It was an electorate which preferred men and women to remain different and to have different activities (item 4.5), and did not want to see the power of the wife and mother reinforced (item 4.3) or to see as many women as men among the deputies and ministers (item 1.13).

Chaban's supporters had a more instrumental attitude to work than Giscard's. They preferred higher salaries to better conditions of work (item 2.8) or to an additional day off (item 2.6). They were less anxious, too, to see changes in the urban environment; they preferred to go off to the country from time to time (item 3.17). They were less in favor of any increase in the organization and power

Table 3-2

EXPECTATIONS OF FRENCH VOTERS CONCERNING
THEIR SOCIETY IN 1980

Item	Voters Favoring: [a]			Total Electorate
	Giscard	Chaban	Mitterrand	
1. Politics				
1.1. Europe is as powerful as the U.S.A. and the U.S.S.R.	88	85	83	81
1.2. There is less difference between the standard of living in the developed countries and that in the developing countries.	85	88	91	86
1.3. French industry is the most powerful in Europe.	79	91	66	75
1.4. The regions are recovering their originality and their strength and are becoming more independent.	65	75	74	74
1.5. Paris is becoming less important, and the provinces more so.	60	66	72	69
1.6. The balanced development of atomic weapons promotes peace.	50	40	3	25
1.7. There is a European president, a European government and a European currency.	34	23	40	33
1.8. The power and cohesion of Europe has increased. / The influence and power of France has increased.[b]	31	−4	43	20

Table 3-2 *(continued)*

Item	Voters Favoring: [a]			Total Electorate
	Giscard	Chaban	Mitterrand	
1.9. The population of France is stable at around 50 million / is over 60 million.[b]	28	5	60	41
1.10. Ministers, deputies, and mayors can be sacked if a certain number of voters so demand.	27	17	78	47
1.11. France devotes a great part of its budget to helping the developing countries.	19	25	34	24
1.12. Mayors, deputies, and ministers exercise their functions for brief periods and then become ordinary citizens again. / Politics has become more and more complex and is in the hands of competent specialists.[b]	2	−17	60	30
1.13. Among the deputies and ministers there are as many women as men.	−1	5	59	29
2. Work				
2.1. The gap between salaries has narrowed; it is only 1 to 4, as against 1 to 20 in 1971.	67	64	95	83
2.2. Adult education enables people to improve in their particular field. / Adult education enables people to change the field they work in three or four times in a lifetime.[b]	66	71	40	52

Table 3-2 *(continued)*

| Item | Voters Favoring: [a] | | | Total Electorate |
	Giscard	Chaban	Mitterrand	
2.3. The right to strike is limited.	62	25	−51	6
2.4. There are fewer foreign workers in France than there used to be.	59	25	16	27
2.5. The major unions have lost power and have been replaced by organizations nearer to the workers.	55	79	25	44
2.6. There are still five working days in the week and the standard of living is higher than in 1974. / There are four working days in the week and the standard of living is the same as in 1974.[b]	53	69	23	40
2.7. After the age of forty no one can be sacked from his job.	52	76	81	69
2.8. The standard of living is higher but the work is still the same. / Work is pleasanter and the standard of living has not changed.[b]	37	63	22	28
2.9. All salaries received are posted in the factories.	26	11	67	50
2.10. The incomes of peasants are guaranteed by the state.	13	19	50	30
2.11. Executives and managers are elected by the employees.	3	41	67	48

Table 3-2 (continued)

Item	Voters Favoring: [a]			Total Electorate
	Giscard	Chaban	Mitterrand	
2.12. Small shopkeepers have virtually disappeared; they are grouped in commercial centers.	− 28	− 27	− 34	− 40
2.13. The salaries of workers vary according to whether the industry is making a loss or a profit.	− 47	− 55	− 55	− 51
2.14. Everyone is a civil servant.	− 82	− 67	− 36	− 56
3. Style of life				
3.1. It is more difficult than it was to obtain a driving license. / One no longer needs a driving license.[b]	97	90	79	84
3.2. Consumers' associations are as powerful as producers and can counter them.	84	71	86	74
3.3. Train and plane fares are cheap and cars are scarcely ever used for long distance traveling.	73	59	67	69
3.4. On the level of local districts people are organized so that they can decide what concerns their district.	65	42	83	66
3.5. Any Frenchman can live and work anywhere in Europe.	56	49	77	62
3.6. Emphasis is put on the protection of the environment / on technical progress.[b]	56	46	75	58

Table 3-2 *(continued)*

Item	Voters Favoring: [a]			Total Electorate
	Giscard	Chaban	Mitterrand	
3.7. Education aims primarily at teaching children to be happy and enjoy life.	34	67	85	64
3.8. Compulsory schooling only lasts until age 14 and young people go to work younger. / Compulsory schooling lasts until age 18.[b]	29	27	1	17
3.9. Teaching is oriented towards professional training / towards culture.[b]	26	66	30	40
3.10. Cars are forbidden in the towns.	23	13	34	23
3.11. There are no longer any private weekend homes; anyone can rent a weekend or holiday house at a controlled price.	16	47	53	35
3.12. Public transport is free / each Frenchman has his own car.[b]	13	10	47	20
3.13. The French have changed their eating habits; they eat less meat and more vegetables.	13	5	10	10
3.14. The use of "tu" rather than "vous" has become general; people communicate more easily; they speak to one another in the street.	7	6	46	26

Table 3-2 *(continued)*

Item	Voters Favoring: [a]			Total Electorate
	Giscard	Chaban	Mitterrand	
3.15. Society has changed; people need less and live more simply. / The consumption society flourishes, and more desires are increasingly satisfied.[b]	3	7	33	23
3.16. Changing one's town of residence three or four times in one's lifetime has become a normal occurrence.	−1	22	19	−3
3.17. Townsfolk can easily go to the country for the weekend. / The towns have become more pleasant, and the townsfolk spend their weekends there more and more often.[b]	−2	33	51	26
3.18. Advertising has been suppressed.	−9	−24	30	5
3.19. Tourists go less often to hotels and more often to "bed and breakfasts."	−22	−49	18	−7
4. *Values*				
4.1. Drugs have virtually disappeared. / Some soft drugs are sold freely, just as tobacco or drink.[b]	95	93	79	88
4.2. The traditional family has regained importance / has been completely changed.[b]	67	67	29	48
4.3. The power of the wife and mother has increased.	41	31	60	48

Table 3-2 (continued)

Item	Voters Favoring: [a]			Total Electorate
	Giscard	Chaban	Mitterrand	
4.4. Prison sentences are more severe for all delinquents.	36	48	20	29
4.5. Men and women remain very different in their attitudes and activities / are more and more alike.[b]	21	42	6	23
4.6. The use of the computer by the civil service has been limited in order to protect private life. / Thanks to the computer, contacts with the civil service have been facilitated.[b]	14	17	41	23
4.7. Murderers are automatically acquitted if their crime is committed in self-defense.	3	2	17	7
4.8. Sex education has become an important part of the school program.	−2	12	44	14
4.9. Half the police are professional policemen, the other half are men doing their national service.	−8	−5	20	−1
4.10. National service is no longer done in the army and is done by both men and women.	−13	−3	7	−8
4.11. There is a tax on capital accumulated by individuals.	−20	−38	26	−3

Table 3-2 (continued)

Item	Voters Favoring: [a]			Total Electorate
	Giscard	Chaban	Mitterrand	
4.12. There is no longer any sort of censorship in politics and entertainment.	−25	−47	38	−1
4.13. Abortion is legal.	−31	−26	41	−2
4.14. The death penalty no longer exists.	−39	−31	22	−11
4.15. Society has become more permissive. / Traditional moral values have gained in importance.[b]	−40	−36	41	−3
4.16. There is complete sexual freedom.	−44	−41	13	27
4.17. The age of majority is now 16; young people can open bank accounts and leave home at 16.	−58	−61	−29	51
4.18. Many families now live together.	−75	−87	−63	−73
4.19. Children are brought up by collective organizations.	−78	−63	−38	−56

[a] Index calculated by the author to give as a single figure the percentage of positive and negative reactions and the number of people responding. The index is equal to the percentage of positive reactions minus the percentage of negative reactions divided by the percentage of negative reactions plus the percentage of positive reactions and multiplied by 100. The index can thus vary from +100 to −100.

[b] In some cases the COFREMCA gave respondents the choice between two alternative statements. In this case the index has been calculated for the first statement indicated. The sign / divides the two statements from one another.

Source: Adapted from a COFREMCA survey conducted between 18 and 22 April 1974 for *Figaro*. The sample was a representative national sample of 500 people over the age of twenty-one.

of the consumers (item 3.2), and they were the most firm partisans of the individually owned car (items 3.3, 3.10, and 3.12). Chaban was strongly in favor of regular discussions with the unions, but his electors were far and away the most eager to see trade-union power limited (item 2.5). When his electors did find themselves in agreement with those of Mitterrand, it was in calling for the protection of the law and the guarantee of employment or of salary, if need be at the expense of necessary change (items 2.7 and 2.13). In other words, Chaban's potential electorate was not very different from that of Giscard, but, insofar as it did differ, it was more conservative and nationalist in almost all fields.

Chaban's failure was inevitable once he had decided to play the new society card rather than that of traditional Gaullism. Not only were the French as a whole less interested in changing their society than in improving the political and, more important still, the economic environment, but Chaban's own potential electors were also the most opposed to change. Once the campaign had started and Chaban had realized his mistake, he tried to modify his strategy. He referred to Gaullism more and more often, which was wise, even if it was rather late in the day. He also attacked Giscard—which was less wise. On 5 May it was not in the Gaullist strongholds that Chaban did best, but in the counties of the Southwest, in Aquitaine, his own region (see Table 3-3). Chabanism had thus regionalized Gaullism. It may even have allowed it to be taken over by Giscardism.

The Victory of Valéry Giscard d'Estaing

Giscard and Gaullism. "Mr. Giscard d'Estaing does not come from the same family as we do and it is therefore not surprising that there are differences between us . . .," [17] Chaban declared at the precise moment when he began to accentuate the differences between himself and Giscard. And yet it is not difficult to enumerate the many occasions on which Giscard has served Gaullism. Giscard himself underlined them throughout the presidential campaign. He was only eighteen in August 1944, but that did not prevent him from taking part in the liberation of Paris, nor from volunteering for the First French Army and taking part in campaigns in France and Germany as a rank-and-file soldier. Elected to Parliament for the first time in 1956 (under the Fourth Republic) as a "moderate," he nevertheless voted in favor of de Gaulle's investiture on 1 June 1958, and thus ratified the general's return to power. His youth—and good luck—caused him to serve only in Fifth Republic governments, a feat neither Chaban nor Mitterrand can boast of. It was he, and not Chaban, whom de Gaulle trusted; de Gaulle made him secretary of state and

---

[17] Jacques Chaban-Delmas, speech, Lyons, 22 April, as quoted in *Le Monde*, 24 April 1974.

Table 3-3

CHABAN'S FIRST BALLOT VOTE (TEN BEST DEPARTMENTS), COMPARED TO THE MAJORITY VOTE OF 1973

Department	Rank [a]	Chaban, First Ballot, 1974 Percent of potential electorate	Difference compared to the average [b] (percentage points)	Majority Vote, Parliamentary Election, March 1973 Rank	Percent of potential electorate	Difference compared to the average [c] (percentage points)
Gironde	1	30.0	+ 17.8	66	26.4	− 2.6
Landes	2	25.6	+ 13.4	48	30.8	+ 1.8
Pyrénées Atlantiques	3	22.0	+ 10.2	30	33.4	+ 4.4
Dordogne	4	21.7	+ 9.5	19	35.1	+ 6.1
Charente	5	20.4	+ 8.2	78	24.0	− 5.0
Charente-Maritime	6	18.9	+ 6.7	22	34.8	+ 5.8
Lot et Garonne	7	18.7	+ 6.5	73	25.4	− 3.6
Corse	7	18.7	+ 6.5	59	27.6	− 1.4
Tarn et Garonne	9	17.3	+ 5.1	67	26.4	− 2.6
Vendée	10	16.2	+ 4.0	2	46.4	+ 17.4

a Out of a total of ninety-five departments.

b 12.2 percent of the electors on the register in metropolitan France.

c 29.0 percent of the electors on the register in metropolitan France.

Source: Author.

then minister of finance. Giscard did not hesitate to emphasize both de Gaulle's and Pompidou's confidence in him:

> I am the only one of the candidates who has some chance of being present on the second ballot of the presidential election to have served only in Fifth Republic governments. I am also the only one of these candidates to whom both presidents of the Fifth Republic have entrusted ministerial functions.[18]

---

[18] Valéry Giscard d'Estaing, television broadcast, 22 April 1974.

It is no doubt his service under de Gaulle that gives him his sense of the utmost importance of the dignity and prestige of France, and of the authority and solidarity of the executive, and his loyal respect for the majority's pact with the electorate. In October 1967, during a debate of censure, he replied to those who reproached the Independent Republicans for saying "yes . . . but" to government policy, but "no" to government crisis: "We refuse to consider crisis as a means of government, and a member of the majority can only censure the government in the case of a grave national crisis." [19]

A national crisis did arise in May 1968. Giscard recognized the fact, but his colleagues did not censure the government because they did not wish to add the terrors of the unknown to the disorder already rife. On 30 May Giscard called for the resignation of Pompidou and the expansion of the government, but he remained firm in his support of the presidential institution and of de Gaulle.

Nevertheless, Giscard has little in common with the Gaullist style and manner. On 17 August 1967, after the government's demand for special powers following General de Gaulle's stand on the Middle East conflict and, more particularly, on Quebec, Giscard broadcast a thundering statement on the "single-handed exercise of power. Discussion does not weaken authority. It can show authority the way and ensure real national cohesion." [20]

A man of distinction who "inherited" his seat in Parliament from his grandfather, Jacques Bardoux, founder of the Independent Republicans, a party full of notable men, Giscard has little affection for the disciplined battalions of the Gaullist party or for the passionate dedication of some of the Gaullist leaders. For instance, Michel Debré is frequently attacked by Giscard's henchman, Michel Poniatowski. It was not the Resistance that brought him into politics, nor grass-roots politics, but ability. A brilliant student first at the *Ecole Polytechnique* and then at the *Ecole Nationale d'Administration*, in 1954 he was called upon by Faure, then minister of finance, to join his private staff (*cabinet ministériel*) under the Fourth Republic. Not unnaturally Giscard remained in the finance ministry, first as secretary of state from 1959 to 1962, then as minister under de Gaulle from 1962 to 1966. He returned to the same post under Pompidou from 1969 to 1974.

Giscard is used to success. At thirty-two, he was the youngest minister of the Fifth Republic; now, at forty-eight, he is almost the

[19] Valéry Giscard d'Estaing, speech in the National Assembly, 20 May 1967, during the debate of no confidence on the special powers of the government, as quoted in *Journal Officiel*, 20 May 1967.
[20] *France Moderne*, no. 309 (7 September 1967).

youngest president France has ever had. (Casimir Perier, elected in 1894, was the youngest.) He has nurtured a deep grudge against the Gaullists for having sacked him "like a servant," as he himself remarked, after the 1965 presidential election. Proudly he rejected the meagre compensation that was offered him, and devoted his energies to building up the party with which, eight years later, he was to conquer the Elysée. Traditionally, the finance minister is both the most powerful and most unpopular minister in France, as in many countries. Giscard managed to remain both powerful and popular. His ability to explain to millions of television viewers the causes of rising inflation or the mechanisms of floating the franc was recognized by all. He became, as it were, the French people's professor of economics, and his capacity in this field was cited (in polls taken 20-22 April 1974) as the main reason for voting for him. The second reason given was that he would include the Center in the majority.[21] In a survey concerning the workers who did not intend to vote for Mitterrand, or were still hesitating on the eve of the first ballot, Giscard was seen—despite the eleven years he had spent in the ministry of finance—as a new man and a highly skilled technician, supremely competent, intelligent and appealing, while Chaban, who had only come to power in 1969 and had been removed in 1972, was thought of as politically worn out on account of his Gaullist label.[22] The majority of the French seemed ready to forgive Giscard anything, from the economic austerity plan of 1963 to the record inflation of 1974, but most of the Gaullists did not forget that, by refusing publicly to vote in favor of regionalization and the reform of the Senate in the referendum of 1969, he had contributed to the "victory of the no's" and to the resignation of de Gaulle. Giscard is without doubt a pillar of the Fifth Republic, but he is by no means a Gaullist.

Giscard and the Center. Giscard's strategy was simple, and, unlike that of Chaban, it was consistent with the facts. France wanted, Giscard believed, to be governed from the center of the ideological spectrum. He, therefore, had to modify Pompidou's majority by

---

21 SOFRES survey, for *Les Informations*, 20-22 April 1974.

22 COFREMCA note concerning the electorate from the lower classes (20 million employees, workers, and retired persons), in particular those who did not vote for Mitterrand—or hesitated to do so—in May 1974. The survey was carried out for the *Nouvel Observateur*. Three days before the vote 57 percent of these electors had decided to vote for Mitterrand, 16 percent hesitated between Mitterrand, Giscard, Chaban, and Royer, and 27 percent had decided not to vote for Mitterrand on either ballot. Giscard was seen by these latter as by far the most capable of fighting inflation, helping the elderly and restoring France to the rank of a first-rate world power.

reducing the power of the UDR within it and widening it to include the centrist reformers belonging to Jean-Jacques Servan-Schreiber's Radical party and Jean Lecanuet's Democratic Center. From 8 April, the day he announced that he was a candidate, Giscard underlined that he was seeking a new majority: "For many years, I have publicly declared that France needs an enlarged majority. In the difficult circumstances in which we find ourselves we must create a wider majority. That is why I call on you all, electors from the UDR, Independent Republicans, centrists, and reformers." [23] But instead of rejecting the UDR, as Chaban rejected the right-wing within the majority, Giscard called on the UDR, invoking both the moral authority of Pompidou and the Gaullist virtue of unity: "I shall do my best to run an exemplary campaign. I shall attack no one, neither the candidates of yesterday's presidential majority nor the candidate of the opposition." [24]

Two days later the political committee of the Democratic Center brought its support to Giscard as its president, Jean Lecanuet, had requested. The centrists—whether they came from the MRP (Christian democrats) or from radicalism—had cut themselves off from de Gaulle and gone into opposition in 1962. As a result of the scorn de Gaulle had poured on European integration, the MRP ministers in Pompidou's government had resigned collectively in May 1962. Later, in October, the Democratic Center, the Radical party, and most members of the National Center of Independents had publicly declared they would vote "no" on the referendum on the direct election of the president.[25] Since then the centrists had been waiting for enough votes and, above all, enough seats in the National Assembly to allow them to play a balance-of-power role. Their relative weakness on the first ballot and the Left-Right polarization on the second ballot had constantly frustrated them both in presidential and general elections. In 1965 Lecanuet obtained only 15.9 percent of the votes cast, managing only to force de Gaulle to a second ballot (a feat not appreciated by many of the Gaullist faithful), while in general elections between 1962 and 1973 the opposition Center had had difficulty in finding the thirty members necessary to form an autonomous parliamentary group. The UDR and the Independent Republicans had

---

[23] Valéry Giscard d'Estaing, statement, Chamalières town hall, Monday, 8 April 1974.

[24] Ibid.

[25] It was on this occasion, in fact, that the CNI divided and enabled Valéry Giscard d'Estaing to place himself at the head of those independents who were in favor of the Fifth Republic and the direct election by the people of the president of the republic.

not, in any case, needed them to form a majority in the Assembly. Far from holding the balance between Left and Right, the Center seemed to be gradually absorbed by the majority. In 1969 one of its leaders, Jacques Duhamel, created a new party—the *Centre Démocratie et Progrès* (CDP)—and joined Pompidou's majority. The CDP won just under thirty seats in the 1973 elections. Pompidou was in favor of joining forces with the Center against the Left, but the years of political struggle between the UDR and the opposition Center had left their mark and reconciliation proved impossible. For years the Independent Republicans had been pressing for the integration of the Center, while the UDR had done all it could to prevent it, either because it was fundamentally hostile to Lecanuet, who was seen as an enemy of de Gaulle and a partisan of an Atlantic supranational Europe, or because it feared any modification of the relative strength of the different groups constituting the majority. Any newcomer would necessarily diminish the power of the UDR. Giscard and Lecanuet were finally to impose a widening of the majority, thus marking the end of the opposition Center's third-force strategy and the disappearance of the political no-man's-land between the Left and the majority, and at the same time reducing the strength of the UDR within the majority.

The electorate of the majority had long been favorably inclined toward the integration of the Center. Thus Lecanuet's support of Giscard, so violently criticized by Chaban and the Gaullists, made Giscard's candidacy popular not only with the centrist electorate but also with that of the electorate of the majority (see Table 3-4).

Table 3-4
THE IMPACT ON PUBLIC OPINION OF LECANUET'S SUPPORT FOR GISCARD

Effect	Total Electorate	Majority Voters	Centrist Voters
More favorable to Giscard	22%	31%	46%
Less favorable	11	8	9
Indifferent	59	55	41
Don't know	8	6	4
Total	100%	100%	100%

Source: SOFRES national opinion poll, 12-16 April 1974, for *Figaro*. The question was: "Mr. Lecanuet has declared that he is supporting Mr. Giscard d'Estaing. As far as you personally are concerned does this make you more or less favorable to Mr. Giscard d'Estaing or does it leave you indifferent?"

Lecanuet's support for Giscard corresponded to the support Duhamel brought Pompidou in 1969, that is, it served as proof of Giscard's desire for renewal, as opposed to the seemingly sectarian rigidity of his rival, Chaban.

The New Majority. The opposition Center had chosen as its slogan in the 1973 elections "change with serenity"; Giscard proposed a modified version, "change without risk." In the press conference in which he defined his presidential program for the first time, Giscard carefully listed the three "securities" and the nine "changes" he was offering the electorate:

> the three securities are security in old age, security in the face of economic perils, security for women and families. The nine changes we must bring into effect are . . . the organization of equal opportunities for the young, the equality of social rights for all the French, employees, peasants, shop-keepers and artisans; . . . the recognition in French society of the rights of women, the improvement of working conditions, . . . the closing of the gap between the highest and lowest salaries, and a study of how best to guarantee a minimum level of income for all . . . the humanization of hospitals and of public transport, and for humane town planning . . . the transfer of resources to local communities . . . the guarantee of the private life of each Frenchman despite the aggression of the modern world. In order to bring all this about, my ninth proposal is the coming of a generation of new men.[26]

After two months as the head of state, Giscard spoke of himself as "a traditionalist who likes change." [27] And he added, "Since France is a traditional country which hankers after change, she and I were destined to recognize one another."

His potential electorate at the outset was both different from that of Mitterrand, in that it refused radical change, and from that of Chaban, in that it was in favor of a certain measure of reform and was more capable of thinking in terms of the future. Giscard's supporters were the most opposed to making civil servants of all the French (see Table 3-2, item 2.14), and the most opposed to collectivization (item 4.19). They were hostile to anything that might change the distribution of power in industry, for instance election by the workers of the cadres and managers (item 2.11), and they were

---

[26] Valéry Giscard d'Estaing, press conference, Strasbourg, 19 April 1974.
[27] Valéry Giscard d'Estaing, press conference, Elysée Palace, Thursday, 25 July 1974.

not unwilling to limit the right to strike (item 2.3). They were relatively uninterested in the developing countries (item 2.4), content with the traditional police and army structures (items 4.9 and 4.10), and firmly in favor of the French nuclear strategy (item 1.6). But they were also, as we have already seen, more European and less nationalist than Chaban's supporters, and more ready to see changes in the framework of city life or in conditions of work. They were as attached as Chaban's electors to the defense of morality and the traditional family, but they were on the whole less rigid on these issues (items 4.4 and 4.12), though by no means permissive (items 4.13 and 4.16). In essence, Giscard's supporters constituted a new majority, with some new electors brought in and some of those who had been included in Pompidou's presidential majority lost.

One of the best illustrations of this is the fact that the rise in Giscard's fortunes during the campaign cannot be entirely explained by the drop in Chaban's popularity. In other words, Giscard did not manage to attract all those who were disappointed by Chaban or by Royer. Mitterrand gained more than Giscard did from the other candidates of the majority in the rural communes—as much as Giscard gained from the falling away of Chaban's women electors— and he gained more than Giscard from the drops in popularity of Royer and Chaban among the shopkeepers and artisans. Among those over sixty-five, however, and among supporters of the majority, Giscard minimized the transfer to the Left of supporters lost by his rivals (see Table 3-5).

The geographical distribution of votes cast on the first ballot in favor of Giscard also shows that his electorate was specifically his own. A comparison of the twenty departments in which Giscard obtained his best results on 5 May 1974, and the departments in which Pompidou's presidential majority obtained its best results on the first ballot of the general election in March 1973, reveals significant information (see Table 3-6). Among the first ten, the differences between Giscard's strong points and those of the former majority are very slight. The only department which seems to be a real exception is the Puy de Dôme, and this can be explained by Giscard's personal links with the region. Elsewhere among these ten departments it is Pompidou's electorate that ensured the success of Giscard. But lower down the list the changes are considerable. Only the Maine et Loire figures both among the strongholds of the former majority and those of Giscard. In the other departments the minister of finance was carried to victory less by the electors of the majority than by the electors of the Center (see Table 3-7).

Table 3-5

CHANGE IN VOTING INTENTIONS, FIRST BALLOT

(percentage points)

| | Candidates | | | | |
Social Categories	Mitterrand	Giscard	Chaban	Royer	Giscard + Chaban + Royer
Electorate as a whole	+2	+3	−7	−1	−5
Sex					
Men	0	+2	−4	−1	−3
Women	+4	+4	−9	−2	−7
Age					
21-34	+1	+3	−6	−2	−5
35-49	+2	+4	−6	−2	−4
50-64	+4	+1	−6	−1	−6
65 and over	+1	+6	−8	−1	−3
Profession of head of household					
Executives, liberal professions	+1	+5	−6	−2	−3
Industrial and commercial employers	+3	+5	−4	−8	−7
Employees	−2	+4	−3	−2	−1
Industrial workers	+3	+2	−6	−1	−5
Retired	+2	+5	−9	0	−4
Peasants	+6	+2	−7	−2	−7
Residence					
Rural districts	+5	+4	−10	−1	−7
Urban districts of less than 20,000	0	+4	−5	−3	−4
20,000 to 100,000	+2	+2	−6	0	−4
over 100,000	+3	+2	−4	−3	−5
Paris and district	+1	+4	−6	−2	−4
Political preferences, 1st ballot, 1973					
Communist	−2	0	0	0	0
Non-Communist Left	0	0	0	−2	−2
Reformers	+4	+6	−8	−5	−7
Majority	−1	+10	−9	−2	−1

Source: IFOP, three surveys, 16, 18, 22 April, compared to three surveys, 24-25, 29 April, and 2-3 May 1974.

Table 3-6

GISCARD'S FIRST BALLOT VOTE (TWENTY BEST
DEPARTMENTS), COMPARED TO THE MAJORITY VOTE OF 1973

Department	Rank [a]	Giscard, First Ballot, 1974			Majority Vote, Parliamentary Election, March 1973		
		Percent of potential electorate	Difference compared to the average [b] (percentage points)		Rank	Percent of potential electorate	Difference compared to the average [c] (percentage points)
Morbihan	1	38.7	+11.0		15	35.9	+ 6.9
Mayenne	2	38.6	+10.9		5	43.2	+14.2
Puy de Dôme	3	38.1	+10.4		52	28.3	− 0.7
Lozère	4	37.9	+10.2		1	47.4	+18.4
Cantal	5	37.7	+10.0		7	41.0	+12.0
Manche	6	37.0	+ 9.3		6	42.9	+13.9
Ille et Vilaine	7	36.9	+ 9.2		9	40.5	+11.5
Vendée	8	36.4	+ 8.7		2	46.4	+17.4
Haute-Loire	9	35.7	+ 8.0		4	44.0	+15.0
Bas-Rhin	10	35.5	+ 7.8		3	45.9	+16.9
Finistère	11	35.1	+ 7.4		26	34.1	+ 5.1
Aveyron	12	34.4	+ 6.7		50	28.7	− 0.3
Maine et Loire	13	34.0	+ 6.3		14	36.6	+ 7.6
Haute Savoie	14	33.6	+ 5.9		42	31.5	+ 2.5
Haut Rhin	15	33.1	+ 5.4		34	32.6	+ 3.6
Rhône	16	32.9	+ 5.2		83	23.5	− 5.5
Alpes Maritimes	16	32.9	+ 5.2		65	26.7	− 2.3
Orne	18	32.6	+ 4.9		27	34.1	+ 5.1
Seine (Paris)	19	32.5	+ 4.8		58	27.7	− 1.3
Moselle	20	32.3	+ 4.6		38	32.0	+ 3.0

[a] Out of a total of ninety-five departments.
[b] 27.7 percent of the electors on the register in metropolitan France.
[c] 29.0 percent of the electors on the register in metropolitan France.
Source: Author.

Table 3-7

EVALUATION OF POLITICAL ORIGINS OF VOTES IN FAVOR OF CANDIDATES OF THE MAJORITY, FIRST BALLOT, 1974

Those Who Voted:	Percentage Who Voted in Favor of:		
	Giscard	Chaban	Royer
1973 General Election, First Ballot			
Extreme Left	0.7	0.9	—
Communist	2.1	6.0	6.9
Non-Communist Left	5.5	7.3	4.1
Reform	17.7	9.3	23.2
Majority	51.3	62.1	31.9
Misc. Right	7.2	4.2	11.1
Non-voters	15.5	10.2	22.8
Total	100.0	100.0	100.0
1969 Presidential Election, First Ballot			
Left (Duclos, Krivine, Rocard, Defferre)	3.5	7.2	6.9
Poher	18.7	11.5	27.0
Pompidou	59.4	69.4	37.5
Others (Ducatel)	1.8	1.0	2.6
Non-voters	16.6	10.9	26.0
Total	100.0	100.0	100.0

Source: Evaluation of IFOP-Europe 1 by the method of Lucien Boucharenc and Jean Charlot, "l'étude des transferts électoraux [aux élections présidentielles de 1974]," *Revue Française de Science Politique*, no. 6 (December 1974), pp. 1205-18.

The renewal of the majority can also be seen if one examines the most solid estimates of transfers of votes between the presidential election of 1969, or the general election of 1973, and this first ballot of the presidential election of 1974 (see Table 3-8). In May 1974 Giscard drew only slightly more than half (51.3 percent) of the 8,253,856 votes cast in his favor in metropolitan France from voters who had voted for the majority on 4 March 1973. Rather less than three-fifths of his electorate (59.4 percent) had voted for Pompidou in 1969. The *réformateurs* (17.7 percent), the 1973 nonvoters

Table 3-8

EVALUATION OF VOTE SWITCHES BETWEEN 1969 AND 1974 AND 1973 AND 1974

Those Who Voted:	Percentage Who Voted on the First Ballot, 1974, in Favor of:						
	Non-voters	Left [a]	Giscard	Chaban	Royer	Others	Total
1973 General Election, First Ballot							
Left	4.4	82.2	6.5	4.9	0.9	1.1	100.0
Reform	7.9	19.6	50.8	11.7	7.3	2.7	100.0
Majority	13.3	8.3	47.7	25.5	3.2	2.0	100.0
Non-voter	43.4	25.1	21.2	6.2	3.4	0.7	100.0
1969 Presidential Election, First Ballot							
Left (Duclos, Krivine, Rocard, Defferre)	1.8	88.6	4.2	3.8	0.9	0.7	100.0
Poher	6.9	50.6	28.5	7.8	4.5	2.3	100.0
Pompidou	12.7	9.3	47.8	24.8	3.3	2.1	100.0
Non-voter	41.0	28.5	20.4	5.9	3.5	0.7	100.0

a Mitterrand, Laguiller, Krivine, Dumont.

Source: Evaluation of IFOP-Europe 1 by the same method as Table 3-7.

(15.5 percent), the Left (8.3 percent), and the various right-wing groups (7.2 percent) completed and widened his electorate. If we take into account the final result, which surpassed that of Chaban (3,646,209 votes) and of Royer (808,825 votes) together, the impact of Giscard is much stronger than that of his rivals in all social and political categories. Over half the *réformateurs* voted for him, as against less than 12 percent for Chaban. Almost half the supporters of the majority (47.7 percent as against 25.5 percent for Chaban) voted for him and on the Left he totalled 6.5 percent and Chaban only 4.9 percent. The minister of finance was clearly seen as the real heir to Pompidou; he obtained 47.8 percent of the late president's votes, while Chaban obtained less than a quarter.

Victory by a Head. On the second ballot it remained for Giscard to beat the candidate of the Left, Mitterrand, since the voting system only leaves two candidates on the second ballot, those who came first and second on the first, unless a candidate is elected on the first ballot with an overall majority. Giscard had to reckon with the trauma felt by the UDR after the severe defeat of its candidate. As had been expected, Messmer, Chirac, and the forty-three immediately gave Giscard unlimited support, but the majority of the Gaullist leaders and deputies merely resigned themselves to calling on their electors to vote against Mitterrand.[28] The meetings of the executive bureau and the parliamentary party of the UDR at the National Assembly on 6 May took place in an atmosphere of conflict and revenge. The representatives of the forty-three were hissed and Prime Minister Messmer was violently attacked.

However, as the fifteen days between the first and second ballots went by, and the danger of a victory of the Left became more imminent from one poll to the next, the Gaullists gradually rallied, willy-nilly, around their victor. Chaban himself, who on the evening of 5 May had refrained from explicitly calling on his supporters to vote for Giscard, modified his position a week later: "Mr. Mitterrand has taken risks we cannot accept. How can we check his undertaking save by voting for Mr. Giscard d'Estaing?"[29]

But the candidates can only point the way; in the end the voters choose themselves. All through the campaign for the second ballot Mitterrand made advances to the Gaullists in the hope of gaining a good number of Chaban's supporters and thus ensuring his own

[28] The text of the only poster the UDR used for the second ballot illustrated this.
[29] Jacques Chaban-Delmas, interview, *Sud-Ouest*, 13 May 1974.

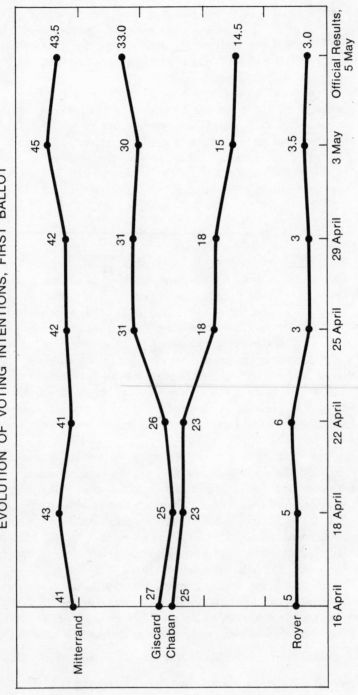

Figure 3-1

EVOLUTION OF VOTING INTENTIONS, FIRST BALLOT

	16 April	18 April	22 April	25 April	29 April	3 May	Official Results, 5 May
Mitterrand	41	43	41	42	42	45	43.5
Giscard	27	25	26	31	31	30	33.0
Chaban	25	23	23	18	18	15	14.5
Royer	5	5	6	3	3	3.5	3.0

Source: IFOP.

victory. His hopes proved founded, in that Giscard did not manage to keep Chaban's entire electorate behind him.

On 19 May 1974 Giscard won by a very narrow margin—344,399 votes in metropolitan France, 424,599 if we include the overseas territories. This means that if Mitterrand had won over a mere 212,300 electors out of the 26,367,807 who voted, France would today have a radical, Socialist-Communist majority. The victory of the new majority was won by a scant 1.62 percent of the votes cast; the verdict could have been different with a transfer of 0.82 percent. The record turnout of almost 88 percent equalled that of democracies where voting is compulsory. It undoubtedly favored the candidate of the majority and Center.

An analysis of the transfers between the first and second ballots shows that out of Chaban's 3,646,209 metropolitan supporters, 9.5 percent (over 346,000) abstained on the second ballot and 11 percent (over 401,000) voted for Mitterrand (see Table 3-9). Had it not been for the turnout of new voters who had not voted on the first ballot, and the transfer of votes from the minor Center candidates and from the right-wing and extreme right-wing candidates eliminated on the first ballot (Emile Muller, Jean-Marie Le Pen, Bertrand Renouvin, Jean-Claude Sébag and Guy Héraud), Giscard would have been beaten. Chaban failed because he wanted to exclude the Right and Center from the Gaullist union. Giscard was almost beaten because he inevitably discouraged, by beating Chaban, those left-wing supporters that Gaullism had so far prevented from joining forces with the Left.

The End of Gaullism?

After Chaban's defeat there were many who tolled the bell for Gaullism as Giscard took up the reins and began by severely limiting the role of the UDR in his new government.[30] The defeat of the Gaullist candidate and its immediate political implications justified a certain pessimism as to the future of Gaullism within the political system set up by de Gaulle after 1958. The most intransigent of the Gaullists, Michel Debré, while hoping that Gaullism would emerge renewed, did not minimize the difficulties that the movement would

---

[30] All the governments, since 1962, had included an absolute majority of Gaullist ministers; since 1968 the Gaullists had held over three-quarters of the posts. In the Chirac government the UDR has fewer than a third of the ministerial posts and even these have practically all been given to Gaullists who were in favor of Giscard d'Estaing.

Table 3-9

VOTE SWITCHES BETWEEN FIRST AND SECOND BALLOTS, 1974

First Ballot, Those Who Voted:	Percentage Who Voted on the Second Ballot in Favor of:		
	Giscard	Mitterrand	Non-voters
Left [a]	3.9	93.7	2.4
Royer	67.6	18.4	14.0
Chaban	79.5	11.0	9.5
Giscard	94.5	3.4	2.1
Non-voters	21.8	14.6	63.6
Total	100.0	100.0	100.0

	Second Ballot Votes as a Percentage of Second Ballot Vote for:		
	Giscard	Mitterrand	Non-voters
Left	3.5	87.1	7.2
Royer	4.4	1.2	3.0
Chaban	22.2	3.2	8.8
Giscard	59.9	2.2	4.5
Non-voters	7.8	5.4	75.3
Other	2.2	0.9	1.2
Total	100.0	100.0	100.0

[a] Mitterrand, Laguiller, Krivine, Dumont.
Source: Evaluation of IFOP-Europe 1 by the method used for Table 3-7.

have to face, nor the temptation to give up, which would inevitably take hold of it: "It is up to the UDR political movement—with its concern for the future of the French people and its respect for a great heritage—whether it makes of this trial the prelude to a betrayal or, on the contrary, an accident in its history." [31]

But to try to assess the impact of the event we must distinguish three levels: the Fifth Republic, the majority, and the UDR, however fundamental the part that de Gaulle and the Gaullists played in the creation of a disciplined majority government system in France and a republic in which the executive is no longer dominated by the legislature but still remains democratically elected.

[31] Michel Debré, *Sud-Ouest*, 24 May 1974.

Giscard's victory in no way threatens the institutions set up by the Gaullists. The successor of de Gaulle and Pompidou does not question the foundations of the Fifth Republic and the primacy of the president of the republic. One might almost say that this victory of a non-Gaullist is a guarantee of the continuation of the system. The new president is no less jealous of his powers than his predecessors, and is perhaps even more inclined to exercise them directly at the expense of his prime minister, who seems more and more the mere executor of presidential directives. Some Gaullists fear that Giscard may be tempted to reintroduce proportional representation for general elections, thus encouraging the multiplication of minor political parties, the reduction of disciplined party groups in Parliament, and the end of the majority system. But the new president of the republic has clearly stated that he is in favor of a majority vote and that the most he could accept would be a slight proportional corrective to the system, which would enable the parties to preserve a certain number of political personalities from the hazards of the constituencies and ensure some slight representation for smaller groups.

Giscard's style of government is obviously not that of de Gaulle. The fundamental liberalism of the new president, his firm desire to reduce the tensions in French political life and to bring the state, the presidency, and the other institutions nearer to the people by limiting pomp and circumstance will no doubt give Giscard his own stamp and will contribute to the strengthening of the political system he has inherited democratically from the Gaullists. The Fifth Republic as such is not in danger.

But if Giscard's victory has not put an end to the regime, nor to the majority system, it has fundamentally upset the balance within the former majority. The psephologists have all underlined the major political change, which the sudden end of the domination of the UDR within the majority coalition represents. The Gaullist candidate only rallied some 15 percent of the electorate, a non-Gaullist is now in the Elysée, a minority of the Gaullists—the least illustrious and the most pro-Giscard—are in the government, and, while the Gaullist parliamentary party is still large, it is too divided, too unsure of its results in the next general election, to speak out loud and clear.[32]

For Georges Vedel, the UDR has ceased to benefit from the advantages given it up until 1974 by the support of the Elysée and

[32] With 181 deputies the UDR still represents within the new majority—which now includes the reformers—roughly 61 percent. If some sixty UDR deputies were to rebel, on one issue or another, the government would no longer hold a majority.

the unity of candidacy on the first ballot: "In fact most of those voters who have abandoned the UDR did not belong to it and had merely been 'lent' in a certain political situation. It is this situation which no longer exists and not Gaullism itself. . . . the percentage of votes obtained by [Chaban] gives the measure of the authentically UDR voters." [33] This interpretation, however, is not borne out by the periodic polls on voting intention, which, at the beginning of 1973, still gave the UDR 22 percent of the votes. It is inaccurate to equate the Gaullism of the voters with Chabanism and not to believe that some people expressed their Gaullism by voting for Giscard. Chabanism is more clearly representative of left-wing Gaullism than of Gaullism as a whole, and there is no proof that part of Giscard's supporters would not vote Gaullist rather than centrist in a general election.

For René Rémond, on the other hand, the change in the French Right is particularly clear and tolls the bell for Gaullism. Just as in 1952, when the *Rassemblement du Peuple Français*, created five years earlier by de Gaulle, broke up when the right-wing leader Antoine Pinay rallied some of the Gaullists, so Giscard is today in the process of federating the right-wing parties now that Gaullism has renovated and modernized the Right: "As for Gaullism as a political family, it is bound to dwindle as time goes by: . . . its survival depends on loyalty and nostalgia. It will no doubt subsist as a diffuse influence, like that of the Christian democrats who can today be found scattered all around the political compass." [34]

This interpretation may well be borne out by events. Nevertheless, the Gaullists have in their hands a certain number of cards which give the Gaullist party some chance of survival, some hope of continuing to make its weight felt within the majority. Their first trump card is that they are at present within the majority and numerous enough to have some influence on what they consider essential. They will also in the normal course of events be there long enough to be able to prepare for the next general election, which may be a decisive clash between the majority groups. In 1952 those who left the RPF to rally round Pinay chose to exercise power in a political system scorned by de Gaulle. Today the Gaullists have no necessity for such heart-searching. They are within a political system they themselves erected; they are part of the majority; and in the very first days of Giscard's presidency, Chirac, the UDR prime minister,

---

[33] Georges Vedel, "mort du gaullisme? . . . Pas sûr!" *Point*, no. 86 (13 May 1974).

[34] René Rémond, "les structures de la droite nouvelle," *Figaro*, 4-5 May 1974.

and Jacques Soufflet, the Gaullist minister of defense, clearly showed their capacity to defend what they considered the essence of Gaullism by forcing the president to exclude from the government Servan-Schreiber, who failed to respect the collective responsibility of the government when he publicly denounced the French nuclear tests. In a matter of weeks the UDR has turned from a frowning vigilance to loyalty to the new president. It seems as if the Gaullist party has decided to win over its brilliant adversary rather than confront him.

But the main advantage of the UDR lies in the fact that the Left is dangerous. By cutting himself off from the Right, Chaban caused the UDR to lose its place in the majority sun. Should Giscard cut himself off from the Bonapartist, popular Gaullism with its own brand of crusty nationalism, its taste for direct democracy, and its lack of confidence in the great capitalists, he would run the risk of losing power and being replaced by the Left. In other words, the federation of right-wing groups cannot hope to rally a majority of the electorate by itself. The social changes within the majority, begun by Pompidou and accentuated by Giscard, have gradually excluded the workers. This has coincided with the rise of the Left (see Table 3-10). In this context it is by no means certain that Giscard

Table 3-10
SOCIAL CHANGES IN THE PRESIDENTIAL MAJORITY

Social Categories [a]	Differences (Percentage Points) in Each Category Compared to the Percentage in the Electorate as a Whole		
	De Gaulle, 1965 [b]	Pompidou, 1969 [b]	Giscard, 1974 [c]
Executives, liberal professions	−2	+2	+24
Commercial and industrial employers			+17
Peasants	−7	+6	+10
Retired persons	+13	+3	+7
Employees	−5	−6	0
Industrial workers	−2	−15	−23
Vote	44%	44%	50%

[a] Profession of head of household.
[b] First ballot.
[c] Second ballot.
Source: Adapted from IFOP.

does not need the Gaullists. In 1978 when—all things being equal—the next general election will take place, the majority will probably not be able to afford to go before the electorate divided. The Independent Republicans may well be denied the opportunity of open conflict with de Gaulle's direct heirs by the president himself.

4

NEVER SO NEAR VICTORY: THE UNITED LEFT'S LONG ROAD TO THE 1974 ELECTIONS

Serge Hurtig

President Charles de Gaulle's defeat in the April 1969 referendum on regionalization and reform of the Senate, his resignation, and the ensuing presidential election caught the Left quite off its guard. Socialists and Communists both presented candidates, neither of whom survived the first ballot. The runoff election was between the Gaullist candidate, Georges Pompidou, and the candidate of the Center, Alain Poher, interim president of the republic by virtue of being president of the Senate, with the Left ignominiously absent.

By contrast, Pompidou's death in April 1974 found the Left miraculously well prepared for the May presidential election. It was only a year after the 1973 legislative election, but also the Left's internal relations had been radically transformed. François Mitterrand, first secretary of the rejuvenated Socialist party, was the obvious choice for a coalition of Socialists, Communists, and left-wing Radicals. Running largely on the 1972 *Common Program of the United Left,* he won 43.3 percent of the votes on the first ballot and 49.2 percent in the runoff election.

Never since 1958 had the Left come so close to victory, never since 1946 had it been as united.[1] While there was bitter disappoint-

---

[1] The Communists and Socialists belonged to the coalition governments led by de Gaulle until his resignation in January 1946. They then continued to cooperate in the *tripartisme* governments with the MRP (*Mouvement Républicain Populaire,* the French equivalent of the Christian democratic parties in other European countries). The alliance became increasingly uneasy, however, after the referendum of 5 May 1946, at which the first draft constitution of the Fourth Republic was rejected by a small margin, with many Socialists voting against their own party's advice. Opposed to both the Socialists and the MRP on many domestic issues, and committed to the U.S.S.R. at a time of growing international tension, the Communists were excluded from the government by a Socialist prime minister in May 1947, and since then have never held any ministerial responsi-

ment at having missed the mark by so little, hope was great: governmental power seemed no longer out of the reach of the Left. All that was needed was another small leap forward.

A Near Victory

The importance of this near victory can be judged only against the background of the almost constant erosion of the Left's electoral power since its peak in the immediate post-World War II period and at the beginning of the cold war. This erosion confirmed the deep splits in the workers' parties that went back as far as the founding of the French Communist party in 1920.[2]

Under the Fourth Republic, the erosion of the Left had been reversed only in 1956, and then for but a short period—and even then in parliamentary more than in electoral terms. At that time, supported for a few months by the Communists, the *Front Républicain* government led by the Socialist leader, Guy Mollet, had proved incapable of ending the war in Algeria, and had participated in the Suez expedition. In the opinion of many, it bore a large share of responsibility for the decline in governmental authority which led to the downfall of the Fourth Republic in May–June 1958.[3]

General de Gaulle's return to power in June 1958 and the triumphal ratification, in September of that year, of the constitution of the Fifth Republic—drafted with Guy Mollet's participation, and approved by the Socialist party, SFIO—eroded the Left even more seriously. The Socialists were badly divided, weakened by defections and the creation of a splinter party, the *Parti Socialiste Autonome* (PSA), which in 1960 became the *Parti Socialiste Unifié* (PSU). Neither in the 1958 legislative elections, as members of de Gaulle's majority, nor in those of 1962, as opponents, were the Socialists able to maintain their previous strength. Adamantly opposed to the Gaullists and to the new constitution, the Communists were in 1958 the major victims of an anti-Communist coalition, and their efforts of many years to reenter the main stream of electoral politics seemed doomed to fail. Their situation was not improved by the fact that

bility. See Philip Williams, *Crisis and Compromise: Politics in the Fourth Republic* (London: Longmans, 1964), pp. 20-25.

[2] François Goguel, "Combien y a-t-il eu d'électeurs de gauche parmi ceux qui ont voté le 5 décembre 1965 pour le général de Gaulle?" *Revue Française de Science Politique*, vol. 17 (February 1967), pp. 65-69.

[3] Williams, *Crisis and Compromise*, pp. 100-2.

Table 4-1

ELECTORAL FLUCTUATIONS OF THE LEFT SINCE 1962[a]

Election	Percentage of Valid Votes
1962, Parliamentary, first ballot	44.5
1965, Presidential, first ballot: F. Mitterrand	32.0
second ballot: F. Mitterrand	45.5
1967, Parliamentary, first ballot	43.5
1968, Parliamentary, first ballot	40.4
1969, Presidential, first ballot: G. Defferre, Socialist; J. Duclos, Communist; M. Rocard, PSU; A. Krivine, Trotskyite	30.9
1973, Parliamentary, first ballot	43.6
1974, Presidential, first ballot: F. Mitterrand, Union of the Left;	43.3
R. Dumont, "ecologist"; A. Krivine and A. Laguiller, Trotskyites	4.0
second ballot: F. Mitterrand	49.2

[a] Continental France and Corsica, excluding overseas departments and territories.
Source: Jacques Ozouf, "L'élection présidentielle de mai 1974," *Esprit*, July-August 1974, p. 37.

de Gaulle's personal and political appeal made inroads among their electorate.[4]

The changes in the internal relations of the Left which occurred after 1962, and especially after 1965, will be described in more detail in the following section. Let us here note simply that, in spite of relative success of the Left in the 1973 parliamentary elections, and in spite of the progress noted in public opinion surveys, enthusiasm was hard to arouse within the Left after Pompidou's death. The ease with which Mitterrand was selected as the sole candidate of the major parties of the Left and the rallying of many labor leaders rapidly created, however, a "dynamics of union" which showed at the polls. And although Mitterrand's supporters were very disappointed that he did not reach the 45 percent mark on the first ballot (many left-wing strategists thought that this could have created an irreversible "dynamics of victory"[5]), the closeness of his position to that of

[4] Serge Hurtig, "La SFIO face à la Ve République: majorité et minorités," *Revue Française de Science Politique*, vol. 14 (June 1964), pp. 526-56.
[5] *L'Election présidentielle de mai 1974* (Paris: Le Monde, 1974), p. 96.

his rival gave rise to the highest expectations in the days preceding the final vote. Victory did not seem out of reach, and although neither public opinion polls nor serious analysts gave much hope to the Left, defeat proved hard to acknowledge on election night, all the harder because the margin was so narrow. With 49.2 percent of valid votes on the second ballot, should the Left rejoice or lament?

The disappointment of left-wing partisans was quite understandable. Considering the political circumstances of recent years, the achievement of the united Left was remarkable and certainly deserves close analysis. Even two or three years ago, who would have dared predict that in the coming presidential election the left-wing parties would work as a team, select an effective candidate, and conduct an effective campaign? The change can be understood only in the light of more than ten years of French history: this was not an exceptional episode, but part of a lengthy and far-reaching process.

Out of the Wilderness: The Long Road to 1974

As has been noted, on the advent of the Fifth Republic the French Left was as divided as ever. The Communist party's line on both domestic and international issues and its intimacy with the U.S.S.R., displayed at the time of the Soviet intervention in Hungary in 1956, made it difficult for the Socialists to accept it as a reliable partner. From the Communist viewpoint, the same was true of the Socialists. Under Guy Mollet's leadership, the Socialist party had waged war in Algeria, participated in the Suez expedition, approved General de Gaulle's return to power, and called for the ratification of the 1958 constitution. The Radicals were divided; most of them had rallied to General de Gaulle. Pierre Mendès-France was the single major figure in opposition.

Slowly, however, the Socialists had been pushed out of the Gaullist coalition. Greatly weakened in the 1958 parliamentary elections, no longer members of the government after January 1959, and bitterly attacked as the grave-diggers of the Fourth Republic and colonialist warmongers by dissidents who broke away to create the PSA, they found it extremely difficult to go into outright opposition as long as the Algerian war lasted. How could they reproach General de Gaulle for trying to win the victory that they themselves had sought from 1956 to 1958, or for acting according to a constitution which they had helped draft and had approved? [6]

---

[6] Hurtig, "SFIO," pp. 537-45.

From Defferre to Defferre: 1962 to 1969. Peace in Algeria and the October 1962 referendum on constitutional revision created a new situation for the Socialists and the other political parties. The Algerian war was no longer a thorn in the Socialists' flesh. But the Socialists disapproved of both the procedure—referendum, rather than the constitutionally stipulated parliamentary vote—and the substance—the popular election of the president of the republic—of the constitutional revision. However, General de Gaulle's proposal was overwhelmingly approved by the voters. In the ensuing parliamentary election, although the Socialists participated in a *cartel des non* [7] to which the Communist party did not belong, Guy Mollet called for the defeat of the Gaullist candidates, even when this meant voting for a Communist.

The SFIO seemed to oppose not only the Gaullist government, as it had since 1959, but also the Gaullist regime, because it was no longer, in the Socialist leaders' view, in accordance with the 1958 blueprint. Could international détente and the evolution of the French Communists make agreement possible between the two major parties of the Left in time for the 1965 presidential election, which would be held under the new rules? Quite understandably, the Socialists hesitated before making their choice.

First there was an attempt at innovation on safe ground: Gaston Defferre, the Socialist mayor of Marseilles, announced his willingness to run, was approved as a candidate in January 1964, and then tried to set up a federation with the SFIO's longstanding allies, the *Mouvement Républicain Populaire* (MRP) and the Radicals, over understandably bitter Communist opposition. Defferre's strategy was to finish second (after General de Gaulle) on the first ballot and force the Communists to vote for him on the second ballot without having negotiated for their support. The MRP and the Radicals, by refusing to enter a "Socialist" federation, however, forced Defferre to drop out in June 1965. The hesitation of the Socialist leadership during the summer ended when a non-Socialist, François Mitterrand, announced his own availability, and rapidly won from the Communists what they had repeatedly claimed they would always refuse: support without negotiation of a common platform. [8]

Mitterrand's brave fight in 1965, despite his defeat by General de Gaulle on the second ballot, the subsequent creation of the Federation of the Democratic and Socialist Left (FGDS), which involved

---

[7] The "democratic parties" which had advocated the defeat of de Gaulle's constitutional proposal.

[8] Georges Suffert, *De Defferre à Mitterrand* (Paris: Le Seuil, 1966), pp. 122-23.

Socialists and Radicals under Mitterrand's chairmanship and the shadow cabinet (*contre-gouvernement*) which he led, were to prove important episodes on the road to the union of the Left. For the first time since 1936,[9] the Left closed its ranks for a major political battle.[10] Although both the FGDS and the *contre-gouvernement* were slowly to fall into oblivion, foundering in May–June 1968, the good showing of the left-wing parties in the 1967 parliamentary elections demonstrated that most of their voters were now willing to accept Socialist-Communist electoral agreements (in return for reciprocal withdrawal of candidates—*désistement*—on the second ballot) which would have been deemed "treasonable" a few years earlier.

This sort of reconciliation within the Left was reinforced by the Communist party's own evolution. Well aware that it was losing support in its traditional strongholds—the industrial workers were no longer increasing in number, and the new foreign proletariat had no voting rights—without winning over the new middle class created by the prosperity and technological changes of the late 1950s and early 1960s, the Communists sought a way out of the political ghetto where they had been stranded since 1947. General de Gaulle's policy of détente with the U.S.S.R. made anticommunism in the style of earlier years somewhat implausible: if an understanding with the U.S.S.R. was considered a reasonable aim, why should the U.S.S.R.'s French admirers be considered lepers, forever to be excluded from the domestic political game?

After 1962, at first tacitly, then quite explicitly, the Communists began to be viewed as legitimate partners by the other left-wing parties, although the Communist party long retained a Stalinist style. In the November 1962 parliamentary election, the Socialists had sided with the Center in the *cartel des non;* the Communists' slogan was then "March side by side, strike together." As noted above, the Socialists welcomed their votes and reciprocated. Gaston Defferre's attempt to federate Socialists, MRP, and Radicals and to run as the presidential candidate of a broad democratic socialist movement was, from 1963 to mid-1965, a stumbling block on the road to Communist reintegration. Defferre's failure and François Mitterrand's 1965 candidacy again made it worthwhile for the Communists to insist that, although revolution remained the final aim, day-to-day efforts could be more productively invested in progress on the electoral road to

---

[9] In June 1936 the parliamentary election was won by the "Popular Front" coalition of Socialists, Radicals, Communists, and minor left-wing parties.

[10] Michel Rocard, the leader of the small PSU, supported Mitterrand on the second ballot.

political power. The builder of the party, Maurice Thorez, was seriously ill, and had been succeeded by Waldeck Rochet. This change made the process easier, for although Thorez had taken the initiative of the rapprochement, he had long embodied the harder line, and he had no friends among non-Communist politicians.

In January 1966, soon after the presidential election, Waldeck Rochet proposed to Guy Mollet the opening of a negotiation between the Communist and the Socialist parties for a common governmental program. The Socialists rejected the idea as premature. Their counterproposal for a "dialogue . . . on the basic issues, including the aims and distinctive features of workers' action in a capitalist regime and the conditions and guarantees of political democracy,"[11] was accepted, and resulted in a series of articles, published in *Humanité* and *Populaire* (the Communist and Socialist daily newspapers), showing efforts by both sides to thresh out the causes of their deep disagreements, but actually underlining them.

The electoral pact signed in December 1966 by the Communist party and the FGDS was to prove effective in the 1967 parliamentary elections. It undoubtedly strengthened the hand of those Communists who supported the policy of joining forces with the Socialists against the Stalinist diehards. After a new dialogue in the Socialist and Communist newspapers and several months of discussion, the FGDS and the Communist party agreed, in February 1968, to a joint declaration which many saw as a first step on the road to a common governmental platform.[12] More important, undoubtedly, than the listing of the many areas of doctrinal or pragmatic agreement and the persistent disagreements—including the major issues of foreign policy—was the fact that this was a joint statement.

The upheaval of May–June 1968 and the Soviet invasion of Czechoslovakia in August temporarily blocked the rapprochement. The failure of the FGDS to act effectively during the crisis, Mitterrand's somewhat erratic initiatives, the pressure of militant radical students and young workers, and the left-wing parties' seemingly wavering analysis (was this a revolutionary situation, or a trap?) resulted in defeat in the June parliamentary elections, and defeat is seldom a factor promoting amicable relations. Although the French Communists publicly and clearly denounced the Soviet intervention in Czechoslovakia, they soon accepted the "normalization" of rela-

---

[11] *Le Monde*, 28 January 1966; Alain Duhamel, "Le Parti communiste et l'élection présidentielle," *Revue Française de Science Politique*, vol. 16 (June 1966), pp. 545-46.

[12] *Le Populaire de Paris*, 27-28 February 1968.

tions between the U.S.S.R. and Dubcek's successors, and they refused to question their own "fraternal relations" with their Soviet comrades. To the Socialists, agreement with the Communists, whom their middle-of-the-road supporters had never ceased to consider agents of the U.S.S.R., and whom many of the younger militants considered Gaullist stooges because of their opposition to *aventurisme*, seemed now far less attractive.

General de Gaulle's resignation in April 1969 moved the parties even farther apart. Never officially dissolved, the FGDS had ceased to exist sometime during the previous months. Negotiations had continued between the SFIO, Mitterrand's small group—the *Convention des Institutions Républicaines* (CIR)—and other minor left-wing formations, for the creation of an entirely new socialist party. Hardly had the date of the unification congress been agreed to than the Left had to face the problems of a presidential election. Mitterrand acted so as to be again, as in 1965, the candidate of the non-Communist Left, in the hope of winning Communist support. When Defferre announced that he was available and hoped to be endorsed by the Socialists, Mitterrand refused to attend the constituent meeting of the new party. The Socialist party which replaced the SFIO in May 1969 was faced with a clear choice. Defferre sought mostly the support of Center and non-Communist-Left voters. The leader of one of the non-SFIO political groups, Alain Savary, offered to be the candidate of a united Left, including the Communists. By a small margin, the convention at Alfortville chose Defferre's line, and Savary, having withdrawn, nominated the mayor of Marseilles to fly the Socialist colors.[13]

Defferre's strategy in 1963–1965 had been simple and plausible: fearing disaster, the Communists would not wish to stand and be counted in a presidential election, for they knew that even their own faithful would prefer a useful vote for a Socialist to a futile act of Communist fidelity. The problem was therefore to entrap the Communists so as to force them to support a Socialist, without any concessions which would alienate the middle-class non-Gaullists. In 1969, however, under vastly changed circumstances—General de Gaulle was no longer in the running and the Communists were much less generally considered lepers—the Communist leaders refused to be trapped. They nominated their popular elder statesman, Jacques Duclos. Their decision proved to be shrewd: on the first ballot Duclos won 21.5 percent of the votes. Despite the support of

---

[13] Stanislas Levif, "Le parti socialiste: quel renouveau?" *Etudes*, May 1972, pp. 722-24.

the respected and prestigious Mendès-France, Defferre's score was a humiliating 5.01 percent.

The postwar imbalance between Socialists and Communists had never been as serious, and some analysts rapidly buried French socialism. Defferre's defeat and the Communist success (even though both candidates of the Left were eliminated from the second ballot) seemed to impair all efforts at union. An agreement was conceivable only if the Socialists did not feel threatened by a far more powerful and disciplined partner, and many Socialists remembered quite vividly the fate of their East European comrades. Nevertheless, the Socialists' change of direction was as rapid as the defeat had been serious: there was no future in appealing to the Center. What the May convention had done was undone in July at the Issy-les-Moulineaux convention of the new Socialist party.[14]

From Socialist Unity to the Union of the Left: 1969 to 1972. The Alfortville convention had been dominated by the policies and personalities of two men, Defferre and Savary. It was Defferre's failure at the polls which led to Savary's victory at Issy-les-Moulineaux; his "union of the Left" strategy received 66 percent of the delegate votes. Although to many Savary was a former renegade—in 1956 he had resigned from Guy Mollet's government over Algeria, and in 1958 from the SFIO itself to help create the PSA and then the PSU— he was elected first secretary of the new party, with Mollet declining to serve on any of the governing bodies.

The "Issy-les-Moulineaux Resolution" outlined a clear policy which was to be unwaveringly pursued by the new leadership. It set the "union of the Left" as the "normal direction of Socialist strategy," and invited an "uncomplacent dialogue" with the Communist party, which could "lead to a political agreement only if satisfactory answers were given to the fundamental questions."[15]

Under Savary's leadership, the new Socialist party soon reversed the decline of previous years. The self-confidence of party workers was restored, and a process of rejuvenation was started which was to lead to a spectacular change in style. While Socialist unity was pursued so as to heal the self-inflicted wounds of the Alfortville convention, a difficult dialogue with the Communists was started, designed both to prevent the Socialists from moving towards the Center

---

[14] Ibid., pp. 724-25.
[15] Christiane Hurtig, *De la SFIO au nouveau parti socialiste* (Paris: A. Colin, 1970), pp. 85-89.

and to make it easier for the Communists to change their line on certain points by invoking the necessity of negotiation.

Bitterly fought by some of the more centrist-oriented leaders (some of whom actually left the party, while others, foremost among them Defferre, led the struggle from within), Savary's policy was generally approved by the Radical party until Jean-Jacques Servan-Schreiber became its secretary-general. The Communists saw in the new policy a major change, and their leaders used this opportunity to speed up their own party's updating.

At the ideological level, the Communist party had taken a new turn in December 1968, when the Central Committee, meeting at Champigny, adopted a manifesto entitled *For an Advanced Democracy, for a Socialist France.*[16] Drafted under the leadership of Waldeck Rochet, who, because of serious illness, was soon to be replaced by Georges Marchais, the "Champigny manifesto" defined a stage midway between capitalism and socialism. Under "advanced democracy," the area of freedom and democracy was to be extended rather than restricted. Violence would be used only in reprisal against bourgeois violence. For "a whole period," small business was to persist. Private property derived from work was to be protected and could be inherited. The manifesto also asserted that the Communist party's leadership must be constantly demonstrated rather than taken for granted.

The manifesto failed to answer many of the basic questions asked by non-Communists: Would opposition parties be accepted? What would happen if the opposition were to become the majority? How would the economy be organized? Nonetheless, it became gradually clear that its adoption had been far more than a minor tactical move. Despite several instances in which the Communist leadership demonstrated that it would not tolerate internal opposition, and that "democratic centralism" remained the organizing principle of the party, there were increasingly open discussions both among Communists and with other organizations. The generational change—for many of the younger Communists, Stalinism was history rather than a personal experience—helped to slowly transform the party from the closed society so convincingly described by its best analysts into a far more permeable one, without any apparent loss of the organizational strengths which still make it unique in French politics.

The dialogue with Savary's Socialist party was to last a whole year, from December 1969 to December 1970. The outcome was a

---

[16] *Manifeste du parti communiste français. Pour une démocratie avancée, pour une France socialiste!* (Paris: Editions sociales, 1969), 79 pages.

mere "statement of agreements and disagreements." The latter concerned mostly foreign policy, but also democracy itself. The Communists refused to accept the Socialists' firm contention that a government of the Left must submit to the verdict of the voters: the hypothesis of electoral defeat was not in their view even to be considered. Slowly, however, with the kind of majesty displayed by such bodies as the U.S. Supreme Court, the Communist party was to accept not only the multiplicity of parties aiming at the construction of socialism, but the existence of a political opposition, as well as the possibility of the alternation of leftist and non-leftist governments. An electoral victory of the Left need no longer be irreversible.

Within the Socialist party itself, the new direction adopted at Savary's instigation was, paradoxically, to become the nearly unanimous position on the occasion of Savary's displacement as leader by Mitterrand. Noting the Socialists' recovery after 1969 and approving their new political line, in 1970 Mitterrand and his friends entered into a long negotiation which led to a new "unifying congress," held at Epinay in June 1971. At this congress, Mitterrand gained the support both of the left-wing, which advocated an outright governmental agreement with the Communists, and the right-wing led by Defferre, which advocated a total break with the Communists. By a small margin, Mitterrand won over Savary, whose line had not changed, and was elected first secretary. By this point the opponents to the very idea of talks with the Communists were silent. The new policy was for the Socialist party to initiate a discussion about a governmental platform on the basis of a Socialist program to be adopted in March 1972.[17]

For the Communists, Mitterrand's election to the leadership of the Socialist party was at first a setback. The dialogue was interrupted for almost a year. The new Socialist leadership depended on the support of men such as Defferre, who both in their constituencies and nationally had always opposed attempts at union. Mitterrand himself, despite the experience of 1965, appeared somewhat unreliable, more preoccupied with the Socialist party's strength and his own ambitions than with a Socialist-Communist agreement. In October 1971, at a time of tension between the two parties, the Communists published their own governmental program, along the lines of the Champigny manifesto. In April 1972, President Pompidou's decision to submit the enlargement of the European Economic Com-

[17] Levif, "Le parti socialiste," pp. 726-30.

munity to a referendum again split the two parties: the Communists advocated a "no" vote, the Socialists abstention or a blank vote.

The desire for unity and the need for an alliance, given the constitution of the Fifth Republic and the existing electoral system, were too strong, however, for the split to widen. The Socialists adopted their own program, an unwieldy and hastily assembled repertory of either vague or minutely detailed proposals.[18] The negotiations could now be resumed. In the eyes of the press and public opinion, they were less unequal than they had been in previous years. Since 1969, first under Savary, then under Mitterrand, the Socialist party had been modernized and strengthened. In a few weeks' time, an agreement between the Socialists and Communists was drafted. Its final version was adopted by the two delegations on 27 June 1972 and ratified by each of the two parties on 9 July. Conversations between the Socialists and the Radicals had been broken off on 18 May, as the Radicals rejected electoral discipline—agreement on common candidates, with all withdrawals in favor of the Left—demanded by the Socialists. This led to a split within the Radical party, with a group led by two well known deputies, Maurice Faure and Robert Fabre, agreeing to the Socialist terms and approving in turn the common program.[19]

The Socialist-Communist agreement, a long document entitled the *Common Program of the United Left,* was quite naturally a compromise between the two parties' previously adopted manifestoes. Some analysts found it actually less doctrinaire, as well as less preposterously detailed than the Socialist one. It explicitly referred to the next five years, rather than presenting the blueprint for a socialist future. In the political and institutional field, while implicitly accepting the general framework of the 1958 constitution, the *Common Program* committed its signers to a vast array of steps for "democratization": reducing the powers of the president of the republic as well as his term of office (from seven to five years), creating an effective supreme court, adopting habeas corpus, guaranteeing by means of a *contrat de législature* (a contract valid for the duration of a legislature) between the government and the parliamentary majority the implementation of the mandate given by the voters. The plurality of political parties was explicitly recognized, as well as the right of the opposition to become an alternative majority. This

---

[18] *Changer la vie. Programme de gouvernement du parti socialiste* (Paris: Flammarion, 1972), 249 pages.
[19] Vincent Wright and Howard Machin, "The French Socialist Party in 1973: Performance and Prospects," *Government and Opposition,* vol. 9 (Spring 1974), p. 143.

was a new and important concession from the Communists, as was the statement, "Should the country refuse its confidence to the majority parties, they would give up power and resume their struggle in the opposition." [20]

The economy was also to be "democratized." A long shopping list of nine industrial concerns (including ITT-France) and whole branches of the economy to be nationalized was included.[21] It was longer than the list in the Socialist platform, shorter than that of the Communists. The "entire banking and financial sector" was to be transferred to the collectivity, and gradual nationalizations were to be "linked to economic development and to the demands of the masses." "Should workers express their will to have their firms enter the public or nationalized sector, the government will have the possibility of proposing such a step to Parliament." "Fair compensation" was promised, with, however, an "essential distinction" between large shareholders and others. This broad program of nationalization was, nevertheless, to permit the "subsistence of an important private sector." A disagreement was noted on the structure and operation of the firms in the public and nationalized sectors, where workers' intervention in management processes might take on new forms "which the Socialist Party views as part of the self-management approach, the Communist Party as part of the permanent development of democratic management." [22] This reflected the Communists' refusal to commit themselves to the demands for *autogestion* (self-management) characteristic of the 1968 movement and deemed unrealistic by them.

On foreign policy several compromises in the interests of peace were noted. The government of the Left would "participate in the construction of the European Economic Community," but would not give up its right of veto, thus excluding the supranationality so strongly favored by the Socialists. The nuclear striking force would be renounced, and France would not rejoin NATO, but no reference was made to withdrawal from the Atlantic alliance itself. The government would merely pursue the simultaneous dissolution of both the North Atlantic Treaty and the Warsaw Treaty.[23]

More important again than the content of the program, which naturally was bitterly criticized as irresponsible and a cover-up by

---

[20] *Programme commun de gouvernement du parti communiste français et du parti socialiste (27 juin 1972)* (Paris: Editions sociales, 1972), p. 149.

[21] Mining, armaments, space and aeronautics, nuclear energy, pharmaceuticals, in their entirety; electronics and computers, chemicals, partially.

[22] All quotations in this paragraph are translated from *Programme commun*, pp. 111 and 115-16.

[23] Ibid., pp. 172 and 175.

the Gaullists and their allies, and as far too timid by the PSU and the Trotskyites, was its political significance: the redirection of the Socialist party initiated in 1969 and the gradual opening up and moderation of the Communists since the mid-1960s had finally produced an agreement. Would it stand the test of the parliamentary elections to be held, at the latest, in June 1973? Would it be an effective tool in the process which was to lead to the presidential election to be held not later than the spring of 1976?

The Union of the Left Stands the Test: 1972 to 1974. Except for minor skirmishes,[24] relations remained quite good within the Left as the parliamentary elections drew near. Despite much internal discontent, the Socialists were able both to nominate many of their candidates as early as July and September, and to announce support for about fifty dissident Radical candidates who supported the *Common Program*. On 20 December, the government announced the date of the elections: 4 and 11 March 1973. United, the Left hoped to gain a large number of seats, perhaps even the majority, and thus create a political crisis which would force the president of the republic's resignation. There remained many ambiguities in its program, and many disagreements were quite clearly camouflaged under vague phrases. Socialists and Communists were undoubtedly rivals for primacy within the Left, at least as much as they were partners in their opposition to Gaullism. But their union, including the left-wing Radicals, was strengthened by the proximity of the elections. Public opinion polls showed that voters were far less frightened by the prospects of a victory of the Left than they had been in previous years.

Both before and during the official campaign, the Left was attacked mainly on two issues, both of which were to remain foremost in 1974: the financial cost of implementing the *Common Program* and the fate of democracy should the Communists share in governmental power. The nationalizations advocated by the Left and the increased expenditure to implement its social policies would, it was claimed, prove an unbearable burden and wreck the economy in a few months' time. If victorious, the Left would not be able to work within the constitutional framework, and would be either unstable and ineffective or dictatorial. Such assertions were energetically denied by both Mitterrand and Marchais. The government's platform,

---

[24] For example, when the Socialists convened a national conference on conditions in Czechoslovakia on 25-26 November, or when the Soviet ambassador wrote to Mitterrand to protest against his statements concerning anti-Semitism in the U.S.S.R.

they claimed, was far more demagogic and costly than that of the Left. They also argued that, because it was solidly united and could rely on labor support, the Left would be stable and democracy would be strengthened rather than endangered. Pompidou nevertheless made it clear that in his view the Socialists and left-wing Radicals, though sincere democrats, were acting as Communist stooges, and that the elections must confirm the mandate which he had won in 1969.

With 21.34 percent of valid votes for the Communist party and 20.65 percent for the Socialists and their direct allies on the first ballot, the Left made substantial progress, but still got well under half of the votes. The final change in the number of parliamentary seats was far more substantial, as the majority system and the second ballot withdrawals accentuated the swing: the Left now had 176 deputies, as against 91 in 1968, and several majority leaders had been defeated. But the 1967 level—193 seats—had not been reached.

The progress of the Socialist-Radical alliance did not please the Communists. Their Central Committee declared on 29 March that the Socialist party had no claim to primacy within the union of the Left. There was also an attempt, by transforming the *Common Program* from a platform for the 1972 elections into a more permanent political charter, to bind the members of the union together and have them travel the road to "advanced democracy," the stage at which the people would be in a position to adopt socialism. Although in all likelihood disappointed by their own performance, the Communists nevertheless retained the policy of alliance. In a vast post-election campaign, they made efforts to win over both those left-wing people who still considered the Communist party wildly revolutionary and those who saw in it a "party of order," far too respectful of bourgeois legality.

Now supported by both Defferre and Savary, and attacked mainly by Mollet's friends and a left-wing group which formally belonged to his own majority, the CERES, Mitterrand saw his leadership and policies confirmed by the Socialist congress held at Grenoble from 22 to 24 June. CERES opposition to the leadership's pro-European policy was defeated in the party's Executive Committee in November, and the policy was confirmed at an ad hoc convention held in December.

As rumors about President Pompidou's illness spread with growing intensity, as the effectiveness of the Messmer government was increasingly doubted, the Left remained remarkably united. The announcement of Pompidou's death, on 2 April 1974, was, despite the rumors, a surprise to the Left, as it was to most of the majority, but the reactions which it produced were far more orderly on the opposition side than those on the government side.

How Near Victory Was Achieved

The Left had no need for the complex and, to many, rather unappealing processes through which three majority leaders finally imposed their candidacy. The coalition of the major opposition groups worked with very remarkable smoothness. Neither the selection of the candidate nor the adoption of a platform gave rise to any embarrassing maneuver. There is little doubt that this contrast served the Left well.

Nominating the Candidate of the Left. No move was made until 5 April, when the *Comité de liaison* of the three signatories of the *Common Program* (Socialists, Communists, left-wing Radicals) announced that Mitterrand would be the "common candidate of the Left." The largest labor unions—the Communist-led CGT and the independent CFDT—soon stated that they would support the candidate of the Left, and, a few days later, the large teachers' union, the *Fédération de l'Education nationale* (FEN) followed suit. The PSU itself, whose leader, Michel Rocard, had been a candidate in 1969, and who had severely criticized the *Common Program*, also announced its support, although this was to produce a new split in the party's ranks. "It is obvious," the Central Committee of the Communist party stated on 8 April, "that the conditions for a majority of the French to vote in favor of a Communist candidate to the Presidency of the Republic are not met. Moreover, a twin candidacy of the Left could encourage the maneuvers of the Right with a view to pulling apart the parties united around the Common Program. This could have resulted in the absence of any candidate of the popular forces on the second ballot." [25] On the same day, a specially convened congress of the Socialist party approved unanimously Mitterrand's nomination. [26]

During the months preceding the election, various political analysts had advocated the twin candidacy rejected in the Communist communiqué. This, they claimed, would prove both the So-

[25] *Humanité*, 9 April 1974.
[26] Many PSU and CFDT militants tried, in vain, to convince a labor leader to stand in Mitterrand's place, or even against him. The two largest Trotskyite groups decided to present their own candidates. With his customary political acumen, Jean-Paul Sartre, the famous philosopher and mentor of the intellectual Left, called the union of the Left "a joke" (*Libération*, 13 April 1974).

cialist candidate's independence vis-à-vis the Communists and his strength. He would get far more votes than any candidate flying the Communist colors. Since only the two candidates who arrived at the top of the first ballot were allowed to run on the second ballot, Communist support would be automatically obtained, as well as that of anti-Communist opponents of Gaullism.

Others pointed out the dangers of such a course. Separate campaigns would stress the differences between the two candidates and be detrimental to the partnership of the Left. What if the Socialist candidate ran second to the Communist, as Defferre to Duclos in 1969? The accepted belief was that on the second ballot a Communist candidate would lose many Socialist votes and gain very few others. And what if, again as in 1969, the first two candidates on the first ballot were a Gaullist and the candidate of the Center—or of the Right? The Left would then, again, be excluded from the runoff election. There was little time, however, to weigh the pros and cons of each of the alternatives: the die had to be cast quickly, and the feeling of unity which the choice of a single candidate was bound to produce was in itself an asset.

The Candidate and the Parties. François Mitterrand was not above criticism. As a prominent member, and after 1953 president, of the UDSR, a small pivotal group very frequently needed to form a viable coalition, he had belonged to no less than eleven different governments under the Fourth Republic, of the Right as well as the Left.[27] From junior ministerial posts in the immediate postwar years he had risen to senior ones, the ministry of interior in the Mendès-France cabinet in 1954–1955 and the ministry of justice under Guy Mollet from 1956 to 1957. This was at the beginning of the Algerian war, and, in the light of his later evolution, he had then taken most unfortunate stands, refusing negotiations with the Algerian rebels, defending the Suez expedition, and requesting repressive emergency legislation. Since 1958 he had been quite adamant in his opposition to the Gaullist regime, which he saw as the product of a military coup, but only in 1962–1963 had he started calling himself a Socialist. In his own constituency in the Nièvre department, he had long run on an anti-Communist platform. Highly literate, an outstanding parliamentary debater, he did not seem very much interested in problems other than those related to his legal training; economics was for a long time a mystery to him, just as to many other French politicians. Finally, in 1959 he had been involved in a bizarre incident, a

---

[27] *L'élection présidentielle de mai 1974*, pp. 73–74.

simulated attempt on his life, which was never quite cleared.[28] To some, Mitterrand seemed dangerously vulnerable.

There were, however, fewer personal attacks on him than in 1965. Most of the press muted its criticism, and there was a tacit (or, perhaps, explicit but secret?) agreement among the three major candidates to refrain from personal innuendo. His successes as leader of the Socialist party and the loyal, though at times unenthusiastic, support of the Communists only confirmed the popularity which public opinion polls had recorded for a long time. His capacity to learn— he had rapidly assimilated the Socialist vocabulary and mannerisms— and his debating talent, as well as remarkable energy and physical resilience, were put to good use during the campaign.

From the very start, as is perhaps inevitable in a presidential election, Mitterrand acted in his own name rather than on behalf of the parties that supported him. He temporarily gave up his secretaryship of the Socialist party, and organized a campaign team composed mostly of his most faithful political friends. Some Socialist leaders complained privately during the campaign that they felt unwanted at his headquarters. As for the Communists, none is known to have participated directly in Mitterrand's campaign, even as an expert or adviser, unlike Mendès-France and Rocard, the secretary of the PSU, who assisted him on economic and financial issues. For many Communists, Mitterrand was the common candidate of the Left only in the sense that each of the components of the union had decided to support him; this implied no common action on his behalf. In the Paris area, for instance, militants were instructed not to belong to any joint campaign committees alongside the Socialists, but rather to set up Communist-led committees. His distance from the parties supporting him gave Mitterrand leeway for a personal campaign. At the very least, the claim that he was a prisoner of the old-time parties did not sound very convincing.

The Campaign. The two major problems which the candidate of the Left had to face were clear enough: he had to divest himself of the rigidities of the 1972 *Common Program* and propose a plausible economic plan by which to fight inflation and unemployment—while proving that he was not, and would not be if elected, a Communist stooge, yet could count on Communist support. The accent on economic problems, a field in which Mitterrand had never felt very

---

[28] Suffert, *De Defferre à Mitterrand*, pp. 117-18; Philip Williams, *Wars, Plots and Scandals in Post-War France* (Cambridge: Cambridge University Press, 1970), pp. 74-77.

much at ease, made it somewhat easier for him to free himself from the *Common Program*. Conditions had changed. The oil crisis, world inflation, and the balance-of-payments problems made it necessary to update the 1972 document, which had been drafted for a parliamentary rather than a presidential election. On 12 April, Mitterrand announced his three-phase plan: during the first six months, the government which he would appoint would fight inflation through price controls, a lowering of indirect taxation of indispensable consumer goods, a ten-billion-franc ($2 billion) government loan, the pegging of savings to the price index, and increased public investment and social expenditure. Phase two was to last a year and a half: the government would restructure industry, develop the most technologically advanced branches, and achieve mastery over credit and banking. Finally, a five-year plan would enable the Left to carry out its own program, reduce inequality, and improve the quality of life, with the help of "a clearly defined public sector." [29]

As for foreign policy, Mitterrand insisted that France belongs to the Western, Atlantic world. It can give up one security system only on the condition of finding another. It must help construct a united Western Europe and live in peace with the other Europe. He would accept no doubts about his own commitment to freedom. To reassure those who feared the Communists, he announced on 16 April that his prime minister would be an unnamed Socialist.[30]

Throughout the campaign, the Communists were to insist that the Left was bound by the *Common Program*, probably in order to reassure their own supporters, while Mitterrand tried to stick to his own plan. Rather favorably received in many sectors—*Le Monde* praised it, and its editor recommended voting for Mitterrand[31]—the Left candidate's economic plan was ferociously criticized by the majority. Mitterrand himself never defended it very convincingly, especially in his debates with Giscard d'Estaing, preferring onslaughts on the Gaullist record (inflation running at the rate of 17 percent a year) to a detailed discussion of his own proposals, especially on nationalizations.

Neither could Mitterrand be very explicit about the political future. Would he appoint no Communist to a major ministerial post?[32] If not, why? Since it was quite unlikely that a government of the

[29] *L'élection présidentielle de mai 1974*, p. 52.

[30] Ibid., p. 60.

[31] Jacques Fauvet, *Le Monde*, 17 May 1974.

[32] "The question of 'major ministries' is no problem for us." G. Marchais, statement on 15 May, quoted in *Le Monde*, 16 May 1974.

Left would get majority support in the National Assembly elected in 1973, would his election not result necessarily in a dissolution and new parliamentary elections? And what if the Left were then not to win a majority? The candidate's answer (that he would necessarily take account of the composition of the Assembly) was more irritating to the Communists, ever afraid of a Socialist betrayal, than it was reassuring to others.

As the campaign progressed and polls showed clearly that the election would be won by either the candidate of the Left or Giscard d'Estaing, Mitterrand's claim that this was a battle of Left against Right, of social justice and progress against conservatism, became increasingly credible. On 5 May, on the first ballot, the Left nevertheless did not reach the 45 percent which it had expected and considered decisive. In fact, in forty-nine departments, Mitterrand won a smaller percentage than the Communist, the Socialist-Radical, and the PSU candidates taken together had registered in the 1973 parliamentary elections. Did this mean that the Left had "a reservoir of votes," as it hoped, or that its situation was hopeless?

The problems of the Left were now fairly simple: getting a better turnout of its traditional supporters, adding the votes which had gone to the Trotskyite candidates, and winning over even a small percentage of the Gaullists. Mitterrand hoped that the bipolar second ballot would activate abstainers and make the extreme Left act responsibly. Would he win all the votes cast on the first ballot for the two Trotskyites, thus rising from 43.24 to 45.93 percent? Would a substantial portion of the 1.10 percent won by the ecology candidate, René Dumont, turn left? How many disappointed supporters of the two defeated candidates of the majority, Jacques Chaban-Delmas and Jean Royer, would join the opposition rather than voting for Giscard d'Estaing or abstaining? The campaign directed at the Gaullist voters was waged mostly by the Communists, who suddenly insisted on their common "commitment to the French nation and its greatness," and their common aspiration to see "a united French people work for a more just and more fraternal society." [33]

In his 10 May televised debate with Giscard d'Estaing, the high point of the campaign, Mitterrand sought to reinforce his image more than to communicate with his opponent. He was the bearer of the underdogs' hopes for social justice, the advocate of a new economic order and stability, and the representative of mass parties and labor unions. They were the majority.

[33] *L'élection présidentielle de mai 1974*, pp. 107-8.

Were they really? Not quite, or barely so, according to the opinion polls.[34] "Not quite" was the verdict on 19 May. Mitterrand found it difficult to acknowledge defeat graciously.

A Near Victory—What After?

Disappointment in the wake of the election was as high as the hopes just before the second ballot. Why had the Left failed? What had gone wrong? What should now be done? Such questioning was understandably widespread, in conversations and in print. Characteristically, however, Mitterrand's performance in the campaign was not criticized: he had done his best, none could have done better.

The assumption, by many on the Left, was that the votes for the Left ought to be a majority, if only Frenchmen voted rationally and if the Left knew how to tap the reservoir. The lessons learned in 1974 would provide the answer, and more favorable circumstances would be the springboard. How plausible is this assumption?

Let us note first that the 1974 circumstances were quite exceptionally favorable to the Left. The election was called during a rare Socialist-Communist honeymoon, with nothing to make an understanding between them difficult. The Socialist leader was unrivalled and almost uncontested in his own party, this in itself being a rather uncommon situation. An accomplished politician, Mitterrand was the only possible choice, which eliminated the necessity for bitter struggles over candidate selection. Giscard d'Estaing, Mitterrand's main opponent, who was running on his record, was a long-time minister of finance—never a very popular position for tax-conscious Frenchmen—at a time when inflation was getting out of hand, and he was the very embodiment of the intelligent but arrogant Right. President Pompidou's death had created a succession crisis in the majority's ranks, and no international crisis made governmental continuity indispensable in the eyes of public opinion. Although one can imagine future elections in catastrophic situations of unemployment or inflation, or both, it is nevertheless clear that the Left could not have hoped for a better deal in 1974.

A careful analysis of the votes shows, not unexpectedly perhaps, that at least a small percentage of the almost 50 percent who voted for Mitterrand were not traditional supporters of the Left. In all likelihood, it was Mitterrand's ability to go beyond the *Common*

---

[34] See the contributions to this volume of Jean Charlot and Alain Lancelot (chapters 3 and 6 respectively).

Program which won him 3 million additional votes: 13 million in 1974, as against 10 million in 1973. Virtually half of France hoped, in 1974, to be ruled by a left-wing coalition including the Communists. For the Left to go beyond the halfway mark, it must simultaneously remain united and push beyond its present borders.

The prospects for union could hardly be better. Both Socialists and Communists are committed to it and have gained from it, even if for the time being the Socialists' gains do create a problem for their partners. (But the Communists are confident that their vastly superior organization and militancy will reverse the process.) The moderation of the course pursued by the two collectivist parties gives their bourgeois Radical allies no cause for alarm. The extreme Left itself feels tempted: much of the PSU, including Rocard, will probably join the Socialist party fairly soon, as will many CFDT militants.[35]

Many political and ideological problems will remain unresolved within the Left, not least the contradiction between the Communists' doctrine and organization and their day-to-day political action. Not until the French Communist party becomes democratic in its internal operations will its partners really trust its commitment to democracy. But, were this to happen, what would differentiate it from a social-democratic party? And would a portion of its militants not wish to maintain a genuine Communist party? Another area where the disagreements are fundamental is foreign policy. Although disagreements are less acute now than they once were, and can to some extent be covered up, unexpected international problems may well reveal them.

Extending the borders of the Left means taking a moderate stand, designed to win over the discontented and the hesitant. It probably means renouncing the claim that almost 50 percent of Frenchmen voted for a new social blueprint *(projet de société)*. Clearly, the Left can impose changes—but not a wholly new society—if it improves its position only by a few percentage points, and its leaders followed with great care the course of the Chilean *Unión popular* to its tragic end. The Communists' capacity for maneuvering places them first in the race for the support of former Gaullists. Their insistent campaign since the election quite logically plays on nationalist and anti-American themes, while revolution is repudiated as an aim for the near future. Marchais's statements in a televised debate of 18 June are quite significant: "We shall go over to socialism when a majority of the people so decide by universal suffrage. . . . There is no majority

---

[35] Their decision was finalized in November 1974.

134

at present for socialism. . . . A majority of Frenchmen want limited changes. The Left must stick to its program of reform." [36]

The Socialists are hampered in appealing to the same clientele by the left-wing phraseology of many of their younger militants and the leadership's reluctance to clearly dissociate the party from extremism. Logically, the Radicals should be in the best position to win over to the Left the dissatisfied middle class, but they are identified with an outdated France and now mostly confined to one region of the country, the Southwest.

The major change brought about by the election is nevertheless the visible strengthening of the non-Communist Left. The poor showing of Defferre in 1969 is now seen to have been an accident, the result of an erroneous policy, rather than an indication of inevitable Socialist decline. The new balance of power within the Left, with the Socialists so visibly stronger than before, makes union with the Communists less dangerous, more acceptable. Several opinion surveys have confirmed that the public feels quite strongly this way.

Some of President Giscard d'Estaing's decisions since his election—for example, lowering the voting age to eighteen, prohibiting illegal wiretapping, liberalizing abortion and contraception laws—and his deliberately informal style have already created a new problem for the Left. The new president, whatever his past and the origins of much of his electoral support, seems quite sincerely to aspire to wide-ranging change. And, after all, is not his own problem extending his majority's boundaries well beyond 50.8 percent? The Left is generally skeptical as to his chances of success, and he may indeed founder on inflation and depression. Precedents are not clear, however. Such situations are most certainly not always favorable to the Left. No political analysis can now tell us if the 1974 score of the Left will prove a high stop in a long climb to the top, or a peak to be remembered with nostalgia.

---

[36] *Le Monde*, 19 June 1974.

5

A CARTOGRAPHIC APPROACH TO THE PRESIDENTIAL ELECTION, MAY 1974

Marie-Thérèse Lancelot and Alain Lancelot

The Method of Analysis

The method of analysis used in this chapter is known in France as "electoral geography." It proceeds from the establishment and comparison of numerous maps. André Siegfried brought the method to perfection with the publication in 1913 of his masterly *Tableau politique de la France de l'Ouest sous la Troisième République,* in which he analyzed the basic trends of public opinion in a large geographic region over a period of several decades. A great many similar studies have followed this example, particularly under the impetus of Siegfried's disciple, François Goguel. Technically, the method is very simple, and it can be defined by its five successive operations.

Selection of a Unit of Analysis. Electoral data can be studied in many varied territorial units, from the voting precinct to the total area. In a study relating to a small geographic entity, it is common to choose the commune (the smallest administrative division in France) as the basic unit, or, more rarely, the voting precinct. (There are 36,593 communes in France, divided into 51,925 voting precincts in 1974.) A regional study might be conducted at the level of the canton (about 3,000 in France). For a study of the nation as a whole, the legislative constituency (473) or the department (95) is usually selected. It is the latter unit that we shall consider here.

Selection of Data. The choice of a unit of analysis is often conditioned by the available data. At the time of writing, for example, the 1974 presidential election data for units smaller than the department have not been published. But the results of the particular election being studied are not the only data taken into consideration in electoral geography. The results of previous elections, or even such nonelectoral data as the vocations, religious affiliations, and income levels of the voting population are often included for purposes of comparison. In the present case only electoral data have been used. These data are: the results in both ballots of the 1974 presidential election and the returns from the presidential elections of 1965 and 1969, the legislative election of 1973, and the referendum of 5 May 1946.

Elaboration of the Data. The selected data cannot be utilized in the raw state in which they are published. The raw data represent absolute values, as dependent on the size of the unit under consideration as on the size of the phenomenon measured. For example, a highly populated department always has more votes for every candidate than a department that is thinly populated. To avoid bias, returns must be studied as proportions. But, here again, it is necessary to select the basis for the percentages. In certain cases the percentages are calculated in relation to the total valid votes. This technique has the advantage of revealing the relative strength of the parties in each geographic unit. But it has the disadvantage of not taking into account the number of abstentions and split votes, for neither the abstention nor the split vote is a neutral phenomenon. These vary from department to department and have complex relationships with the valid votes. They also vary considerably from one election to another. For these reasons, we find it preferable to calculate the percentages in relation to the number of registered voters—all the citizens who have the right to vote. In principle, registration on an electoral roll is obligatory for citizens aged twenty-one and over.[1] But since there is no penalty for not registering, a certain number of citizens (about one million) neglect to register and so are excluded from our calculations. Inversely, a certain number of electors figure on the commune lists who should have been struck off because of death or change of residence. This is a genuine problem, but it is limited. We believe that it is decidedly compensated for by the advantages of studying election returns in relation to the number of registered voters. Aside from percentages, various deviations and indices can be calculated from election data, but in this chapter we are mainly concerned with the addition and subtraction of percentages.

---

[1] In July 1974 Parliament accepted the reduction of the voting age to eighteen.

Cartographical Representation. For mapping purposes the data (percentages, deviations, indices, and so on) are classified and each classification is designated with a particular sign. The choice of categories—or, if one prefers, of lines of demarcation between units— is delicate. Often one hesitates between a classification following the particular phenomenon to be classified (the Communist vote, for example), centered on the average for that phenomenon, and an a priori classification, which allows several phenomena to be treated in the same way (the Left and the Right, for example) and thus facilitates comparison. The second solution is used here. Each unit covers five percentage points (for example, from 10 to 15 percent of registered voters, or from 15 to 20 percent) except for candidates with small electorates, for which smaller units have been chosen (2.5 percentage points). As for the signs identifying the various categories, they must respect the rules of unity and progression, so that the visual pattern corresponds to the electoral pattern it charts; that is, the progression from the lowest to the highest value must correspond to the program from the lightest to the darkest signs.

Interpretation. The interpretation involves description, which generally leads to explanation. Simple description is by no means without its value. The electoral variable, when crossed with a detailed regional variable, allows the variations in the phenomenon under consideration to be measured. But its essential interest is to suggest an explanation. In general, electoral geography calls three factors into play in order to explain electoral behavior: geographical factors, sociological factors, and historical factors. The first seeks to explain electoral behavior according to voter residence: climate and topography may hinder participation; a local paper may influence its readers; proximity to the residence of a candidate may bring into play the "friends and neighbors" reflex analyzed by V. O. Key, Jr., in *Southern Politics*. The sociological explanation seeks the reason for the behavior of a given unit in its social structure. The historical approach looks for the explanation of voting patterns on a given occasion in voting patterns of previous occasions: it examines a second ballot in the light of the corresponding first ballot result, or a presidential election in the light of the preceding parliamentary elections. In this chapter we will rely on the latter type of explanation almost exclusively. For us it is less a question of establishing a table of the electoral structures of France under the Fifth Republic to seek their causes—which has already been done in numerous publications—than of highlighting the specificity and originality of the presidential election of May

1974 in contrast to the previous elections. Consequently, our analysis gives more space to particular circumstances than to structural factors.

As we have just described it, electoral geography is infinitely more simple and less costly than psychosociological methods of analysis based upon opinion polls. Yet our method, too, has its limitations. Some are purely technical, having to do with the difficulty of acquiring data at the level chosen. For example, the results of a presidential election are not published by constituency, nor do we have any detailed geographic data on union affiliation, television viewing, average income, and so on. In certain cases the difficulty may arise because the variable is too uniformly distributed over a region for it to be taken into account, regardless of its importance in electoral behavior. This is the case with sex, for example. Finally, the censuses which furnish the basic data of electoral geography are intrinsically incapable of recording certain variables. These are the psychosocial variables—attitudes, party identifications, and so on—which constitute the raw material of opinion poll surveys.

But beside the limitations having to do with data, there are also two drawbacks to the method itself. The first is that it gives emphasis to territory over population. This is characteristic of all cartographic methods in which the units are represented according to their surface area rather than their population. For example, Nord is only very slightly larger than the department of Lozère, yet it contains twenty-six times as many registered voters. Doubtless this is an extreme case, but one must always bear in mind that electoral geography tends to give undue emphasis to rural zones in relation to urban zones. This was not an especially serious distortion in the days of André Siegfried, but it is certainly of significance today.

The second is the danger of confusing geographic correspondence with causality. The fact that two phenomena are similarly distributed over a given region does not necessarily mean that they are linked in a causal relationship and does not illuminate the meaning of that relationship if it exists. The problem is especially masked when data on two different phenomena are put into relation one with the other (for example, votes and religion or votes and union affiliation). The problem is too important for it not to deserve a mention here.

The method of analysis just described will now be applied to the presidential election of May 1974, taking the first and second ballots in order. (Map 1 shows the main regions cited in the analysis and the departments of metropolitan France. The maps displaying electoral data will be found at the end of this chapter, beginning on page 157.)

Map 1: DEPARTMENTS AND MAIN REGIONS CITED IN THE ANALYSIS

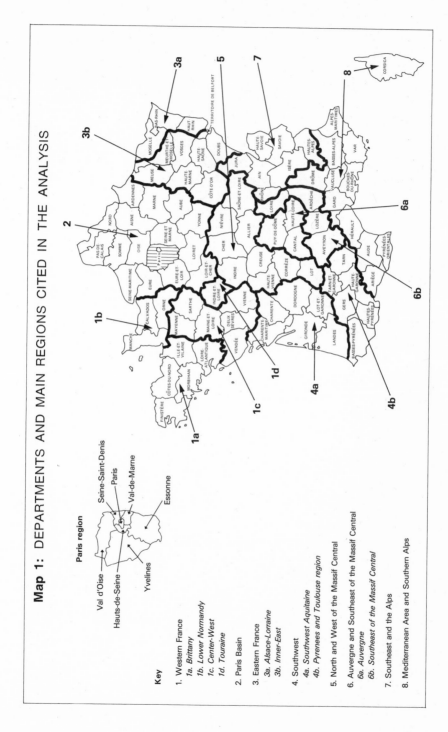

Key

Paris region

Val d'Oise
Seine-Saint-Denis
Hauts-de-Seine
Paris
Val-de-Marne
Yvelines
Essonne

1. Western France
   1a. Brittany
   1b. Lower Normandy
   1c. Center-West
   1d. Touraine

2. Paris Basin

3. Eastern France
   3a. Alsace-Lorraine
   3b. Inner-East

4. Southwest
   4a. Southwest Aquitaine
   4b. Pyrenees and Toulouse region

5. North and West of the Massif Central

6. Auvergne and Southeast of the Massif Central
   6a. Auvergne
   6b. Southeast of the Massif Central

7. Southeast and the Alps

8. Mediterranean Area and Southern Alps

Geography of the First Ballot, 5 May 1974

Nonvoting. On 5 May the rate of abstention for metropolitan France was 15.08 percent. Consequently, the first ballot of the presidential election of 1974 failed to beat the participation records established in 1958 and 1965. But the gap was slight. The rate was 15.06 percent in the referendum of 28 September 1958 (on the foundation of the Fifth Republic), and it was 14.98 percent in the first ballot of the first presidential election with universal suffrage (5 December 1965). On the 5 May ballot the abstentions were fairly evenly distributed. Only two departments exceeded 20 percent: Corsica (32 percent) and Creuse (20 percent). On the other hand, only two attained a figure of less than 12 percent: Somme (10.3 percent) and Pas-de-Calais (11.7 percent). It is a vivid indication of the permanence of collective attitudes toward elections that the poles of abstention and participation were the same for the last three elections:

	23 June 1968 (Parliamentary)	1 June 1969 (Presidential)	4 March 1973 (Parliamentary)	5 May 1974 (Presidential)
Maximum				
Corsica	37.4%	39.1%	32.4%	32.0%
Creuse	26.6	29.5	25.4	20.1
Minimum				
Somme	13.3	15.7	12.6	10.3

The general distribution is almost as stable. The abstentions for 5 May 1974 (Map 2) are practically identical with the abstentions for 4 March 1973. We see the same contrast between the election-conscious North and West and those departments in the eastern section which are less concerned with their civic responsibilities. The resemblance is true down to the details. We see in both elections, for example, that Charente-Maritime and Gironde and most of the Pyrenean departments constitute islands of comparatively high abstentionism against a background of more active participation.

If a more distant reference is chosen, the presidential election of 5 December 1965 (Map 3) also suggests a remarkable permanence in general structures. At most, we notice a slight increase in civic apathy for the 1974 election in east Lorraine—which had been canvassed in 1965 by Charles de Gaulle, who wore the cross of Lorraine as his symbol for thirty years—and a slight falling-off of abstentionism in the Southwest and Center-West.

Corsica is an exceptional case. Contrary to what one might think, the rate of abstentionism does not reflect a desire for home rule. It only indicates that the majority of Corsicans who have moved to the mainland remain registered in Corsica, where, thanks to correspondence voting, they constitute an electorate that is highly valued by local clans. But all those who are registered do not vote, even by correspondence, and thus the level of abstentionism is artificially high. The department of Creuse, where a considerable rural exodus has taken place, suffers from the same phenomenon, though to a lesser degree.

It is also noticeable that abstentionism is generally higher in the major cities than in the rest of the departments where they are situated. Such is the case with Paris (17 percent) in relation to the greater Paris area, Marseilles (23 percent) in relation to the rest of Bouches-du-Rhône, and Lyon (17 percent) in relation to the rest of the department of Rhône. This is partially explained by the fact that electoral lists are more difficult to maintain in large cities than in smaller towns, and are therefore less up-to-date. A number of voters who are counted as abstainers no longer live in the place where they are registered.

The Left. First we will consider the votes for François Mitterrand, then those for the lesser candidates of the extreme Left. Mitterrand, the joint candidate of the left-wing parties (Communist party, Socialist party, Left Radicals, and PSU), led the first-round balloting with 36.5 percent of the registered voters (43.4 percent of the valid votes cast). Map 4 shows the departmental distribution of these votes. Here we see that Mitterrand—who received a majority of valid votes in eleven departments—attained 45 percent of registered voters in six departments: Nièvre, for which he has been deputy since the war practically without interruption (48 percent), Aude and Ariège, rural departments of Southwest Languedoc and the Pyrenees (47.9 percent and 46.9 percent), Seine-Saint-Denis, a working-class suburb and Communist bastion north of Paris (46.2 percent), Haute-Vienne, the ancient rural stronghold of the Communist and Socialist parties in Limousin (45.4 percent), and Pas-de-Calais, a highly urbanized department in the North, partly comprised of coalfields (45 percent). Inversely, Mitterrand obtained his worst results (under 25 percent of the registered voters) in the traditionally Catholic right-wing departments of Haut-Rhin in Alsace (23.9 percent), Vendée (24.1 percent), and Mayenne (24.7 percent) in the West.

The geography of Mitterrand's support is a matter of tradition. The vote corresponds to left-wing geography as it has stood for thirty-five years. It is composed of three major strongholds. The first of these is northern France and the Paris Basin, a vast diamond-shaped region bordered by Dunkerque (Nord), Le Havre (Seine-Maritime), Orléans (Loiret), and Briey (Meurthe-et-Moselle), linking up the rich agricultural plains of the North with the intensely concentrated labor force of the Paris region, the North, and the East. The second is the northern and western belts bordering the Massif Central, from the departments of Nièvre and Allier in the North to Lot in the South—a green country with Red peasants. The third is Mediterranean France, with its extensions into the Pyrenees and the lower Alps, linking the important wine-producing departments to those in the lower Rhône valley that are undergoing rapid industrialization. In 1974 the southern left-wing stronghold also covered the southwest area—with the exception of Pyrénées-Atlantiques—and the main part of the southeast Alps.

The regions least favorable to the Left were western France (with the exception of the Sarthe, whose industrial concerns [Renault] orient it more and more towards Paris, and the Côtes-du-Nord, where the peasants are traditionally open to revolutionary currents), Alsace and the Vosges in the East, the northern Alps, and the Southeast of the Massif Central. All these regions are characterized by entrenched Catholicism.

Contrary to what has happened in the United States, the heart of the cities has remained residential, and is generally less favorable to the Left than the suburbs, where the workers are crammed together. The example of Paris, where real estate operations are little by little emptying the city of its working-class element, makes this clear. The city of Paris, which had almost 300,000 fewer registered voters in 1974 than in 1965, voted for Mitterrand at the rate of 30.8 percent of registered voters, while three entire departments in the nearby suburbs voted Left at the rate of 41.2 percent. The same phenomenon may be observed in all the big cities, counterbalanced by the fact that the residential suburbs to the west of the cities are usually extensions of the conservative "nice neighborhoods."

Mitterrand was a candidate against de Gaulle in 1965. On that occasion he took the votes of 27.1 percent of the registered voters on the first ballot (32.3 percent of valid votes). Map 5 shows the distribution of his votes at the time of that election. The general level is lower but the structures are very similar. Nièvre (44.3 percent), Aude (42.1 percent), and Ariège (40.5 percent) are already in the top group; Haut-Rhin (11.4 percent), Mayenne (13.4 percent), and Vendée (14.9 percent) are already among the most reticent; but it is Bas-Rhin which shows itself least favorable with 8.4 percent. Undoubtedly the most appreciable difference is in the eastern part of the Paris Basin where, in 1965, Mitterrand was far less attractive to the workers than de Gaulle and where Mitterrand made spectacular progress in 1974. He increased his margin in terms of registered voters by 19.5 percentage points in Moselle (from 16.0 to 35.5), 17.2 percentage points in Meuse (from 18.2 to 35.4) and 13.1 percentage points in Meurthe-et-Moselle (25.9 to 39). The increase in the strength of the Left is equally pronounced in Paris and in the greater Paris region.

In order to understand the geography of the joint candidate of the Left in 1974, it is helpful to examine the geography of the parties that backed him. Such is the object of Maps 6, 7, and 8. Map 6 illustrates the geographical distribution of the Communist votes in the first ballot for the parliamentary elections of March 1973. Map 7 illustrates that of the votes received by the Union of the Democratic and Socialist Left, an electoral cartel grouping the Socialist party and the left-wing of the Radical party. A comparison of these two maps is instructive. It shows that the non-Communist Left was more uniformly distributed than the Communist party. The two sides of the Left coincide in the urban zones of the North (Nord and Pas-de-Calais), the borders of the Massif Central, and the southeast Mediterranean. They are complementary, to the benefit of the Socialist party, in the Southwest and Center-West and, to the benefit of the Communist party, in the Paris Basin. Map 8 illustrates the distribution of the sum of the votes for the Left (PC, UGSD, and PSU) in the first ballot of 1973. Nationally, this grouping represents 35.1 percent of registered voters (17 percent for the Communist party, 16.5 percent for the UGSD, and 1.6 percent for the PSU), which add up to a little less than the votes cast for Mitterrand (36.5 percent). In percentages of votes cast, the relationship is inverted, 44.1 percent in 1973, 43.4 percent in 1974, an indication that the electoral mobilization benefited Mitterrand a little less than his opponents. From the geographical point of view, the structures are in the main very similar. The presidential election, by nature less sensitive to the diversity of the candidates than parliamentary elections, is a little more uniform. In 1973 the entire left-wing varied between a minimum of 15.6 percent (Bas-Rhin) and a maximum of 50.7 percent (Pas-de-Calais), making a gap of 35.1 percentage points as against 24.1 percentage points in the presidential election.

To make a systematic comparison of the Left during the parliamentary and presidential elections we have drawn up Maps 9 and

10. Map 9 shows those departments where Mitterrand did better in 1974 than the Left in 1973. Map 10 shows those where his results were poorer. The "gains map" corresponds rather to the weak zones of the Left and demonstrates the phenomenon of standardization or "nationalization" mentioned above. Mitterrand, a national leader campaigning along national lines, attracted support even in the regions where the leftist parties are so weak that they have trouble finding candidates, much less good ones. The "losses" map corresponds closely enough to the distribution of the Communist party.[2] This geographic correspondence may be explained by the defection of some of the Communist party supporters or even by the defection of some of the non-Communist Left where the Communist party is so strong that Mitterrand could have been taken to be the Communist candidate. In any case, we note that the losses are particularly striking in regions of strong Communist-Socialist competition, such as Pas-de-Calais, Haute-Vienne, Gard, and even Bouches-du-Rhône.

Against the left-wing coalition candidate there were three candidates representing extreme-left-wing positions. Arlette Laguiller campaigned on labor, Trotskyist, and feminist platforms, Alain Krivine, the strictly Trotskyist platform, and René Dumont, the ecology platform. Among them they took 3.4 percent of registered voters (4 percent of the valid votes), in contrast to 1.1 percent won by the extreme Left without the PSU in 1973.

Map 11 shows the distribution of the extreme Left in 1974. This map has been drawn up on a finer scale, the better to reflect variations in the distribution of this tiny minority. Three areas of strong support stand out: the Paris Basin, the southeast Alps and the Massif Central. It is characteristic of these areas that they comprise industrial departments *and* highly rural departments. In the first case, we see the result of working-class and ecological themes, whereas in the second the extreme-Left vote is more a protest vote. Both the ideological vote and the protest vote won by the extreme Left, notably by Arlette Laguiller, were doubtless to the detriment of Mitterrand. It is possible that these platforms tempted voters, particularly women, who had been in the habit of abstaining because no candidate had taken their specific problems into consideration.

Gaullism. The Gaullist party was represented on 5 May by the candidacy of Jacques Chaban-Delmas, one of the "barons" of the move-

---

[2] Particularly, if we except those few departments where Mitterrand's failure to win is explained by the candidacy of a local man (Giscard in Puy-de-Dôme, Chaban in Gironde, and Royer in Indre-et-Loire).

ment. The former prime minister entered the campaign as the favorite. On the night of the first ballot he came in third, far behind Mitterrand and Valéry Giscard d'Estaing, with 12.2 percent of registered voters (14.6 percent of valid votes), the worst showing for the Gaullists since the foundation of the Fifth Republic in 1958.

Map 12 shows the distribution of the votes in favor of Chaban-Delmas, revealing its even distribution at a very low level, less than 15 percent of registered voters in eighty-three departments and a small concentration in Southwest Aquitaine.

In regard to the first point, one notices that Chaban-Delmas's vote is particularly weak in the personal strongholds of the principal candidates: Puy-de-Dôme, associated with Giscard d'Estaing (3.7 percent), Indre-et-Loire with Jean Royer (6.3 percent), and Nièvre with Mitterrand (8.1 percent). So far as the concentration for Chaban-Delmas in the Southwest is concerned, it corresponds to his own regional support, as mayor of Bordeaux, which extends beyond Gironde (where the level reaches 30 percent of registered voters) into neighboring departments. Outside this region, the only department favorable to Chaban-Delmas is Corsica, the loyal island, where Bonapartism has not completely disappeared.

Chaban's support, combining, as it does, a residual political phenomenon with a personal phenomenon, does not lend itself to cartographic analysis. In any case, it will be noted that the partisans of the "new society" were not recruited particularly from the leftist departments, nor from the major cities, in contrast to the Mendès-France supporters of 1956 to whom they have sometimes been compared. Chaban-Delmas did not match his national average (nor even that for the whole of France less Gironde, which was 11.9 percent) in any of the fifteen largest French cities except Bordeaux.

The geographic patterns of the Chaban-Delmas vote are very different from the habitual support patterns of the Gaullist party as they appear on the reference maps we have drawn up, Map 13 showing de Gaulle's vote in the first ballot of the presidential election of 1965, Map 14 for the Pompidou vote in the first ballot of 1969, Map 15 for the majority (UDR, Independent Republicans, and the centrists of the CDP) who backed Pompidou and Pierre Messmer in the first ballot of the parliamentary elections of March 1973. These three reference maps have a certain air of kinship. We find the same strongholds in Western France, Eastern France, and the Southeast of the Massif Central, and the same weak zones in the left-wing regions of the Paris Basin, central and southern France. We note, however, that de Gaulle was clearly superior to his political heirs in the industrial North and East. From 1965 to 1969 the center of gravity in the Gaullist party moved slightly towards the South, a shift in keeping with the geographic origin of Pompidou, former deputy of Cantal. In 1973 this phenomenon continued to the extent that the majority penetrated the strongholds of the republican South at the same moment that it lost its dominant position in certain departments of the East and the Paris Basin.

To have a more precise view of the evolution of Gaullism from the majority of 1973 to the Chaban-Delmas vote of 1974, a map showing the divergences (in percentages of registered voters) between these two phenomena has been drawn up (Map 16). They are all negative for Chaban-Delmas, with the exception of Gironde, yet by only 0.8 percent of registered voters. This map is such a faithful reproduction of the map of the majority in 1973 (Map 15) that one cannot but consider the Chaban vote as a residual vote, except in the Southwest and, to a lesser extent, in the North.

Giscard d'Estaing and the Center. With 27.7 percent of registered voters (32.9 percent of valid votes) Giscard d'Estaing easily carried the first ballot election against Chaban-Delmas among those hostile to the united Left.

Map 17 gives the geographical distribution of his votes on 5 May 1974. These votes vary between a maximum of 38.6 percent (Morbihan) and a minimum of 12.1 percent (Gironde). Three regions are particularly favorable to Giscard: Western France (six departments above 35 percent), the southeast Massif Central (four departments above 35 percent), and Eastern France (one department over 35 percent). Outside these strongholds, there were also high percentages in Paris and in the south Paris Basin as well as in the southeast Alps. The least favorable regions were the Southwest, where the influences of the left-wing and Chaban-Delmas come together, Royer's Midwest and the northern part of the country, where Gaullism was reconquered by the Left.

Backed from the start of the campaign by the centrist party of Jean Lecanuet and benefitting from the neutrality of Jean-Jacques Servan-Schreiber, Giscard presented himself as the spokesman of the Center. The map of the distribution of his votes does not, however, establish any correlation with that of the votes for Alain Poher (Map 18), who wore the centrist colors in the presidential election of 1969, in which he took 18.1 percent of the registered voters in the first ballot. South of the Loire their positions are reversed. Poher enjoyed successes in Southwest Aquitaine and the Toulouse region (where Giscard is particularly weak) thanks to the moderate Socialists who voted for him, but he did not manage to penetrate the Center support faithful to Pompidou and which rallied en masse to Giscard d'Estaing in 1974.

Since the geography of centrism was profoundly altered in 1969 by the collapse of the non-Communist Left (whose supporters, anticipating a rally in time for the second ballot, abandoned Gaston Defferre in order to back Poher on the first ballot), it would doubtless be better to select a different point of comparison. Politically, the map of the centrist *Réformateur* movement for 1973 is indispensable (Map 19). But the difference in level is such between the 1973 *Réformateur* vote and Giscard's 1974 vote that a comparison does not reveal much. With only 9.9 percent of registered voters in the first ballot of the parliamentary elections the centrist party is very far from Giscard's score. Its successes, a little more marked in the East and West, suggest networks of supporters rather than any ideological influence.

The map showing the divergences between the Giscard vote in the 1974 first ballot and the *Réformateur* vote of March 1973 (Map 20) is, nonetheless, instructive. This map makes it clear where the main part of the Independent Republican leader's votes came from. This map is reminiscent of Maps 17 (votes for Giscard) and 15 (the majority in 1973). In other words, it was among the Gaullist majority of 1973 rather than centrists that Giscard found the voting base for his ascendancy in the 1974 election.

Map 21, showing the divergences between the majority of 1973 and the Giscard vote, provides a "counter-proof." On the whole, the divergences are much less important than divergences which appear on Map 20. Giscard d'Estaing was slightly stronger than the 1973 majority in twenty-eight departments which, with a few exceptions, were favorable to the Center in 1973.[3]

Royer. Running first among the lesser candidates, Royer resigned from his position as minister in charge of the postal and telecommunications service in order to campaign—or rather crusade—on behalf of the small family business and austere principles that are threatened by the permissive society. On 5 May he took 2.7 percent of registered voters (3.2 percent of valid votes). The geographic distribution of his votes appears on Map 22, which again has been

---

[3] The exceptions are the left-wing departments where Giscard's candidacy was able to mobilize centrist and moderate supporters who were reduced to abstaining in the parliamentary elections of 1973. Map 21 also shows the Southwest and Center-West departments where Giscard was most strongly challenged by Chaban-Delmas and Royer among majority supporters.

drawn up on a finer scale than the other maps to make possible a graphic representation of Royer's small vote. Royer took above 5 percent of registered voters in only nine departments, while he scored less than 1.5 percent in six, and in Corsica dropped as low as 0.5 percent. The Royer phenomenon is a striking example of regional influence. As mayor of Tours and deputy of Indre-et-Loire, the former minister had considerable local success. In Tours he led the field with 28.9 percent of registered voters (35.3 percent of valid votes), and was hard on the heels of Mitterrand in the overall vote in Indre-et-Loire (28.5 percent of registered voters as opposed to 29.6 percent). His support progressively decreases the further one gets from his center of popularity. He received more than 7.5 percent of the vote in three departments bordering on Indre-et-Loire, more than 5 percent in a slightly wider area and, finally, more than 2.5 percent in the whole of the Center-West. Outside this conglomeration of twenty-two contiguous departments, only five departments accorded him more than 2.5 percent of registered voters. It would be difficult to find a better defense and illustration of electoral geography.

From the Majority of 1973 to the Majority of 1974. Chaban-Delmas, Giscard d'Estaing, and Royer were all members of the 1973 majority. Thus it is legitimate to consider their votes together. Map 23 gives the geographic distribution of this amalgam, which represents 42.7 percent of registered voters (50.7 percent of valid votes) on 5 May 1974, a proportion comparable to that attained by the sole candidates for the majority in 1965 and 1969. In 1965 de Gaulle took 36.7 percent of registered voters on the first ballot (43.7 percent of valid votes). In the first ballot of 1969 Pompidou obtained 33.9 percent of registered voters (44 percent of valid votes). By comparison, let us remember that on the first ballot of the parliamentary elections of 1973 all the candidates claiming to represent the majority totalled 30.1 percent of registered voters (37.9 percent of valid votes) among them.

Whatever their differences of level, these successive states of the electorate of the majority retain the same geographical structures. Map 23 does not break with that tradition. It is very similar to Maps 13, 14, and 15. We find the same strongholds in the West, East, and in the Southeast of the Massif Central. Also the same are the less favorable zones in the North and the West of the Massif Central, along the Mediterranean, in the northern part of the country, and in the working-class suburbs. An exceptional density of "majority" votes can be observed in the West, where eight out of the nine departments giving above 50 percent (Vendée 58.1 percent) are situated. Inversely, only eight departments go below 35 percent (Ariège 30.7 percent).

In order to give a true appreciation of the advances and retreats of all the majority candidates of 1974 in respect to 1973, Map 24 has been drawn to show the divergences between their individual votes and the total votes received in 1973 by the parties that backed either one or the other in 1974. This map allows us to distinguish two kinds of progression. The first concerns the left-wing strongholds (Bouches-du-Rhône and Haute-Vienne, for example) where the Right and the Center are very weak, if not absent, in parliamentary elections. In a presidential election, the appeal of the right-wing candidates, who are national leaders, is much greater. The second progression takes place in the areas where the majority candidates exerted personal influence (Auvergne for Giscard d'Estaing, Aquitaine for Chaban-Delmas, Touraine for Royer). So far as the minor losses from 1973 to 1974 are concerned, it is mostly a question of left-wing inroads into the zones of Right and Center parliamentary domination. This is the counterpart of the right-wing successes in the parliamentary strongholds of the Left. This twofold phenomenon of interpenetration is linked to the nature of the presidential competition, animated by national leaders, which greatly contributes to the "nationalization" of electoral behavior.

Geography of the Second Ballot, 19 May 1974

Nonvoting. On 19 May 1974 the level of abstentionism sank to a record low, 12.1 percent for metropolitan France. Never in the history of French universal suffrage had such a proportion been approached. When account has been taken of the enforced abstentions resulting from circumstances outside the voters' control or from errors on the electoral lists, which together affect from 5 percent to 7 percent of registered voters, the proportion of abstentions resulting from indifference, hesitation, or hostility is very slight.

This residual abstentionism is very evenly distributed over the entire country, as Map 25 demonstrates. Only in two departments does the level rise above 15 percent, Corsica (22.6 percent), which has never before scored such a high level of participation, and Bouches-du-Rhône (15.3 percent). On the other hand, the level descends below 10 percent in ten departments. Five of these are situated in the northern half of the country (where Somme beats all records with 8.2

151

percent) and five are in the Southwest, where the rising level of participation has been very striking for some fifteen years.

Nor did the major cities remain untouched by this exceptional mobilization. The rate of abstention was 14.7 percent in Paris, 15 percent in Lyon, and a little under 18 percent in Marseilles. But the cities as a whole voted to a slightly lesser extent than the rest of the country.

Map 26 shows the drop in abstentionism, or, if one prefers, the increase in the relative proportion of votes between the two ballots. It demonstrates that the level of participation rose greatly where it had not been high on the first ballot (the southeast quarter of the country). With regard to departmental geography it is difficult to say who profited from this mobilization. Some signs indicate that it was probably Mitterrand. In towns of more than 30,000 inhabitants, for example, Giscard d'Estaing took 0.2 of a percentage point fewer registered voters on the second ballot than the sum of the right-wing and lesser candidates had taken on the first ballot (42.5 percent as against 42.7 percent), while, in terms of registered voters, Mitterrand gained 2.5 percentage points (from 39.8 percent to 42.3 percent) more than did all the left-wing candidates on the first ballot. Abstentions and spoiled ballots went down by 2.3 percentage points (from 17.5 to 15.2).

Giscard d'Estaing. Elected on 19 May by a small lead (50.7 percent of valid votes in metropolitan France), Giscard received the votes of 43.9 percent of registered voters. Although his election was more difficult than those of his two predecessors, he received almost as many votes as de Gaulle and many more than Pompidou, thanks to the high level of participation:

	Out of 100 votes cast	Out of 100 registered voters
19 December 1965, de Gaulle	54.5	44.7
15 June 1969, Pompidou	57.6	37.2
19 May 1974, Giscard d'Estaing	50.7	43.9

Map 27 shows the distribution of Giscard's votes on the second ballot. Taking an absolute majority of valid votes in fifty-one departments, Giscard obtained above 50 percent of registered voters in sixteen. He pulled in below 35 percent of registered voters in only four departments, Ariège, least enthusiastic with 31.5 percent, Nièvre, Seine-Saint-Denis, and Aude.

Three strong zones stand out: (1) Western France—where the pro-Giscard vote hits its highpoint in Vendée with 59.4 percent—stretching as far as the western sector of the Paris Basin and into Paris (with the exceptions of Côtes-du-Nord and Sarthe, the pro-Giscard vote was above 45 percent of registered voters in the departments of this region), (2) Eastern France, from Meuse to Doubs and from Haute-Marne to the Rhine, and (3) the heart of the Massif Central, stretching as far as the northern Alps by way of the Catholic area around Lyon. The zones of weakness were: (1) the north and the center of the Paris Basin, (2) the North and West of the Massif Central, (3) the Southwest, with the exception of the Catholic Basque regions, and (4) the Mediterranean region, with its extensions into the lower Rhône valley and upper Provence.

The progress made by Giscard d'Estaing between the first and second ballots is particularly appreciable in those departments where his rivals from the majority were hailed with enthusiasm on 5 May. This appears clearly on Map 28, where the united zones of influence of Chaban-Delmas and Royer are shown. In certain departments it is also apparent that many of those who abstained on 5 May turned out for Giscard on 19 May.

Because of the closeness of their average values, it is interesting to compare the maps showing the votes of de Gaulle and Giscard d'Estaing at the final ballots of 1965 and 1974. The map representing the vote for de Gaulle (Map 29) shows slightly greater contrasts, varying between a maximum of 63.5 percent of registered voters in Bas-Rhin and a minimum of 28.2 percent, a gap of 35.3 percentage points, while the gap is only 27.9 percentage points between the most and least favorable departments for Giscard. But the geography is on the whole the same. The only qualifying factor is that de Gaulle was stronger in the north and center of the Paris Basin—where he took votes from the Left—while Giscard is better established south of the Loire.

In order to illustrate the permanence of electoral structures one might compare Map 28 with earlier references, maps showing the votes of the Center and Right under the Fourth or even the Third Republic. The election we have chosen is the referendum of 5 May 1946, in which the "no" of the Right and Center narrowly won the day over the Socialist-Communist "yes" (53 percent of valid votes against 47 percent, 41.7 percent of registered voters against 36.9 percent) and thus threw out the first draft constitution of the Fourth Republic. Map 30 shows the geography of the "no" vote, which varied between a maximum of 59.7 percent (Manche) and a minimum of 23.3 percent (Haute-Vienne). After twenty-eight years and many political upheavals, and in spite of a veritable socioeconomic transformation, the map for the Center and Right of 1946 and that of 1974 seem virtually copied one from the other. This would make a fine lesson in modesty for the sociologists and economists who, obsessed with socioprofessional categories and growth rates, seem to be ignoring history. In France voting patterns are truly as much the result of geographically entrenched political tradition as the result of social conditions.

Mitterrand. Taking 49.3 percent of valid votes in metropolitan France, which represents 42.8 percent of registered voters, Mitterrand carried the Left to a level that it had not before achieved under the Fifth Republic. Map 31 shows the geographical distribution of votes cast in his favor on 19 May 1974. The candidate of the Left attained an absolute majority of recorded votes in forty-four departments and in seven a majority of registered voters, with his best turnout in Ariège (55.6 percent). In only four departments did he score less than 30 percent of registered voters, Bas-Rhin, the lowest with 27.8 percent, Haut-Rhin, Mayenne, and Vendée.

The map seems practically the opposite of that showing Giscard d'Estaing's vote. There are four main areas of strength: the north of the Paris Basin extending into the working-class suburbs of the capital, the North and the West Massif Central, Southwest Aquitaine and the Pyrenees, and the Mediterranean South and Rhône areas.

Since departmental geography tends to focus excessively on the rural areas of France, we have sought to ascertain Mitterrand's results in the urban areas. First let us consider the fifteen largest cities. The left-wing candidate outdid Giscard in only four, Marseilles, Toulouse, Le Havre, and Grenoble. In the other eleven, including Paris, he came in second. In the towns with population figures above 30,000, Mitterrand obtained 42.3 percent of registered voters in the final ballot, but here too he was beaten by Giscard, who obtained 42.5 percent.

From the first to the second ballot, Mitterrand gained 6.3 percentage points in terms of registered voters nationwide. This advance was far from being uniformly distributed, as Map 32 demonstrates. The left-wing gains are a little more marked in a strip of territory which slowly widens as it stretches from the north of the Paris Basin to the Pyrenean Southwest. These gains are largely the result of the transfer of extreme-left-wing voters whose candidates backed Mitterrand on the final ballot. But Map 33, which presents the divergences between the total left-wing vote on the first ballot and the vote for

Mitterrand on the second one, shows that this explanation does not suffice. A certain number must be added, coming from the abstentions on one hand and from eliminated majority candidates on the other. In this last case, it is sometimes less a case of real progress by Mitterrand than a return to the Left of voters who had been temporarily won over by the local appeals of Chaban-Delmas and Royer (see Map 9).

In the final ballot of the presidential election of 1965, Mitterrand took 37.3 percent of registered voters, 5.4 percentage points less than he took on 19 May 1974. This overall shift can be seen by comparing Map 31 and Map 34, which gives the votes cast in Mitterrand's favor at the final ballot of 1965. Here the left-wing candidate only achieved an absolute majority of registered voters in five departments (maximum, Aude with 55.4 percent). He dropped below 25 percent in six departments (minimum, Bas-Rhin with 16 percent). Except for this difference of level, the patterns are the same, allowing for the fact that in 1974 the Left reconquered northern France, where de Gaulle had given the Left a hard time in 1965.

Here, yet again, we can easily find references going back to 1956, 1936, or even 1849 that demonstrate the permanence of left-wing traditions in certain regions of rural France. For reasons of symmetry, we will look only at Map 35, which charts the geography of the "yes" vote in the referendum of 5 May 1946. The similarity between this and the Mitterrand vote on 19 May 1974 is striking. There are the same strong zones (49.1 percent in Aude) and the same weak zones (20 percent in Manche, 20.5 percent in Vendée, 20.6 percent in Bas-Rhin). The stronghold of agricultural and industrial France in the North, weakened in 1965, shows up clearly, a sign that the Gaullist penetration of that region was only a parenthesis.

Once again electoral geography brings us back to a consideration of history and to the political traditions which are passed on within given regions from generation to generation. It is this, finally, that seems to be its principal lesson. It cannot claim to rival opinion polls when it comes to measuring the influence of psychosocial variables or sociological criteria. But only electoral geography allows us to estimate the importance of the unconscious feelings of fellowship which condition voting in both space and time.

The Maps

The maps which follow are drawn up by department within the framework of the ninety-five departments as they exist at present.

The two exceptions are Maps 30 and 35, dealing with the referendum of 1946. On these maps the Paris region is composed of three units: the department of Seine-et-Oise (now three departments: Yvelines, Essonne, and Val d'Oise), Paris, and the department of the Seine (now three departments: Hauts-de-Seine, Seine-Saint-Denis and Val-de-Marne). *All values on the maps are in percentages of* registered *voters or, where vote divergences are under consideration, in differences of percentages in relation to* registered *voters.*

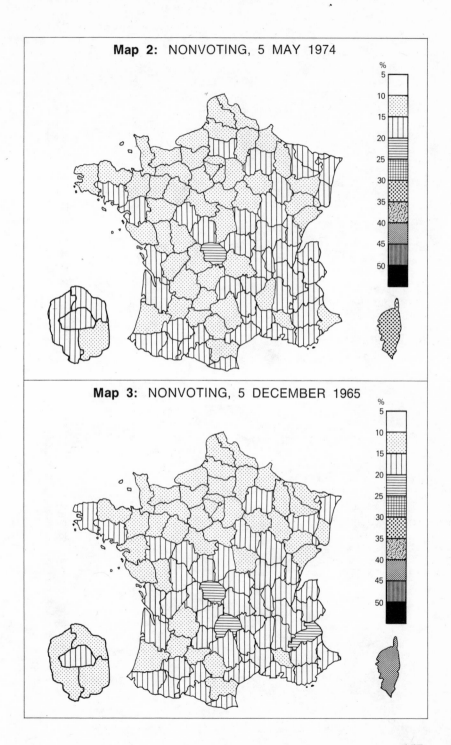

Map 2: NONVOTING, 5 MAY 1974

Map 3: NONVOTING, 5 DECEMBER 1965

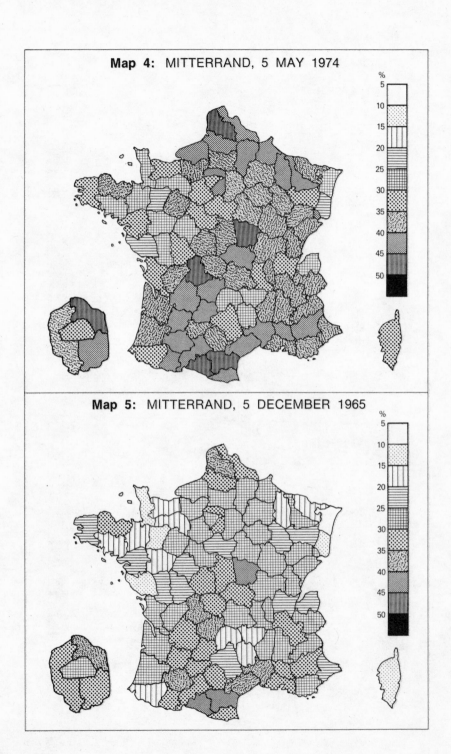

Map 4: MITTERRAND, 5 MAY 1974

Map 5: MITTERRAND, 5 DECEMBER 1965

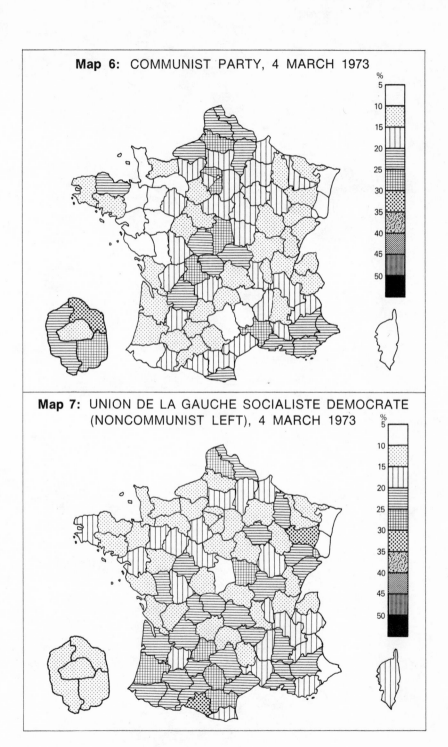

Map 6: COMMUNIST PARTY, 4 MARCH 1973

Map 7: UNION DE LA GAUCHE SOCIALISTE DEMOCRATE
(NONCOMMUNIST LEFT), 4 MARCH 1973

159

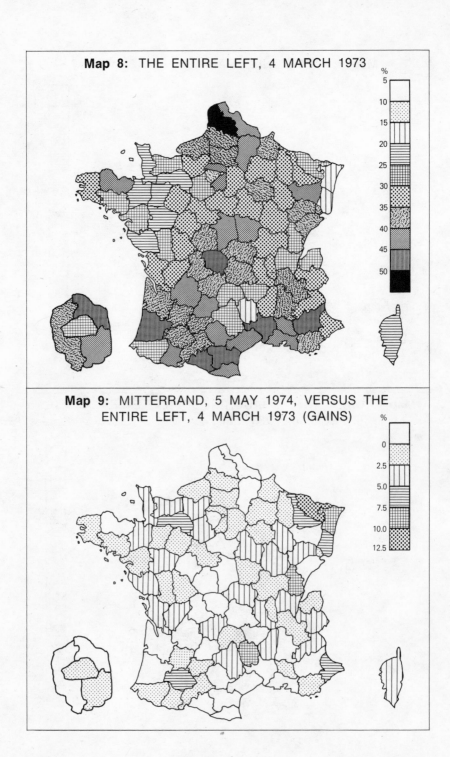

Map 8: THE ENTIRE LEFT, 4 MARCH 1973

%
5
10
15
20
25
30
35
40
45
50

Map 9: MITTERRAND, 5 MAY 1974, VERSUS THE ENTIRE LEFT, 4 MARCH 1973 (GAINS)

%
0
2.5
5.0
7.5
10.0
12.5

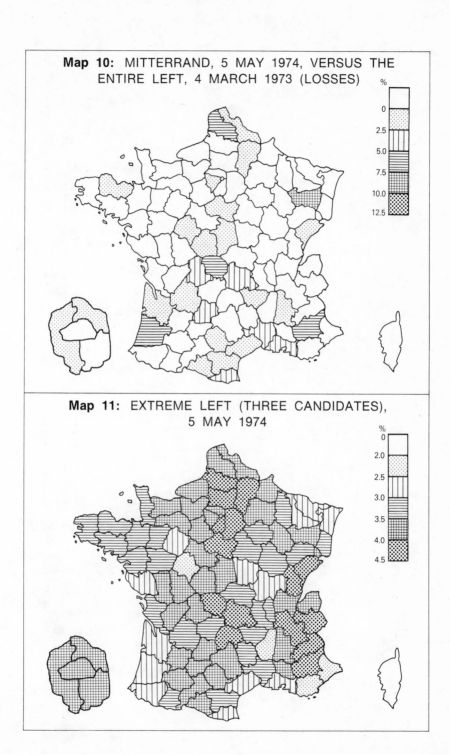

Map 10: MITTERRAND, 5 MAY 1974, VERSUS THE ENTIRE LEFT, 4 MARCH 1973 (LOSSES)

%
0
2.5
5.0
7.5
10.0
12.5

Map 11: EXTREME LEFT (THREE CANDIDATES), 5 MAY 1974

%
0
2.0
2.5
3.0
3.5
4.0
4.5

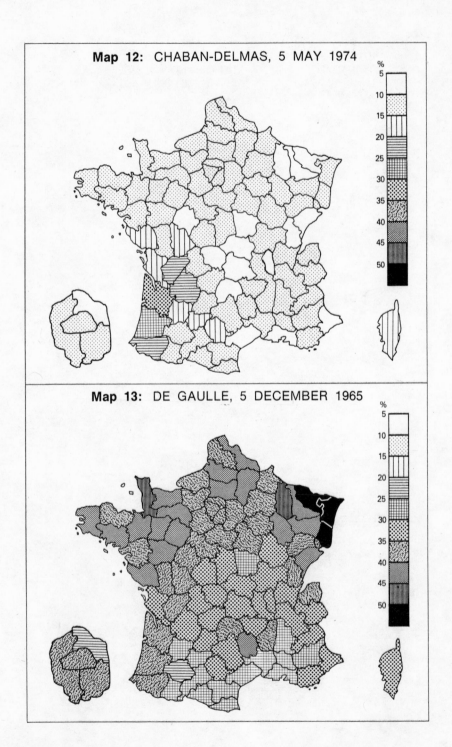

Map 12: CHABAN-DELMAS, 5 MAY 1974

Map 13: DE GAULLE, 5 DECEMBER 1965

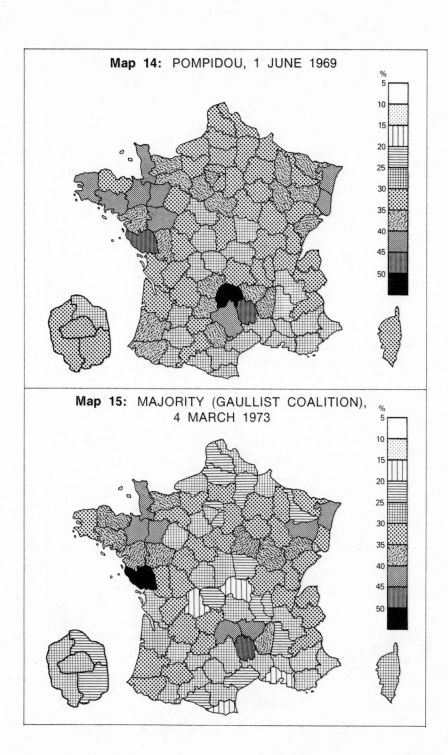

Map 14: POMPIDOU, 1 JUNE 1969

%

Map 15: MAJORITY (GAULLIST COALITION),
4 MARCH 1973

%

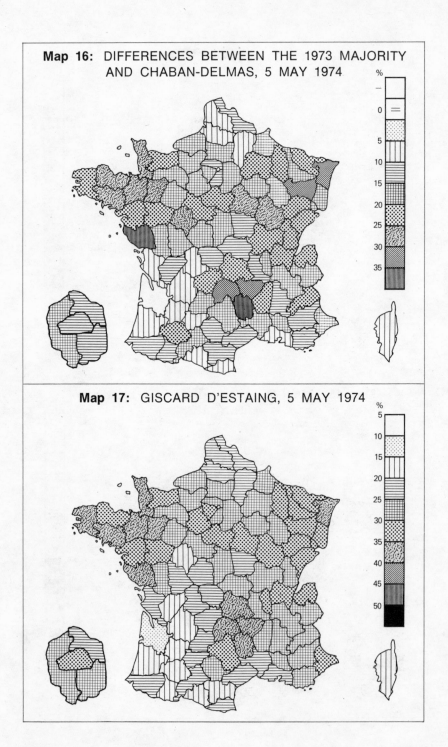

Map 16: DIFFERENCES BETWEEN THE 1973 MAJORITY AND CHABAN-DELMAS, 5 MAY 1974

%
—
0
5
10
15
20
25
30
35

Map 17: GISCARD D'ESTAING, 5 MAY 1974

%
5
10
15
20
25
30
35
40
45
50

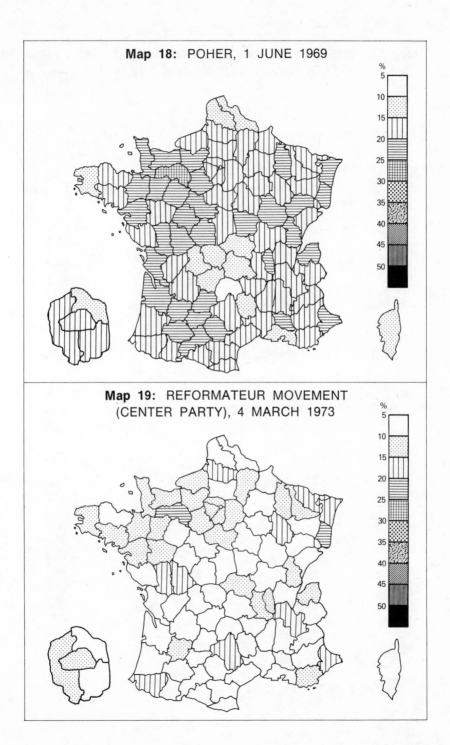

Map 18: POHER, 1 JUNE 1969

%

Map 19: REFORMATEUR MOVEMENT (CENTER PARTY), 4 MARCH 1973

%

165

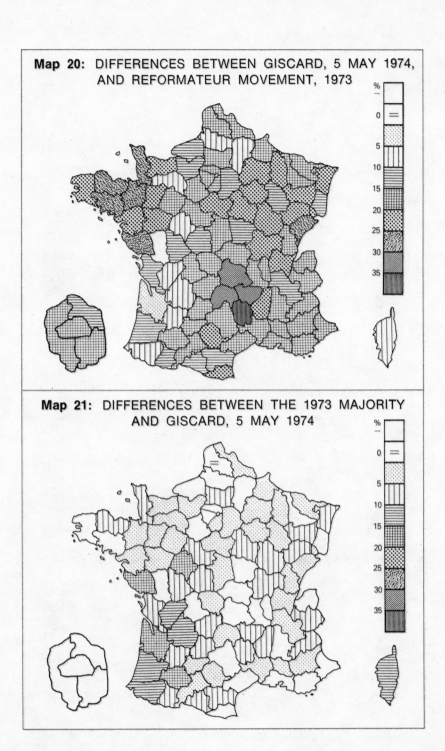

Map 20: DIFFERENCES BETWEEN GISCARD, 5 MAY 1974, AND REFORMATEUR MOVEMENT, 1973

Map 21: DIFFERENCES BETWEEN THE 1973 MAJORITY AND GISCARD, 5 MAY 1974

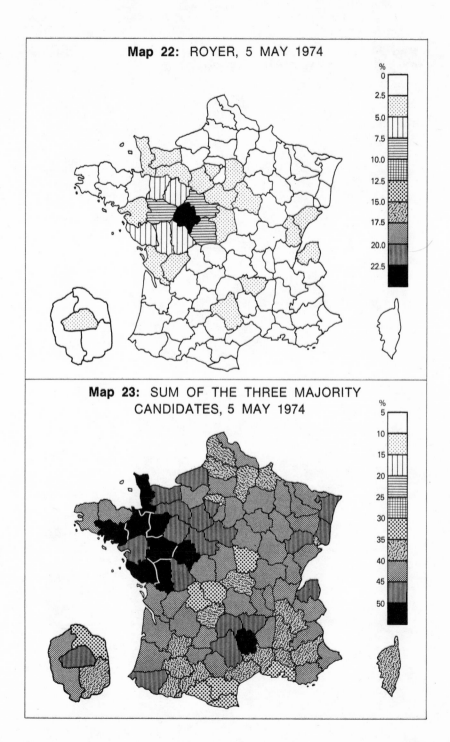

Map 22: ROYER, 5 MAY 1974

%

Map 23: SUM OF THE THREE MAJORITY
CANDIDATES, 5 MAY 1974

%

Map 24: DIFFERENCES BETWEEN THE TOTAL MAJORITY
VOTE & THE TOTAL MAJORITY & REFORMATEUR VOTE, 1973

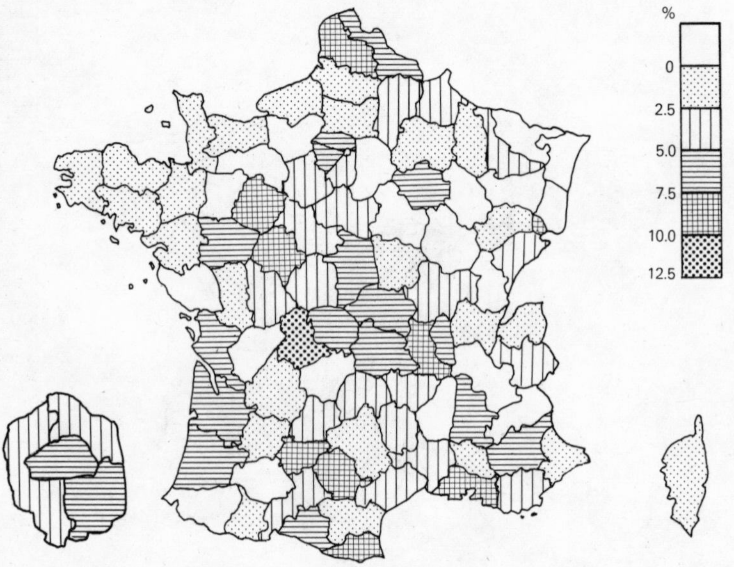

Map 25: NONVOTING, 19 MAY 1974

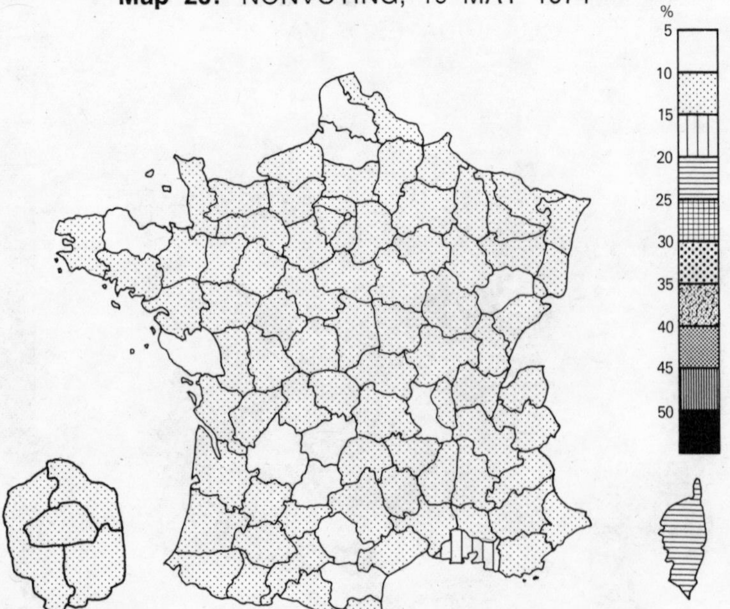

168

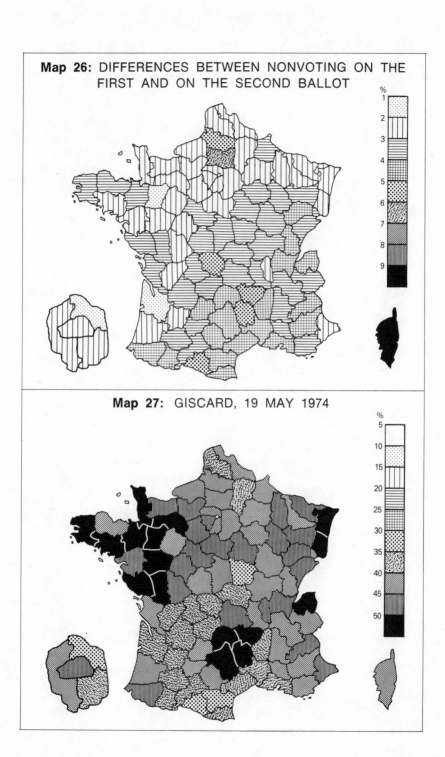

Map 26: DIFFERENCES BETWEEN NONVOTING ON THE FIRST AND ON THE SECOND BALLOT

Map 27: GISCARD, 19 MAY 1974

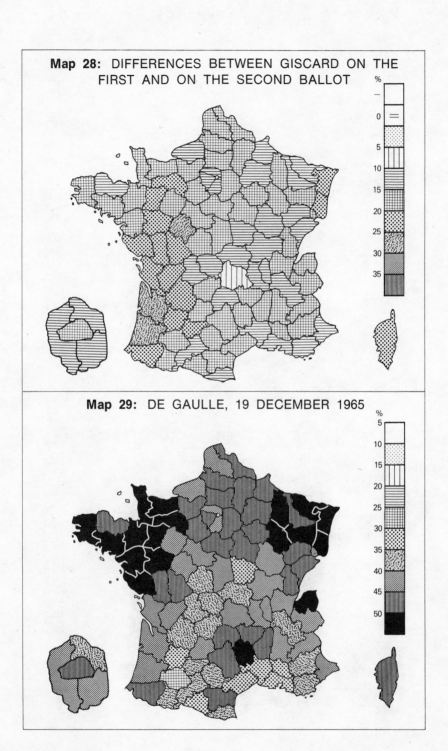

Map 28: DIFFERENCES BETWEEN GISCARD ON THE FIRST AND ON THE SECOND BALLOT

%

—
0
5
10
15
20
25
30
35

Map 29: DE GAULLE, 19 DECEMBER 1965

%

5
10
15
20
25
30
35
40
45
50

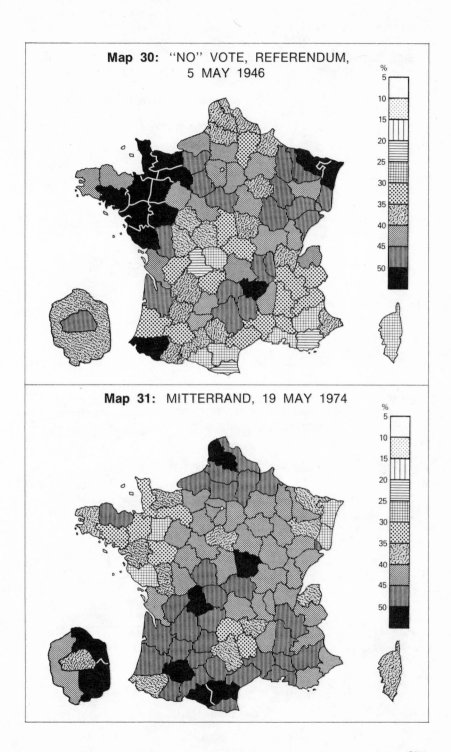

Map 30: "NO" VOTE, REFERENDUM, 5 MAY 1946

Map 31: MITTERRAND, 19 MAY 1974

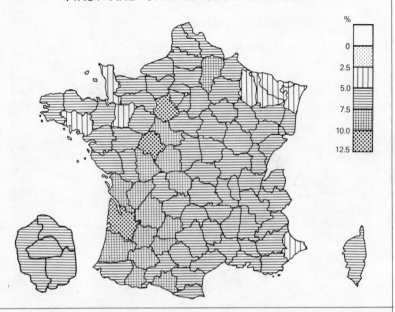

Map 32: DIFFERENCES BETWEEN MITTERRAND ON THE FIRST AND ON THE SECOND BALLOT

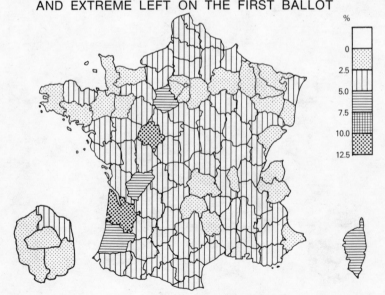

Map 33: DIFFERENCES BETWEEN MITTERRAND ON THE SECOND BALLOT AND THE SUM OF MITTERRAND AND EXTREME LEFT ON THE FIRST BALLOT

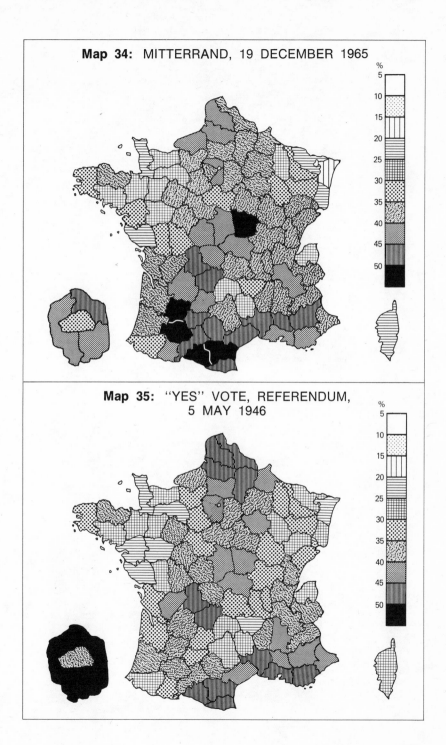

Map 34: MITTERRAND, 19 DECEMBER 1965

Map 35: "YES" VOTE, REFERENDUM, 5 MAY 1946

173

6
OPINION POLLS AND THE PRESIDENTIAL ELECTION, MAY 1974

Alain Lancelot

Opinion polls have been used in France since just before World War II, but they did not come into the limelight until 1965, when the first presidential election by universal suffrage was held. The personalization of this type of ballot, along with its novelty value in 1965, strongly aroused public interest in the opinion polls, whose audience had never previously exceeded the circle of party officials and administrators. Since 1965, opinion polls have become part of the established routine. All election preparations and campaigns have been punctuated by polls—often long in advance of election day—and the polls have been indispensable in the interpretation of election results. This is so because of the incontestable accuracy of the polls. Since 1965 the deviation between the registered vote and the predictions published on election eve has always been minimal. This fact deserves to be underlined, particularly because polls in other countries are not always so accurate and because the French political situation is seemingly not especially favorable to the use of polls, due to the multi-party system and the existence of a large Communist party whose supporters are suspicious of all surveys.

The success of the polls, however, is not without its counterpart. Certain opinion leaders—politicians and journalists—have become unhappy with survey techniques which seem to dispossess them of the monopoly they enjoyed when it came to translating (and interpreting) the feelings and desires of the electorate. Consider, for example, the following passage taken from a *Le Monde* editorial on the results of the 5 May 1974 election:

> There is an uncontested winner in the primary election: the opinion polls as a whole. From one election to another, their technique and success excite our admiration. Then we begin

to feel uneasy. Even to doubt the necessity of universal suffrage and a democratic government. Computer experts in the service of technocrats will end up by supplanting them, if that has not already happened. The polls are also winners in other ways. Like all other information media, they are incapable of starting off a political trend themselves, but they can amplify or deaden its effects . . . and their force of conviction and pressure is all the greater because of their scientific character, even if their presentation and utilization are at times highly empirical.[1]

This critical mood has undeniably become widespread, and the already endemic controversy over the political use of polls has been awakened to such an extent that it is impossible to deal with the presidential election of 1974 without some reference to it. This will be included later in our discussion.

The Protagonists: A Note on the Opinion Poll Institutes and the Electorate

Before letting the polls speak in their own way on the presidential election of 1974, it may be of some value to give our "stars," the poll institutes and the electorate, a brief introduction.

In France there are many private research centers that conduct regular surveys by polling, but of these only a very small number become involved in elections. In order of importance these are: SOFRES, IFOP, and COFREMCA. In recent years, two other firms, Publimetrie and Inter-Opinion, both very small, have entered the field. Taking into account that COFREMCA had relatively little to do with the 1974 presidential election, and that the small firms are too new for us to assess the validity of their results with any exactitude, we will limit ourselves to a commentary upon the results of SOFRES and IFOP. Both are private companies and their profits come more from market research than from political and sociological polls. Their services are funded from time to time by the media (in particular *Figaro*, *Nouvel Observateur*, and *Express* for SOFRES, and *France-Soir*, *Point*, and Europe 1 for IFOP), by the government and the civil service bureaucracies, and sometimes by political candidates and parties. The firms employ similar research techniques, SOFRES leaning often toward a psychological approach (in-depth interviewing, small samples, heavy interview guides, et cetera) and IFOP inclining rather toward purely quantitative methods (surveys based on large

---

[1] Jacques Fauvet, "Un Vaincu," *Le Monde*, 7 May 1974, p. 1.

samples). The electoral opinion polls we are going to study were conducted on samples of between 1,000 and 2,000 persons chosen according to a quota system designed to represent the entire voting public of metropolitan France.

The electorate, which consists of everyone aged twenty-one and over who is registered on an electoral roll, totals a little under 30 million persons. No precise statistical description of the French electorate has ever been made. An approximation has been found satisfactory by most researchers—namely, the *entire* population of voting age, whether or not registered on an electoral roll. The deviation from the actual electorate is slight, but it is not uniformly distributed, there being a greater number of unregistered persons among women, the aged and those of modest means. Despite this source of slight error, the approximation provides us with an accurate general description of the French electorate: A majority is female, and there is also a majority of persons with only a primary education. Significantly large proportions are comprised of persons over fifty years of age, the nonemployed,[2] the self-employed (farmers, shop-keepers, craftsmen, small employers), and residents of small towns and rural areas (see Table 6–1).

This, then, is the sociological picture of the electorate. The political picture is of four panels. Following the legislative elections of 1973, the electorate roughly divided into four main political tendencies: Communist (21.4 percent of valid votes in 1973), non-Communist Left (24 percent, if we add to the Socialist party the PSU and the left-wing splinter groups), the Right-Center opposition party (15.4 percent) and the majority coalition (37.9 percent). There is also a small Trotskyite element of the extreme Left, which retains its independent position and is often highly critical of other left-wing parties (1.3 percent).

The State of Public Opinion on the Eve of the Death of Georges Pompidou

In March 1974, one year after the legislative elections that saw a clear victory for the coalition led by Georges Pompidou, public opinion underwent a veritable crisis of confidence. In March 1973 a poll conducted by SOFRES concluded that 46 percent of the French public believed that circumstances in France tended towards improvement, whereas 25 percent believed that they did not. One year later

---

[2] "Nonemployed" is a French usage meaning in the main retired persons and housewives.

Table 6-1

FRENCH NATIONALS AGED TWENTY-ONE AND OVER, METROPOLITAN FRANCE

Category	Percent
Sex	
Male	48
Female	52
Age	
21-34	27
35-49	32
50-64	23
65 and over	18
Education	
Elementary	56
Secondary	23
Technical or commercial	11
Higher education	10
Profession of voter	
Farmers and agricultural workers	9
Shopkeepers and craftsmen	6
Executives, industrialists, professionals and businessmen	5
Office workers, white-collar employees	17
Laborers	21
Nonemployed	42
Profession of head of family [a]	
Farmers and agricultural workers	11
Shopkeepers, craftsmen	7
Executives, industrialists, professionals and businessmen	8
Office workers, white-collar employees	19
Laborers	28
Nonemployed	27
Residence	
Towns of under 2,000	27
2,000-20,000	15
20,000-100,000	16
Above 100,000 except Paris	25
Greater Paris	17

[a] This distribution breaks down the nonemployed according to the profession of the head of the family at the time he is working. It corresponds, then, more to the notion of social background.

Source: SOFRES, from census data.

the figure had sunk to 12 percent (as against 76 percent). This tremendous rise in pessimism was partly the result of immediate causes—the energy crisis and the consequent surge of inflation—but there were also deeper reasons. In fact, a year after the election of 1973 the French despaired of seeing put into effect the "bold reforms" which had been promised during the electoral campaign. Instead, had they not seen the government show more and more signs of hesitation and conduct a lifeless economic policy without conviction? The polls conducted at the time reveal the concerns of the electorate in the face of this state of affairs. At the beginning of April 1974, a SOFRES poll revealed that the two major concerns of the electorate were the struggle against rising prices and the necessity for improving the situation of the economically under-privileged (see Table 6–2). Next, and quite a way behind, came the smooth running of the economy in respect to production and employment, protection against political and social disorder, and the defense of liberties. Foreign policy concerns and the desire to "throw the rascals out" seemed secondary by comparison.

The public's preoccupation with rising prices and the persistence of social inequalities translated into political terms as a veritable crisis of confidence in the national executive. Unlike his predecessor, Jacques Chaban-Delmas, Premier Pierre Messmer never was popular with the public. But his inability to rise in public esteem was more

Table 6-2
CONCERNS OF THE FRENCH ELECTORATE

	Top Priority	Very Important
Control rising prices	67%	26%
Improve the lot of the underprivileged	53	34
Assure the smooth running of the economy (production and employment)	37	42
Avoid political and social disorders	37	39
Protect and develop public liberties	23	41
Conduct a foreign policy in keeping with the voters' aspirations	15	38
Give fresh impetus to the construction of Europe	15	29
Make radical changes in the political personnel in power	19	18

Source: SOFRES poll, 10-16 April 1974.

than obvious at the moment when Pompidou solemnly placed him at the head of the government for the third time. According to a SOFRES poll taken in February 1974, only 20 percent of the French public considered the prime minister to be one of the politicians with a highly promising future. A few weeks later Messmer beat all records of unpopularity: 47 percent were unhappy with him as prime minister, and only 42 percent felt satisfied with him (IFOP, March 1974). Pompidou, on the other hand, was still very popular, with 56 percent of the respondents in the same poll declaring themselves satisfied with him as president of the republic. But the percentage of dissatisfieds (37 percent) was the highest since his election to the presidency in 1969. Furthermore, the state of the president's health finally began to have an effect on public opinion. Fifty-eight percent of those interviewed between 23 and 25 March, eight days before Pompidou's sudden death, thought that there could be a presidential election before the end of 1974 (IFOP, *France-Soir*, 28 March).

Would this be the moment of change awaited for two years? Some expressed their desire to see the united Left assume power at this point, but they remained in a minority during the first months of 1974. Actually, the economic program of the Left was found more disquieting than reassuring at this difficult moment in the nation's history, as the results of a SOFRES poll of 8–14 February show:

Question: With which of these two opinions are you most in agreement?

- Given the present critical condition, now is not the time to bring the Left to power 43%
- In order to confront the present economic problems, the best solution at this time is to bring the Left to power 32
- No opinion 25

TOTAL 100

Those who did not believe that relief would come from the Left looked to the Center, where little more than squabbles between individuals separated the Democratic Center party of Jean Lecanuet from the centrists of the majority. When Pompidou and Messmer refused to make an overture to the Center, persisting in their conception of a closed majority, the hopes of public opinion fixed themselves on other leaders, in particular Chaban-Delmas and Valéry Giscard d'Estaing. From October 1973 to February 1974 the percentage of those considering Chaban-Delmas to be a politician with a bright future went from 37 percent to 46 percent over the entire population.

At the same time opinion concerning Giscard d'Estaing went from 59 percent to 60 percent. Among majority supporters, Chaban-Delmas was close to Giscard d'Estaing (in February 1974, 61 percent as against 65 percent), but he trailed badly among the supporters of the *Réformateur* movement (47 percent as against 71 percent), who seemed to have fixed upon Giscard d'Estaing as the man to free them from the ghetto to which they had been relegated by the deadlock of the centrist third party and the ostracism of Pompidou. No doubt Chaban-Delmas seemed too closely allied to the UDR for centrist supporters to back him without compromising themselves. Giscard d'Estaing, who had never ceased to lay claim to a certain independence within the majority coalition, probably seemed to them the most likely to federate a new majority. The sudden death of Pompidou made it possible for these latent trends and more or less confused expectations to come out into the open.

The First Ballot Campaign

Importance of the Preelection Polls. In the month between the death of Pompidou on 2 April and the first ballot of the presidential election on 5 May, sixteen national polls dealing with voting predictions were made public. A similar number of surveys on questions allied to the presidential election (predictions for a particular category of voter or region, motives of the electorate, the public image of candidates, et cetera) were published during the same period. Never before had the presence—not to say pressure—of opinion polls been so massive.

And this, so to speak, was but the visible tip of the iceberg. In order to appreciate the total role played in the presidential election by the polls, we must also take into consideration the confidential surveys conducted on behalf of candidates, political parties, and the government. It is difficult to know exactly how many such surveys were conducted, but surely the number is not less than fifteen.

To get a better idea of the significance of these polls, let us consider for a moment the types of survey that a presidential candidate can order from the research centers:

Detailed analysis of declared voting intentions. (Poll taken on national samplings of 1,500 to 2,000 persons.)

In-depth analysis of voting intentions of one category: youth, women, farmers, Catholics, et cetera. (Poll taken on a specific sample of between 500 and 1,000 persons.)

In-depth analysis of the candidate's public image and those of his adversaries. (In-depth interviews, 10 to 20 persons; surveys with open-ended questions, about 100 persons; national poll of about 1,000 persons.)

Analysis of motives. (In-depth interviews of 10 to 20 persons.)

Tests of campaign slogans, posters, and television broadcasting. (Surveys on questions of opinion, about 100 persons; group meetings; standard polling.)

Simulation of effects of different campaign strategies based on a model of the behavior of the voters.

Several models of this type were used during the campaign. The most sophisticated is without doubt the one that was developed for SOFRES by Denis Lindon and Pierre Weill from a model that had been used during the legislative election of 1973.[3] To simplify somewhat, we may say that this model was based on the principle that a vote is the result of a more or less conscious and systematic confrontation between the voter's own aspirations and the candidate's image (and that of the party that backs him). But the process of confrontation and decision is often complex. It often happens that none of the candidates lives up to the voter's ideal image. In this case a set of individual mechanisms of consideration and arbitration comes into play, and it is these mechanisms that the survey on which the model is based makes it possible to discover. By combining a precise knowledge of the expectations of each voter, of the image he has built up of each candidate, and of the mechanisms of consideration and arbitration, it is possible to determine the probability of his voting for a given candidate. The electorate can then be broken down according to this voting probability, distinguishing between the proportions that are favorable, critical, and hostile. During the campaign, the images of the candidates undergo modification in the minds of the electors in these different categories. The number of critical voters upon whom the choice of a particular campaign strategy will have a positive effect can be determined from the model.

Even if every candidate did not commission all of the survey types on the above checklist, the sheer volume of work financed by the candidates is considerable. The expense, even if it is not a large proportion of total campaign expenditures, is also considerable. It probably runs between 200,000 and 400,000 francs, depending on the candidates, for the first ballot campaign.

---

[3] Denis Lindon and Pierre Weill, Le choix d'un député, un modèle explicatif du comportement électoral (Paris: Editions de Minuit, 1974).

The Evolution of Voting Intentions. From the mass of public and confidential opinion polls we shall now attempt to select the most interesting data to explain the evolution of the voting public between early April and early May 1974. If we consider the published polls of SOFRES and IFOP, we will see that the declared voting intentions developed as shown in Tables 6–3 and 6–4.

Even if the voting predictions made by IFOP are a little more erratic than those of SOFRES (owing to their closer time spacing, which renders them more sensitive to any minute, transient variation in the public mood), the lessons to be drawn from the two sets of data follow exactly the same lines and may be summarized as follows: (1) The field was restricted from the start to the three principal candidates, who split nine-tenths of the declared voting intentions in every poll. (2) The Left was slow in mobilizing its supporters, but did so at a fairly steady rhythm. (3) Within the majority, the respective positions of Chaban-Delmas and Giscard d'Estaing, very nearly equal at the start of the campaign, later modified considerably in favor of the latter.

This last point constitutes the most spectacular and important element in the first ballot campaign. Tables 6–3 and 6–4 allow us to see this phenomenon unfold precisely and chronologically. If we ignore the polls of 9 April, when uncertainty about who would be in the running still fogged the results, three phases can be distinguished. The first phase lasts until 22 April. During this phase

Table 6-3
EVOLUTION OF VOTING INTENTIONS BEFORE THE FIRST BALLOT (SOFRES)

	9 April	12–16 April	22 April	29–30 April	Result, 5 May
Extreme Left	a	a	a	2%	3%
Mitterrand	36%	40%	42%	44	43.5
G. d'Estaing	27	28	28	31	33
Chaban-Delmas	26	26	24	17	14.5
Royer	a	5	4	3	3
Other	11 b	1	2	3	3
Total	100	100	100	100	100

a The response was not measured or not distinguished from "other."
b Eight of the eleven percentage points are for Edgar Faure.

Table 6-4

EVOLUTION OF VOTING INTENTIONS BEFORE THE FIRST BALLOT (IFOP)

	9 April	16 April	18 April	22 April	25 April	29 April	2–5 May	Result, 5 May
Extreme Left	2%	2%	1%	1.4%	3%	3%	2.5%	3%
Mitterrand	40	41	43	41	42	42	45	43.5
G. d'Estaing	27	27	25	26	31	31	30	33
Chaban-Delmas	29	25	23	23	18	18	15	14.5
Royer	—	5	5	6	3	3	3.5	3
Other	2	2	2	2.5	3	3	4	3
Total	100	100	100	100	100	100	100	100

the gap that placed Chaban-Delmas behind Giscard d'Estaing widened slowly but consistently. The second phase spans the days 25 to 30 April. This is the decisive turning point, for it sees a difference of thirteen percentage points suddenly open up between the two candidates. The third phase, from early May until the day of the ballot, is the phase of the final lunge or the keeling over, depending on whether one's eyes are upon Giscard d'Estaing or the unfortunate Chaban-Delmas. What could explain such a drastic swing in public opinion, a swing that won Giscard d'Estaing 1,250,000 supporters in three days? A first indication can be furnished by a detailed analysis of the "turning-point" phase, from 22 to 25 April, in the various social categories which comprise the electorate.

Sociological Analysis of the "Turning Point." Let us consider the distribution of declared voting intentions in favor of Giscard d'Estaing and Chaban-Delmas as they were measured by IFOP on 22 and 25 April, as shown in Table 6–5. The outstanding point in this table is that Giscard d'Estaing, while making progress in all categories, leaps forward in most spectacular fashion in those categories which are least politically conscious and most favorable to the Right and Center, that is, women, the aged, the nonemployed, industrialists and businessmen, and executives and professionals. Everything came to pass exactly as though the party of the "happy medium" had decamped en masse from Chaban-Delmas to rally behind Giscard d'Estaing. The distribution of the change in declared voting intentions according to party preference confirmed the defection of centrist voters. Giscard d'Estaing gained fifteen percentage points among the *Réformateur* movement supporters (from 44 percent to 59 percent), while Chaban-Delmas lost nineteen percentage points (28 percent to 9 percent). Giscard also gained eight percentage points among majority supporters (from 42 percent to 50 percent), while Chaban-Delmas went down by four percentage points (42 percent to 38 percent).

Influence of Polls and Television. The foregoing sociological analysis allows us to appreciate the relative influence of the two factors which have often been put forward as the causes of Chaban-Delmas's lack of success, the polls and television. So far as the polls are concerned, it is certain that they played a role in bringing to the attention of the French electorate the fact that, contrary to general expectation, Giscard d'Estaing had at least as good a chance of carrying the vote as did Chaban-Delmas. But, contrary to the suggestions of some,

Table 6-5

POLL RESULTS: GISCARD VERSUS CHABAN, 22 APRIL–25 APRIL 1974

	Giscard d'Estaing			Chaban-Delmas		
	22 April	25 April	Difference	22 April	25 April	Difference
Total	26%	31%	+5	23%	18%	−5
Male	25	28	+3	19	17	−2
Female	27	34	+7	27	20	−7
Age						
21-34	21	26	+5	19	13	−6
35-49	29	31	+2	18	15	−3
50-64	25	30	+5	26	22	−4
65 and over	30	38	+8	31	25	−6
Executives and professionals	44	50	+6	19	11	−8
Industrialists and businessmen	27	38	+11	24	14	−10
Farmers and agricultural workers	32	37	+5	30	29	−1
White-collar, office employees	28	32	+4	15	15	0
Laborers	14	16	+2	21	14	−7
Nonemployed	29	38	+9	29	27	−2

Source: IFOP polls, 22 and 25 April 1974.

Table 6-6

PERSONAL QUALITIES OF THE THREE
PRINCIPAL CANDIDATES[a]

	Giscard	Chaban	Mitterrand
Intelligence	+136	+70	+68
Competence	+73	+16	+10
Proximity to people's problems	+63	+45	+114
Seriousness	+56	−4	+2
Energy	+53	+47	+20
Absence of status motive	+40	−56	−11
Honesty	+39	−24	−8
Tolerance	+16	−44	+5
Absence of pretention	+15	−82	−36
Sincerity	+10	−45	−29

[a] This index was computed from the rating of each candidate on each quality or ability. The process of rating varied according to the wording of questions. SOFRES used three scales with four levels, from "excellent" to "really bad" and from "applies exactly" to "does not apply at all" for each personal quality, and from "entirely able" to "not at all able" for each ability.
Source: SOFRES poll, April 1974.

they could not have played the primary role. They could not, indeed, have been responsible for the sudden swing in opinion that they recorded between 22 and 25 April. As for the influence of television, we will examine it through the study of the images of the candidates.[4]

The Image of the Candidates. The first surveys conducted by SOFRES and IFOP at the start of the campaign had revealed that Giscard d'Estaing was benefitting from a much more favorable image than Chaban and, though to a lesser extent, than Mitterrand. Giscard's superiority comes out most clearly in the matter of individual characteristics and personality traits, as Table 6–6 demonstrates.

In those questions concerning statesmanship, where respondents are asked to make a political judgment, Giscard d'Estaing's superiority is not as absolute, especially as compared with Mitterrand, who projected the image of a man well able to solve social problems. But

[4] For a more complete discussion of the influence of the polls, see pp. 198-200, and of television, see Chapter 8.

Table 6-7

ABILITIES OF THE THREE PRINCIPAL CANDIDATES TO SOLVE TODAY'S PROBLEMS

	Giscard	Chaban	Mitterrand
Control rising prices	−8	−35	+41
Improve the lot of the underprivileged	−18	−30	+75
Assure the smooth running of the economy (production and unemployment)	+89	+37	+9
Avoid political and social disorders	+2	+17	−6
Protect public liberties	+42	+31	+24
Conduct a foreign policy in keeping with the wishes of those interviewed	+52	+33	−9
Give fresh impetus to the construction of Europe	+79	+55	+3
Make radical changes in the political personnel in power	−14	−50	+117

a This index was computed in the same way as that of Table 6-6.
Source: SOFRES poll, April 1974.

as opposed to Chaban-Delmas, Giscard's image was still outstanding (see Table 6–7).

The data in Table 6–8 indicate that the social program of the Left had rendered obsolete Chaban's call for a "new society," so dear to him when he was prime minister. The UDR candidate was perceived more as one dedicated to the maintenance of order than as one who would launch a generous social policy. Of the three candidates, he is the one who least fulfilled the electorate's hopes for change.

Chaban-Delmas was also seen as rather further from Center and more to the Right than Giscard d'Estaing (see Table 6–8). Therefore those centrists who were hopeful of an opening up of the majority were not inclined to support Chaban.

Overall, the advantage won by Giscard d'Estaing over Chaban-Delmas in the declared voting intentions after 25 April is not, therefore, really surprising. It is only the expression of the virtual

Table 6-8

RESPECTIVE POSITIONS OF THE THREE PRINCIPAL
CANDIDATES ON THE LEFT-RIGHT AXIS

	Mitterrand	Giscard	Chaban
Extreme Left	10%	—	––
Left	44	—	—
Left Center	38	2%	3%
Right Center	1	33	36
Right	1	29	32
Extreme Right	—	10	10
No opinion	3	7	7
Total	100	100	100

Source: SOFRES poll, April 1974.

superiority of Giscard d'Estaing [5] which was hidden at the opening of the campaign by the support accruing to Chaban-Delmas from his UDR and CDP backers. Dissension within the UDR following the maneuvers of Jacques Chirac and Messmer, Chaban's poor television broadcasts, and the polls that revealed his fragility all contributed to weaken the Gaullist candidate. But one should realize that his position was already undermined in advance by the conjunction of two additional factors: when compared with Giscard d'Estaing he did not carry enough weight as a person, and he did not appear capable of assuring that an overture to the Center would be made. The less politically conscious voters, who judge according to personality (and generally lean towards the Right), and the real centrists, who dreaded the weight of the UDR, finally came down on the side of Giscard d'Estaing.

The Results of the First Ballot, 5 May 1974

The fifth of May was a day of honor for the poll institutes for two reasons. First, the final results of the first ballot were very close to the poll predictions made several days before the ballot. Second,

[5] The SOFRES model indicated that virtual superiority from mid-April. At that date the "probable votes" in favor of Giscard and Chaban rose respectively to 34 percent and 16 percent, while the declared voting intentions still stood at 28 percent and 26 percent.

the predictions made on election night were borne out with extra-ordinary precision. We will consider these operations, whose sensational aspect did much for the renown of the firms concerned, before moving on to a commentary—less sensational, but more important—on what the post-electoral polls reveal about the French ballot.

The Election Night Predictions. Estimation of first ballot results was conducted on behalf of the principal radio-television networks existing in France. ORTF (public) employed the services of SOFRES and its allied data-processing service, SIA. Europe 1 (private) turned to IFOP, and Radio-Télé Luxembourg, RTL (private), employed a team of political science researchers and the firm of Honeywell-Bull.

At 8:00 p.m., closing time for the ballot in the large cities, the following estimates were broadcast:

	ORTF	RTL	Europe 1	Actual Result
Mitterrand	44 %	43 %	43.6%	43.4%
Giscard d'Estaing	33	33	32.6	32.9
Chaban-Delmas	13.6	14.5	14.5	14.5
Royer	3.5	4	3.6	3.2
Laguiller	2.4	2.4		2.4
Krivine	0.5	0.3		0.4
Dumont	1.2	1.2		1.3
Le Pen	0.7	0.6		0.8
Muller	0.7	0.7		0.7

According to the firms concerned, each used different estimating procedures. The procedure followed by IFOP combined an a priori estimate based in part on the results of the preelectoral opinion polls with a running correction as the results from 473 sample voting precincts came in. This procedure was the subject of an article in the IFOP review in 1965.[6]

---

[6] Lucien Boucharenc, "L'operation Europe No. 1, IFOP," *Sondages*, vol. 27, no. 4 (1965). The procedures followed by SOFRES-SIA and Honeywell-Bull can be described in the following manner:

1. Establishment of a sample of 300 to 400 precincts, representative at national and regional levels, although overrepresentative of voting offices closing at 6:00 and 7:00 p.m. (small towns and rural areas).

2. Compilation of the results from several reference elections in each precinct.

3. A priori estimate in terms of several hypotheses concerning the voting evolution between the reference elections and the election to be estimated. These

The Opinion Polls and the First Ballot. On 20 and 21 May SOFRES conducted a post-election survey of about 2,000 persons. While this survey will be used here largely in the study of the final vote, it also offers valuable insight into the vote of 5 May. The number of people interviewed is sufficiently great and the descriptive variables are sufficiently varied to permit a sociological analysis of the three principal candidates' supporters.

The most significant results of the survey are shown in Table 6–9. We will comment upon it, examining each variable in succession. The sex factor reveals some important differences, especially on the Left. Mitterrand has far more impact on men than on women. Likewise, from the point of view of age we note that there is an inverse relationship between Mitterrand's supporters, who grow in number as their age decreases, and those of Giscard d'Estaing, who grow in numbers as they grow in years. Since Chaban-Delmas is a little better accepted among the young, the difference between his position and that of Giscard d'Estaing is only nine percentage points in the twenty-one-to-thirty-four age bracket, while it is thirty percentage points in the over-sixty-five bracket.

From the point of view of profession, we note that Mitterrand led among the working class, and in general gets his best scores among wage earners, whether working or retired. His opponents, on the other hand, are more successful among the self-employed. Contrary to the expectations of many, Chaban's supporters were no more numerous in the working class than those of Giscard d'Estaing. In fact, conservative workers showed a marked preference for the

---

estimates lead to the calculation of probable or "dummy" votes for each candidate in each sample precinct.

4. Calculation for each dummy vote and precinct of the deviation from the national average.

5. When the true result comes in from a given precinct that result is corrected by the deviation from the calculated mean for the dummy vote corresponding; thus one obtains an estimate of the national result for each precinct.

At a given time the published estimate is obtained by calculating the arithmetic mean of the estimates calculated by precinct.

6. In reality there are several possible estimates (from 2 to 8) for a candidate varying with the number of dummy votes calculated by a priori methods. To find the best, a coefficient must be calculated to measure the correlation between each series of dummy votes calculated a priori and the actual result. The estimate chosen is that for which the correlation is the highest. The whole procedure is known as Max Allen's algorithm.

While such estimates fit more into show business than scientific research, their implications for political science are important. The calculation of a priori estimates (dummy votes) allows real models of electoral behavior to be established, models which are put to the test on the day of the ballot. More important, the sample precinct information can be processed for various statistics operations after the election.

Table 6-9

SOCIOLOGICAL DESCRIPTION OF THE ELECTORATE ON THE FIRST BALLOT

(percent of valid votes in each category)

Category	Mitterrand	Giscard	Chaban
Total vote	44	33	15
Male	47	32	13
Female	41	34	16
Age			
21-34	49	25	16
35-49	44	33	15
50-64	41	34	14
65 and over	38	43	13
Profession of head of family			
Farmers and agricultural workers	27	48	17
Shopkeepers and craftsmen	29	35	17
Executives, industrialists, professionals and businessmen	32	40	25
White-color employees	46	35	13
Laborers	58	19	13
Nonemployed	42	38	13
Profession of interviewee			
Farmers and agricultural workers	23	49	19
Shopkeepers and craftsmen	25	38	15
Executives, industrialists, professionals and businessmen	40	42	16
White-collar employees	45	30	17
Laborers	62	18	12
Nonemployed	43	35	14
Monthly income of household			
Less than 1,000 francs	41	40	14
1,000 to 2,000	52	25	13
2,000 to 3,000	48	27	15
Above 3,000	36	40	15
Education			
Elementary	46	31	13
Secondary	38	35	18
Technical or commercial	41	36	16
Higher education	43	37	12

Table 6-9 *(continued)*

Category	Mitterrand	Giscard	Chaban
Religion			
Catholic (devout)	19	51	19
Catholic (practicing a little)	43	32	16
Catholic (nominal)	67	17	11
Other	53	31	6
None	79	12	3
Political allegiance[a]			
Extreme Left	92	1	1
Left	84	5	4
Center	15	56	20
Right	4	58	31
Extreme Right	3	60	25
"Marais"	28	43	16
Vote in 1973 (first ballot)			
Communist party	93	1	—
PSU and extreme Left	77	—	—
Socialist party and Left Radical	85	3	3
Réformateur movement	17	57	18
Majority	5	60	30

[a] The political allegiance was determined by asking the interviewees to place themselves on a Left-Right axis. Those who could not do so, or who claimed to be centrist but uninterested in politics, comprise the "Marais." See, for example, Emeric Deutsch, Denis Lindon, and Pierre Weill, *Les Familles politiques, aujourd'hui en France* (Paris: Les Editions de Minuit, 1966).
Source: SOFRES survey, 20-21 May 1974.

minister of finance over the former champion of the "new society." The comparison between the occupation of the head of the family of the person interviewed is interesting in that it reveals the conservatism of laborers' wives, the importance of Gaullism among women and eldest sons of managerial personnel, as well as the sympathy with the Left among small shopkeepers and the rural unemployed.

Consideration of voter preferences by income category brings to light a phenomenon already familiar to us: the poorest category almost always votes as far to the Right as does the richest category. The Left was strongest in the intermediate categories. From the point of view of education, on the other hand, the Left was strong at the two ends of the scale.

Religion continued to be strongly linked to the vote. The more Roman Catholicism was practiced, the less votes there were for Mitterrand and the more for Giscard. Other religions, Protestant in the main, were, on the contrary, solidly behind the left-wing candidate.

Finally, the analysis according to party preference shows that Mitterrand had practically compensated in the Center for his small losses on the Left (to the extreme revolutionary left-wing as well as to his principal rivals). Likewise, it shows that Giscard d'Estaing received twice as many votes among the majority as Chaban-Delmas and three times as many from the centrist *Réformateur* party.

The Final Election Campaign

The day after the first ballot, 58 percent of the electorate proclaimed itself satisfied with the results and 28 percent expressed disappointment, according to a SOFRES poll taken 6–7 May. Although it may not come as a surprise to find that 56 percent of Chaban-Delmas's supporters were disappointed, it is interesting to note that the most euphoric voters were those who supported Giscard d'Estaing, who were more satisfied (67 percent against 64 percent) and above all less disappointed (19 percent against 29 percent) than the supporters of Mitterrand. We find the same difference of satisfaction in the estimate that each supporter made of his own candidate's chances after the first ballot. Eighty-one percent of Giscard's supporters thought that the result increased his chances (as against 58 percent of the total electorate). Only 60 percent of Mitterrand's supporters felt quite so optimistic about the chances of their candidate. Forty percent of the total electorate judged that his chances were better as a result of the first ballot, and 34 percent thought they were worse.

The Candidates' Images. Compared with the results registered at the start of the first ballot campaign, the surveys conducted on the public images of the candidates on the day following the 5 May election show that a certain repositioning had taken place in favor of Mitterrand and to the detriment of Giscard d'Estaing. In the two-candidate election of the final round, the centrists would have the decisive voice, and Mitterrand seemed to them to have moved a little more towards center and Giscard a little more to the right, compared to their positions before the first ballot (see Table 6–10). Perhaps here we see the combined effects of Chaban-Delmas's campaign to force Giscard further to the right and Mitterrand's campaign of

Table 6-10

POLITICAL CHARACTERIZATION

	Mitterrand		Giscard	
	Before the first ballot	7–8 May	Before the first ballot	7–8 May
Extreme Left	10%	4%	—	—
Left	44	37	—	—
Center Left	38	49	2%	2%
Center	3	4	19	15
Center Right	1	1	33	36
Right	1	—	29	33
Extreme Right	—	—	10	9
No opinion	3	5	7	5
Total	100	100	100	100

Source: SOFRES polls, April and May 1974.

recovery on the evening of 5 May, which he aimed at the Gaullist supporters.

The same swing can be observed in the personal quality categories (see Table 6–11). Giscard d'Estaing, seen as being more to the Right, remains highly superior regarding competence, intelligence, energy, and seriousness, but he is less easily credited than before with the qualities traditionally attributed to the left-wing (tolerance, empathy—even sympathy). Mitterrand, for his part, was rewarded for his hard-hitting, yet respectable, campaign before the first ballot. His personal image progressed on all points except those in which he already had the advantage over Giscard. However, this slight change of position did not materially affect Giscard's image of general superiority over Mitterrand.

Now let us consider political abilities. The effects of political polarization are even more appreciable here than in connection with personal qualities (see Table 6–12). Giscard d'Estaing either consolidated or retained his credit in all that concerns the economy and foreign policy, but he appeared less credible than he did before the first ballot regarding social questions (the safeguarding of purchasing power and the reduction of inequalities) and even in the avoidance of social disorders—a probable consequence of the threatened strike by which the unions "held the nation at ransom" in order to impede

Table 6-11
PERSONAL QUALITIES[a]

	Giscard		Mitterrand	
	Before the first ballot	Before the second ballot	Before the first ballot	Before the second ballot
Intelligence	+136	+127	+68	+88
Competence	+73	+64	+10	+26
Proximity to people's problems	+63	+16	+114	+99
Seriousness	+56	+52	+2	+15
Energy	+53	+62	+20	+32
Absence of status motive	+40	+10	−11	−5
Honesty	+39	+28	−8	+6
Tolerance	+16	−8	+5	+22
Absence of pretension	+15	−6	−36	+6
Sincerity	+10	+4	−29	−14
Sympathy	+4	+2	−22	+9

a This index was computed in the same way as that of Table 6-6.
Source: SOFRES poll, 7-8 May 1974.

the election of a right-wing president. This repositioning with regard to personal image was to have its impact on declared voting intentions.

The Evolution of Declared Voting Intentions. The polls published between the two elections by SOFRES and IFOP produced the results shown in Table 6–13. As the table shows, the outcome of the final election remained uncertain during the two-week campaign. The only moment when it was possible to believe that the decision had been made was on 11 May, following the televised confrontation of 10 May.

The Televised Confrontation of 10 May. On the evening of Friday, 10 May, two French presidential candidates were brought face-to-face in a televised confrontation for the first time. It has been claimed that the debate was viewed by 81 percent of the electorate. The effects of the broadcast were measured that very evening by an IFOP poll, and were found favorable to Giscard d'Estaing. The validity

Table 6-12

ABILITY TO SOLVE THE PROBLEMS OF TODAY[a]

	Giscard		Mitterrand	
	Before the first ballot	7–8 May	Before the first ballot	7–8 May
Control rising prices	−8	−40	+41	+53
Improve the lot of the underprivileged	−18	−32	+75	+108
Assure the smooth running of the economy	+89	+94	+9	+36
Avoid political and social disorders	+2	−19	−6	+49
Protect and develop public liberties	+42	+37	+24	+53
Give fresh impetus to the construction of Europe	+79	+75	+3	+20
Form a firm government so as to avoid political instability	b	+35	b	−14
Defend the prestige of France abroad	b	+101	b	+4

a This index was computed in the same way as that of Table 6-6.
b Not asked before the first ballot.
Source: SOFRES poll, 7-8 May 1974.

Table 6-13

EVOLUTION OF VOTING INTENTIONS BETWEEN THE FIRST AND SECOND BALLOTS

	Giscard	Mitterrand
SOFRES		
6–7 May	51%	49%
11 May	51.5	48.5
14 May	50	50
IFOP		
7 May	51	49
13 May	50	50
Actual election result		
19 May	50.7	49.3

of the poll has been much debated, because of the circumstances of the survey and the size of the sample taken. But a poll conducted by SOFRES the following day came down just as strongly in favor of an "on points" victory for Giscard d'Estaing (see Table 6–14).

One can understand that under these conditions the voting intentions measured in the same poll seemed to incline in favor of Giscard d'Estaing. But the image of the candidates' political abilities had not really been affected by the debate, which seemed to indicate that Giscard's advantage would not be decisive (see Table 6–14).

The Controversy over the Opinion Polls. The controversy about the polls, which arose at the time of the first ballot campaign, really began to rage between 5 and 19 May. It is nonetheless difficult to accuse the polls of influencing the electorate, since the fact that they all predicted 50 percent of the vote for each candidate gave equal

Table 6-14
IMPACT OF THE 10 MAY TELEVISION DEBATE

Question	Giscard	Mitterrand	Don't Know	Neither
If you had to choose a winner in the debate, would you pick Giscard d'Estaing or Mitterrand?	47%	35%		18%
Which candidate seemed to be:				
the one most made of presidential material?	52	30	18%	
the clearest?	52	32	16	
the most sympathetic?	42	38	20	
the most sincere?	40	34	26	
the most democratic?	34	42	24	
Has this debate made you:				
more favorable to . . .	33	26		
less favorable to . . .	22	28		
no change	44	44		
no opinion	1	2		
In the light of the candidates' statements, which one would you have most confidence in to:				
oppose rising prices?	36	43	21	
avoid unemployment?	38	41	21	
keep peace in society?	36	45	19	
defend the prestige of France?	55	27	18	

chances to both. But the rapid rate at which they were published was no doubt excessive. "All at once we pass from the age of the photograph to the age of movies," as Francis Balle said in *Le Monde* of 19–20 May.

As was observed above, the minipoll conducted by IFOP on the evening of the televised confrontation powerfully contributed to this resurgence of criticism. Specialists in the calculation of probabilities, statisticians and sociologists—generally favorable to the Left or extreme Left—gave vent to their anger with a greater or less degree of seriousness and sincerity, and Mitterrand decided to lodge a complaint against IFOP.

For its part, IFOP published the results of a poll on opinion polls, which had been conducted on 9 May with a sample of 1,951 voters, and which demonstrated that the polls exercised only a slight influence. Only 3 percent of persons interviewed claimed that the polls were their most important source of information, as opposed to 48 percent for television and 20 percent for radio. Ninety percent declared that the publication of polls on voting intentions had not caused them to alter their own original intention, as opposed to 6 percent who said it did. And finally, 52 percent estimated the polls were of more value published in newspapers, whereas 27 percent said they should be reserved exclusively for the eyes of politicians.

Despite this last result, the publication of the final IFOP poll (conducted on 17 May to appear in *France-Soir* the next day, the eve of the ballot) was prevented. Alain Poher, interim president of the republic, "strongly insisted" that the editor of *France-Soir* should forego publication, on the grounds that such publication "would occur after the closing of the electoral campaign." [7] Although *France-Soir* was in the habit of publishing its last poll on the eve of the ballot, and no legal impediment stood in its way, the editor of the paper gave way and IFOP suspended processing of the survey data.

It is clear that this case could constitute an annoying precedent in the publication of opinion polls. *France-Soir* declared that it would not abandon "a democratic means of information," but added, "even if we admit that the use and frequency of polls during electoral periods could be the object of prior discussion with the interested parties." [8] The Constitutional Council took up the same idea, declar-

---

[7] *France-Soir*, 18 May 1974.

[8] Ibid.

ing in the report of 24 May which accompanied the official proclamation of the election results that

> the opinion polls conducted and published during the course of the presidential election of 1974 have held a place of considerable importance in the commentaries devoted to this campaign . . . as, it appears, in the minds of a large number of citizens. This situation incontestably poses a problem. It would therefore be proper that the conditions in which polls are conducted and their results made public should be covered by a deontological code to guard against influencing the choice of citizens by a possibly erroneous prediction of the respective chances of the candidates.

And the council expressed the wish that it would see "the establishment of a . . . statute to govern the practice of opinion polls during electoral periods."

The poll institutes were led to attach all the more importance to such statements because in 1973 it was only thanks to the reticence of the government that a proposition adopted by the Senate to ban poll publication in preelectoral periods had not been adopted by the National Assembly. Therefore it is likely that the next electoral campaign will be decisive for the future of preelectoral opinion polls and their publication.

Results of the Second Ballot, 19 May 1974

The results of the second ballot showed yet again that the predictions made by the polls are far from being erroneous. This achievement was further heightened by the success of the election-night broadcasting of estimates. At 8:00 p.m. IFOP and Europe 1 predicted that the outcome would be 50.63 percent for Giscard and 49.37 percent for Mitterrand; in the end, the final count was 50.66 percent and 49.33 percent. SOFRES-SIA (ORTF) predicted 50.9 percent and 49.1 percent; Honeywell-Bull (RTL), 51 percent and 49 percent.

But, here again, the essential contribution of the polls is less their spectacularly accurate predictions than the indispensable information they provide on French voting behavior. In the presentation of this information we will again refer to the post-electoral survey conducted by SOFRES on 20–21 May for the *Nouvel Observateur*.

Comparison of the First and Second Ballots. The first lesson drawn from this poll concerns the path followed by the electorate between the first and second ballot (see Table 6–15). The Gaullist supporters

Table 6-15
COMPARISON OF VOTING IN
FIRST AND SECOND BALLOTS

Those Who Voted on First Ballot for:	Voted on the Second Ballot for:		
	Mitterrand	Giscard	Neither
Mitterrand	96%	2%	2%
Giscard	2	97	1
Chaban	11	83	6
Royer	10	80	10

decided en masse in favor of the candidate of the majority. However, the proportion that voted for Mitterrand was not negligible. Eleven percent of Chaban-Delmas's votes and 10 percent of Royer's together represent 480,000 voters. If the percentages had been 16 percent and 15 percent respectively, Mitterrand would have been elected.

Sociological Description of the Second Ballot. The principal results of the post-electoral survey made by SOFRES appear in Tables 6–16, 6–17, and 6–18. It is important to note that the ballot of 19 May is very significant because of the record turnout and the clear-cut Left-Right confrontation. The returns illuminate the really essential structures of the French electorate, and will doubtless be used as points of reference in the future.

From the point of view of sex and age the results of the second ballot confirm those of the first: men and young people vote for the

Table 6-16
PRESIDENTIAL VOTING BY AGE AND SEX

Age Group	Mitterrand		Giscard	
	Men	Women	Men	Women
21-34	59%	58%	41%	42%
35-49	54	44	46	56
50-64	47	45	53	55
65 and over	43	38	56	62

Source: Based on data from SOFRES survey, 20-21 May 1974.

Table 6-17

SOCIOLOGICAL DESCRIPTION OF THE ELECTORATE
ON THE SECOND BALLOT
(percent of valid votes in each category)

Category	Mitterrand	Giscard
Total Vote	49%	51%
Male	53	47
Female	46	54
Age		
21-34	59	41
35-49	49	51
50-64	46	54
65 and over	40	60
Profession of head of family		
Farmers and agricultural workers	31	69
Shopkeepers and craftsmen	36	64
Executives, industrialists, professionals, businessmen	34	66
White-collar employees	51	49
Laborers	68	32
Nonemployed	44	56
Profession of voter		
Farmers and agricultural workers	28	72
Shopkeepers and craftsmen	33	67
Executives, industrialists, professionals, businessmen	44	56
White-collar employees	53	47
Laborers	73	27
Nonemployed	45	55
Monthly income of household		
Less than 1,000 francs	46	54
1,000 to 2,000	60	40
2,000 to 3,000	55	45
Above 3,000	40	60
Education		
Elementary	51	49
Secondary	43	57
Technical or commercial	49	51
Higher education	49	51

Table 6-17 *(continued)*

Category	Mitterrand	Giscard
Religion		
Catholic (devout)	23	77
Catholic (practicing a little)	49	51
Catholic (nominal)	74	26
Other	64	36
None	86	14
Political allegiance		
Extreme Left	97	3
Left	89	11
Center	16	84
Right	4	96
Extreme Right	2	98
"Marais"[a]	34	66
Votes in 1973 (first ballot)		
Communist party	97	3
PSU and extreme Left	92	8
Socialist party and Left Radical	90	10
Réformateur movement	24	76
Majority	8	92

[a] See note to Table 6-9.
Source: SOFRES survey, 20-21 May 1974.

Left, while women and the elderly vote for the Right. The tables are based on a sufficiently large sample for it to be possible to combine these two criteria (Table 6–16).

As might be expected, the most staunchly pro-Giscard category is that of elderly women, but the gap dividing men and women is almost nil for people under thirty-five years of age, and reaches its maximum in the thirty-five-to-forty-nine bracket.

In the occupation, income, and education categories, we are also brought back to the same conclusions reached after the first ballot, and here they are even more pronounced. The Left is in the majority among wage earners, the Right among the self-employed and non-employed categories. The poorest and richest vote for the Right, while the intermediate section support the Left. The Left is most powerful among wage earners in the public sector and in big business. Union affiliation likewise has marked effects on voting behavior.

Table 6-18

VOTING PATTERN OF WAGE EARNERS

(percent of valid votes in each category)

Category	Mitterrand	Giscard
Total vote	61%	39%
Private sector	57	43
Public sector	70	30
Size of firm		
Under 50	59	41
50-200	64	36
200-500	60	40
More than 500	63	37
Union affiliation		
CGT	90	10
CFDT	73	27
FO	52	48
Other	64	36
Nonunion	53	47

Source: SOFRES survey, 20-21 May 1974.

Members of the CGT and CFDT—unions backing Mitterrand—voted much more to the Left than did the members of FO (who were individually free to select their candidate) or nonunion members, although even in these categories the Left was in the majority (see Table 6–18).

Crossing sex with occupation demonstrates that employed female workers are hardly less leftist than employed male workers (67 percent to 74 percent). Nonworking wives of workers, on the other hand, are a little more favorable to the Right.

The ballot of 19 May has often been referred to as a class vote. It is true that the electoral structures are very strongly correlated with social structures, but this does not alter the fact that the most important political phenomenon to emerge from this ballot is the persistence of a conservative wage-earning electorate. Because there are more conservatives among laborers and office workers than there are radicals among the middle classes, Giscard d'Estaing was elected president of the republic.

So far as religion is concerned, the second ballot demonstrates an even more precise correlation (see Table 6–17). In 1973 it was widely argued that socialism was increasingly accepted among Catholics. The results of the presidential election make that conclusion considerably less clear-cut. Mitterrand still has a long road ahead if he wishes to convince practicing Catholics that he is not an enemy of religion.

From the *political* point of view, Mitterrand took practically all the Left and extreme Left and Giscard d'Estaing all the Right and extreme Right. And, of course, the Center overwhelmingly supported Giscard. It is, however, noteworthy that one-third of the "moderate" and one-quarter of the *Réformateur* movement supporters finally came down on the side of the left-wing candidate (see Table 6–17).

The Psycho-Sociological Explanation of Giscard d'Estaing's Success

The SOFRES explanatory model allows us to go beyond the description of electoral structures to pin down more precisely the reasons for the final decision.[9] On the day following the first ballot the electorate could be broken down into three groups, one won over by Mitterrand (43 percent), one won over by Giscard (43 percent), and one uncertain (14 percent), the latter being the crucial group. Contrary to what the similarity of the figures might lead one to believe, this latter group was not composed of supporters of Chaban-Delmas. On the evening of the first ballot, two-thirds of Gaullist party supporters joined in backing Giscard d'Estaing and a little less than one-tenth of them supported Mitterrand. The remainder—a little over one-quarter— hesitated between the two candidates. Besides these Gaullists, the critical group contained some wavering supporters of Giscard and Mitterrand and those who had backed the minority candidates in the first ballot.

At the social level, these voters came from modest backgrounds; most were workers. Politically, they belonged to the Left-Center. But more important, they were generally not very politically minded. The day after the first ballot, according to the poll, they hesitated between the two candidates, with a slight advantage for Mitterrand. On 19 May they voted 60 percent for Giscard d'Estaing. How can this evolution be explained? By the anti-Communist campaign of the right-wing? It seems not. Only 12 percent of crucial voters held a highly unfavorable attitude to the Communist party, and 27 percent were simply unfavorable.

The decisive factor seems to have been the superior personal image of Giscard d'Estaing. His intelligence, competence, seriousness,

---

[9] See Denis Lindon and Pierre Weill, "Pourquoi M. Giscard d'Estaing a-t-il gagné," *Le Monde*, 22 May 1974.

prestige, and even his social aloofness, made the crucial voters see the right-wing candidate as presidential material. At the moment of decision they voted for the man rather than for the political program.

An ironic factor in the second ballot—outstanding on account of the record voter turnout and the most clear-cut Left-Right confrontation in thirty years—is that the outcome was decided for reasons of personal image by the least politically conscious segment of the electorate. It is not the least interesting aspect of opinion polls that they were able to provide a key to explaining the presidential election of 1974 that no other method of inquiry could have revealed.

7

THE ROLE OF THE PRESS, RADIO, AND TELEVISION IN FRENCH POLITICAL LIFE

Alfred Grosser

To understand the role of the mass communication media in the 1974 electoral campaign in France, it is necessary to have a solid knowledge of the media's habitual role in French political life. Hence this chapter will offer a general description of the media in France, illustrating essential features with references to the French presidential campaign and to points of similarity and difference in the American media situation.[1] Only at the end will there be direct analysis of the press in the recent campaign.

---

[1] There are very few helpful studies on the French media and their influence. The best way to collect serious information (including up-to-date statistical data and excellent monographs on newspapers, TV programs, et cetera) is to read the small but very informative monthly, *Presse-Actualité*, published by the Catholic press center Bayard-Presse (5, rue Bayard, 75008 Paris). The general study by Roland Cayrol, *La Presse écrite et audio-visuelle* (Paris: Presses Universitaires de France, 1973), is very helpful in providing an understanding of the French situation through a comparison with similar ones. It also contains an extensive bibliography. Short but precise information on each French daily (with good additional statistical material) is found in Emmanuel Derieux and Jean C. Texier, *La presse quotidienne française* (Paris: A. Colin, 1974). Interesting information on the role of money and the status of newsmakers, especially in the United States and France, can be found in *Le pouvoir d'informer* (Paris: R. Laffont, 1972), by Jean-Louis Servan-Schreiber, the editor of the best French economic monthly, *Expansion*.

Some important newspaper directors and journalists have published memoirs or collections of their best columns: Pierre Brisson, *Vingt ans de "Figaro" 1938-1958* (Paris: Gallimard, 1959); Hubert Beuve-Méry, *Onze ans de règne 1958-1969* (Paris: Flammarion, 1974); Françoise Giroud, *Si je mens . . .* (Paris: Stock, 1972), and *Une Poignée d'eau* (Paris: Laffont, 1973), a collection of editorials from *Express*; Jean Daniel, *Le temps qui reste: Essai d'autobiographie professionnelle* (Paris: Stock, 1973); Jean Lacouture, *Un sang d'encre* (Paris: Stock, 1974); and Pierre Viansson-Ponté, *Des jours entre les jours* (Paris: Stock, 1974), a collection of the long columns published every Saturday in *Le Monde* since 1972, including those published during the 1974 electoral campaign.

The books that have already been published on the 1974 electoral campaign contain a little information on the press: Michèle Cotta, *La VIᵉ République* (Paris:

The Press and Its Problems

After the liberation in 1944, newspapers that had continued publication during the German occupation saw their assets confiscated and organs born of the Resistance installed in their place. *La Croix*, the Catholic daily, and *Figaro*, which had ceased publication in Lyon a few days after the Germans entered the nonoccupied zone in November 1942, escaped. The main concern at the time was to guarantee the press independence of both political power and moneyed interests.

For many reasons, this goal was never fully realized, and the new papers became by degrees and in different forms "normal" commercial enterprises. However, the events of 1944 and, before that, the division of France in 1940 had changed the press profoundly. Before the war, the Parisian press had many readers in the provinces, but since 1945 the provincial press, clearly more prosperous than its Parisian counterpart, has become dominant. Only a few people in the regional intellectual, economic, and political elites read *Le Monde*, *Figaro*, or *La Croix*. *France-Soir* also has a limited circulation outside Paris, but it is really the regional press that most influences the mass of the population outside the Paris urban area.

It should be remembered, however, that the Parisian megalopolis represents approximately one-fifth of the French population. Moreover, the news in the provincial dailies is largely inspired by the issue of *Le Monde* appearing the preceding afternoon, and, most importantly, the weekly press is almost exclusively Parisian, so much so that the regional editions which *Express* has launched in the Rhône-Alpes and Mediterranean areas have failed to establish themselves. And yet the French press cannot be understood with reference to the

Flammarion, 1974); Michel Bassi and André Campana, *Le grand tournoi* (Paris: Grasset, 1974).

There are also some allusions to the press in a brilliant parody written in the form of a classical French tragedy of the seventeenth century: Frédéric Bon, Michel-Antoine Burnier, and Bernard Kouchner, *Les Voraces: Tragédie à l'Elysée* (Paris: Balland, 2nd ed., revised, 1974).

The problems of the impact of public opinion polls are excellently analyzed in a book published at the time of the campaign: Frédéric Bon, Michel-Antoine Burnier, and Nonna Mayer, *Les sondages peuvent-ils se tromper?* (Paris: Calmann-Lévy, 1974).

The available material about television is very poor, but the official volume, *ORTF 73* (Paris: Presses de la Cité, 1973), offers a good general view of TV organization and activity. There are also some polemical works on different stages of the chronic television "crisis": Roger Louis, *L'ORTF, un combat* (Paris: Le Seuil, 1968); Jacques Thibau, *La télévision, le pouvoir et l'argent* (Paris: Calmann-Lévy, 1973); and Arthur Conte, *Hommes libres* (Paris: Plon, 1973), which tells the story of the author's short career as president-director-general of ORTF, the official French television network.

Parisian press alone, however many interpreters try to evaluate it that way.

The two most important press phenomena of the postwar period are the same for France as for other Western European countries: "departification" and consolidation. In 1946, the large parties owned and directly controlled the important dailies. Today the party newspapers have been in crisis for a long time. Beginning in 1945 the Radical party lost, simultaneously with its electoral power, its two pillars of the press, *Progrès* in Lyon and *Dépêche de Toulouse*—which, however, in becoming *Dépêche du Midi*, retained its radical tendency and actively opposed Gaullism under the Fifth Republic in the Southwest. Of the three large parties at the Liberation, one, the MRP (Christian democrats), lost its principal press outlet, the daily, *Aube*, which disappeared in 1951. The second, the Socialist party, managed to keep *Populaire* alive as a daily until 1966—though its circulation had fallen to 20,000 copies in 1955 (as against 270,000 in January 1946). The third, the Communist party, circulates 151,000 copies of *Humanité* every day—for more than five million Communist voters. By this standard, the other large party of the Fifth Republic, the Gaullist UDR, is even worse off; its daily, *Nation*, has only four pages and a circulation of 12,000. However, its editorials are quoted by other newspapers and by radio and television newscasts.[2] Furthermore, the Fifth Republic governments of Presidents de Gaulle and Pompidou, and Chaban-Delmas's candidacy, had massive support from the large circulation daily *France-Soir*, albeit support masquerading as purely objective news.

As for the consolidation of the French press, the figures in Table 7–1 show its rate and extent. These figures show, first of all, the decline of the daily press. Total circulation is going down while population rises. (The number of registered voters grew from 25 million in 1946 to 30 million in 1974—and eighteen to twenty-one-year-olds, not yet voters but generally already newspaper readers, are much more numerous today than they were then.) Furthermore, the Frenchman is not a great reader of daily newspapers—and what he turns to when he does read it is not necessarily political news.

Secondly, while Paris is still better off in the number of newspapers it has than London or, especially, New York, it has been losing papers over the last half century and has fewer than many large foreign cities.

---

[2] *Nation* went out of business in July 1974 after Giscard's government team cut off its secret subsidy because of the paper's criticism of the "ungaullist" behavior of the new president.

Table 7-1

CONSOLIDATION OF THE FRENCH PRESS, 1914–1972

Year	Paris News-papers	Paris Circulation	Provinces News-papers	Provinces Circulation	Total Circulation[a]
1914	60	5.0	242	4.0	9.0
1939	31	6.0	175	6.0	12.0
1946	28	6.0	153	9.2	15.1
1956	14	4.4	111	7.0	11.5
1966	14	4.4	91	7.8	12.2
1972	11	3.9	78	7.5	11.4

[a] Average daily circulation in millions.
Source: Emmanuel Derieux and Jean C. Texier, *La presse quotidienne française* (Paris: A. Colin, 1974), p. 292.

The consolidation of the provincial press has gone even farther than the table leaves one to suppose. Many nominally independent papers belong to chains, which means that only the local news is independently reported. Even the larger papers sometimes collaborate more than they compete. In the Rhône-Alpes region, for example, the two large dailies, *Progrès* and *Dauphiné Libéré*, have divided zones of influence between themselves and have pooled their news-gathering resources in a press association called AIGLES. In Marseilles, *Provençal*, headed by Socialist leader Gaston Defferre, bought out its principal rival, *Méridional*, leaving it enough editorial latitude to express moderate right-wing views, but nevertheless bringing all newspaper political expression under monolithic control.

Consolidation has created veritable monopolies in large areas of France. *Sud-Ouest* in Bordeaux is one. *Ouest-France*, published at Rennes, has a circulation of close to 700,000 and hardly any competitors in a good ten departments out of the ninety-five that make up metropolitan France. The disadvantages of this state of affairs have been seen in other countries. At the same time, there are some advantages; when everybody reads the same newspaper, social communication is easier than when each ideological group reads only the newspaper expressing its views. It can be argued, for example, that cable television results in the establishment of veritable ghettos of the like-minded, telling audiences only what falls within a rigid opinion frame. Yet it is quite possible for a monopolistic newspaper to be fair to more than one point of view. During the presidential campaign of 1974, for example, *Ouest-France* was quite remarkably balanced, serious, and impartial in telling readers about the candidates and their programs.

The independence, or lack of it, of staff on individual newspapers varies in France as in other countries, with members of the press chains, of course, having comparatively less. Here are several examples. Robert Hersant, centrist deputy from the Oise, edits eight regional dailies, of which one, *Centre Presse*, resulted from the merger of eleven newspapers; he controls a whole series of weeklies and monthlies of all sorts, such as *Auto-Journal* and *Bonne Cuisine*. The case of Jean Prouvost is quite different. At ninety, this great wool industrialist, creator of the two unprecedented journalistic successes, *Paris-Soir* and *Match*, before the war, is as energetic as ever. He not only controls the now declining weekly *Paris-Match*, which he launched in 1939, but, with Hachette, controls the largest radio-television weekly, *Télé 7 Jours* (which has a circulation between 2.5 and 3 million). He also acquired control of *Figaro* in 1972, after having been co-owner since 1950, and, thanks to a rather complicated stock distribution, he exercises considerable influence on Radio-Luxembourg. Prouvost has less power than the Hachette group, but seems to use it more directly on the editors. The press is only one concern of many for La Librairie Hachette, created in 1826. Through its publishing houses (Hachette, Fayard, Grasset, Stock), it controls about a fifth of French publishing, including school texts and the chief French paperbacks. By holding 49 percent of the shares of the NMPP (News Delivery Service of the Parisian Press), of which five other newspaper cooperatives hold the remaining shares, Hachette has a central place in the distribution of newspapers in France. It is similarly strong in advertising, record distribution, the production of television films, the development of video cassettes, and printing. Among news periodicals, Hachette controls totally or partially weeklies and monthlies of all sorts, but only one daily, *France-Soir*, which has declined consistently since the rise of television. The most directly political weekly of the group is *Point*, launched in 1972 by a team of journalists who had just left *Express*.

Hachette has no real equivalent in the United States and neither has Bayard-Presse, the most important Catholic publisher in the world. This organization controls eighteen periodicals, most of them vigorous and innovative. Bayard publications range from the monthly *Notre Temps* for people over fifty to the best French publication on the problems of the press, *Presse Actualité*. The daily, *La Croix*, previously known for its clerical preoccupations and political conservatism, has become, notably at the time of the Algerian war when its positions were particularly firm and courageous, an organ noted for its liberalism and its balance.

Does outside control of a newspaper mean that the editors have no freedom? Not quite. In September 1971, Simon Nora, an important public official, up to that time the principal counselor of Prime Minister Chaban-Delmas, became director-general of Hachette. When *Point* was launched the following year, it manifested no open hostility toward Chaban-Delmas. However, Simon Nora has never shaped all the magazine's political positions. The editorial staff exercises considerable autonomy and during the electoral campaign an attentive reader could detect many of its editors' sympathy for Mitterrand behind the paper's ostensible support for the Gaullist candidate. On the other hand, *France-Soir* took a stand, clearly discernible in the slant of its news and commentary, for the mayor of Bordeaux. This seemed to confirm the tendencies revealed when, just before the death of President Pompidou, the editor, a former member of Pompidou's team, was replaced by an excellent journalist, Henri Amouroux, until that time editor of *Sud-Ouest*, Bordeaux's large daily. During this period, Jean Prouvost selected a new editor for *Figaro*, the writer Jean d'Ormesson, who was a supporter of Valéry Giscard d'Estaing. In any case, Jean Prouvost is a man much more concerned about directly influencing the content of the newspapers that he financially controls than is, for example, the industrialist Marcel Boussac with *Aurore* or the former co-owner of *Figaro*, the sugar industrialist Ferdinand Beghin.

In an attempt to protect their freedom and to fight against the power of the owners, who buy and sell newspapers (writers and all) like industrial goods, editors have tried, probably earlier and more often than their counterparts in other countries, to obtain certain guarantees. Until 1969 the editorial staff of *Figaro* was very well protected by a system of management at several levels. The editors of *Paris-Normandie* (Rouen) and those of the largest political weekly, *Express*, were granted significant safeguards of their independence in principle. But the direction was reversed; Jean Prouvost is very much the master of *Figaro*, as is Jean-Jacques Servan-Schreiber of *Express*. No association of editors has obtained any truly decisive results, and the situation of *Le Monde* remains unique, even though the editorial staff of *La Croix* is equally independent.

The *Le Monde* corporation, founded on 11 December 1944 as a limited liability corporation, is unique in its field. Its capital of 1,000 shares is divided into three categories. The 400 shares of A stock are owned by individuals, 155 by Hubert Beuve-Mery, who was editor from 1944 to 1969, and by one of his sons; the rest by ten or so influential university professors, union leaders, and so on. The 490 shares of B stock are owned by associations of the employees, 400 by the journalists' association, 50 by that of the executives, 40 by that of the clerical staff. Finally, the 110 shares of C stock are owned by the current management, 70 by the editor, Jacques Fauvet, and 40 by the business manager. Because Le Monde continues to increase its circulation and to attract advertising, making it a sound and profitable business venture, the question of raising new capital does not arise, and the journalists' association can enjoy a privileged position in controlling, if not in actually managing, the newspaper.

To what extent does advertising limit a newspaper's freedom? It is hard to say. Sensitive issues are not always directly political, but the list of economic and social problems that interest advertisers can be long. To be sure, editors do not necessarily bow before the advertisers' interests, but the fact remains that the advertising portion of the budgets of French newspapers is particularly large compared with that of newspapers in other countries, because fewer French readers subscribe. The expenses of distribution for newsstand sales are so heavy that they virtually cancel out the receipts coming from regular subscribers.

Here are several significant figures for 1972: for its circulation of 360,000 (a figure to be distinguished from a total printing, which includes unsold copies amounting regularly to more than a quarter of the Parisian press's output), Le Monde had only 77,000 subscribers; Figaro had 99,000 out of 408,000; and France-Soir, 6,000 out of 724,000. Only La Croix distributes almost solely to subscribers (114,000 out of a total circulation of 131,000), which compensates for La Croix's severe lack of advertising receipts, a lack that is due to the fact that La Croix readers are not considered significant consumers by the advertisers.

The "revolution" in the press in 1945 ought to have led the state to protect newspapers from money pressures to some degree. There is a certain amount of government aid to the press in the form of subsidies for the purchase of paper, which permit the French press to buy paper below the world price. The press also enjoys lower postal rates and tax benefits. But this aid has two serious disadvantages. First, it favors the rich. The big papers, which use more paper and send heavier issues through the mail, get proportionally more than the small. (In 1973 some help was given to the papers with the least advertising, but not enough to make up for the "surplus aid" the large publications receive for their advertising, which, in addition, is freer of tax burdens than the news space!) At the same time, its control of postal rates and of the price of paper gives the government formidable power over the press.

ORTF and the "Périphériques"

The government's powers in the field of radio and television are considerable, and certainly more direct than those exercised over the print media. Paradoxically, political discussion of these powers became more intense in 1959, 1964, and 1972, as new structures were established to ensure radio and television greater autonomy.

In part, the change in scale of the televisual media explains heightened public interest in them. When the Fifth Republic was instituted in 1958 there were fewer than a million television sets in France. The 5 million mark was passed in 1964. In 1967 the owners of television sets were for the first time more numerous than those who had only radios. In 1969 there were more than 10 million TV sets, and at the time of the presidential election of 1974 the figure was approximately 14 million.

A second factor bringing government power over radio and TV to the political forefront has been governmental stability. Under the preceding republic, government and party influence on radio and television was veiled by the instability of the former and the competing multiplicity of the latter. As order replaced chaos, the power structure became more visible.

Finally, General de Gaulle's habit of addressing the French directly by television reinforced the belief, rather generally accepted in the world in the early sixties, that television exercised a decisive influence on the political behavior of citizens. This is a belief more widespread today among politicians than among political scientists, who now think TV has more impact on long-range attitudes than on current opinions.

In 1946, after the withdrawal of the broadcasting licenses granted to private corporations before the war and the affirmation of the monopoly, Radiodiffusion Française (later to become Radiodiffusion-Télévision-Française, RTF) was created as an individual agency, directly under the ministry of information. An important first step was taken at the beginning of the Fifth Republic with the ordinance of 4 February 1959, which made RTF a public institution. It became a separate administrative unit, but continued to depend directly upon governmental authority, which meant that the real director of RTF was not the man who had the title, but the cabinet minister.

Whether he wanted to or not, the most liberal of ministers was bound to influence the news as well as the cultural and artistic programming of RTF. Since the minister had discretionary power over the content of all broadcasts, every newscast and every program was thought of as carrying his permission and approval. The law of 27 June 1964, transforming RTF into ORTF, was supposed to put an end to this situation. It restricted the minister's administrative and financial power and created a board of directors and a director-general to run the organization on a day-to-day basis. While this somewhat resembles the situation in Great Britain and in the Federal Republic of Germany, the effects are different. The BBC remains independent even though the government appoints its directors.

It would seem that in Great Britain and Germany the national interest is less easily confused with the political power of a majority than in France. In 1969–1970 it was curious to see the newspapers and the parties speculating on how President Pompidou would react to Prime Minister Chaban-Delmas's liberal policy for ORTF—for the law forbade the government to have any policy, liberal or otherwise, on the matter and made the board of directors and the director-general the only legally responsible officials.

The statute of 1964 was rather suddenly transformed in 1972 when the parliament hastily passed a law inspired by Pompidou and his advisers. It was this law of 3 July 1972 that governed ORTF at the time of the presidential campaign. It says specifically:

> The national public service of the Radiodiffusion-Télé-vision-Française has, within the boundaries of its authority, the mission of meeting the needs and aspirations of the population for news, culture, education, entertainment, and all the values of civilization. Its aim is to provide for the general interests of the collectivity. . . . [Article 1]
> The national public service . . . is a monopoly of the state. [Article 2]
> . . . ORTF is a public institution of an industrial and commercial character. It is administered by a Board of Directors presided over by a President-Director-General. . . . [Article 4]
> The Board of Directors of the Office defines the general policy for the institution. It guarantees the high quality and the morality of the programs. It watches over the objectivity and the accuracy of the news broadcast by the

Office. It ensures that major intellectual trends and currents
of opinion are expressed. . . . [Article 7]

Since the government now names the board's director-general, the
board has lost some power. On the other hand, the president-
director-general (PDG) now has a degree of independence because
he has a limited term—three years—whereas before he was constantly subject to removal. Arthur Conte, the first PDG, completed
less than half of his term. Although originally a supporter of the
president, he found himself in conflict with the minister of information in October 1973, and was fired by the government on a probably
illegal technicality: the PDG must be chosen from among the members of the board of directors, and board members of the category to
which Conte belonged were subject to removal, so he was removed
as a member, and thereby disqualified from serving as PDG!

A bright civil servant was chosen to succeed Conte, the politician.
The new PDG, Marceau Long, explained immediately to the press
that he regarded his new post as just another government job.

It must not be deduced from this that all ORTF journalists are
"government men" and that they are subject to constant, overt
censorship. Most of what happens is self-censorship—the bureau-
crat's natural wariness of controversy. It is not merely fear of displeasing the government, but also fear of displeasing the mass of
television viewers or the social groups of which they are composed.
Hence, inexhaustible caution. Caution, timidity even, especially on
any subject connected with contemporary history; only the established truths about the wartime period or the Fourth Republic, for
example, appear on the screen. Timidity, too, in discussing political
and social issues—the deeper an investigation tries to go, the less
likely it is to be shown on television. Doctors, professors, farmers,
veterans, and the public agencies watch to see that they are not overly
criticized. At a special session called by the government in July 1974,
Parliament passed a new law that completely restructured the state
radio-television system. ORTF was divided into six public corporations, with all six corporate presidents appointed by the government.

The same thing is true of the press in a monopoly situation. A
sort of self-restraint not directly imposed from outside leads it to
avoid sensitive subjects and to aspire to the blandness of the lowest
common denominator. The effect, of course, is conservative. This
can be more important than government control of news, especially
during an electoral campaign when special laws, backed up by a
regulatory commission, place the candidates temporarily on an equal
footing.

216

In April–May 1974, this produced several absurdities. The serious candidates had no more TV time than the fringe candidates. Furthermore, no confrontation between candidates was possible before the first round of voting. The "peripheral" radio stations exploited this situation to great advantage.

What are the "périphériques"? Since the immediate postwar period, Paris-owned transmitters located near French borders have breached the ORTF monopoly. There is Radio Monte Carlo, nominally owned by the Principality of Monaco, but in reality controlled by a corporation belonging to the French state, SOFIRAD (Société française d'information et de radiodiffusion). Since 1973 it has been headed by Denis Baudoin, previously press secretary to the president of the republic, then governmental representative for information. Radio Monte Carlo also engages in telecasting by means of a new transmitter which is located illegally inside French territory and which reaches a fairly wide audience.

Most important are the two large stations that compete both between themselves and with France-Inter of ORTF—Europe 1, whose transmitter is located at Felsberg in West Germany, and Radio Luxembourg, whose transmitter is at Beidweiler in Luxembourg. Europe 1 is controlled by a powerful self-made man, seventy-four-year-old Sylvain Floirat, who holds an equal number of shares with SOFIRAD, each having about a third of the stock. At Radio Luxembourg, bitter and intricate struggles are going on between Belgian and French financial groups (including Hachette and Havas, the advertising agency owned by the French state) over the future succession of Jean Prouvost, a minority stockholder who is, however, in actual control.

Europe 1 and Radio Luxembourg have much more flexibility than ORTF. Although they too are restricted by taboos (both stations are supported exclusively by advertising), their commentators can speak freely, while ORTF tolerates no personal commentary, and they can broadcast extemporaneous debates and reports from any place where something is happening that will hold an audience's interest (and make it hear advertisers' messages).

The Scope of the Media

But what is it, precisely, that interests the public? The French are not very great consumers of newspapers, especially by comparison with the British. Fewer than 60 percent of all households subscribe to or regularly buy a daily newspaper, and only one out of two regularly reads a weekly of any kind. Shock events make circulation climb. On 3 April, the day after the death of Georges Pompidou, *France-Soir* printed 1,500,000 copies (500,000 more than average), *Parisien Libéré* 1,274,000 (up 500,000), *Le Monde* 819,000 (up 300,000), *Figaro* 695,000 (up 200,000), *Ouest-France* 895,000 (up 210,000), and *Sud-Ouest* 508,000 (up 65,000). Even though the television viewer rarely follows political debates, the audience for the great Mitterrand/Giscard confrontation that took place between the two electoral rounds was a record 86 percent.

Assuming that the essential function of a newspaper is to inform, what type of information is the most easily disseminated? In the provinces, the answer is rather simple: the newspaper's first priority is local news at its least politicized. When a strike prevented *Sud-Ouest* from appearing in February 1972, it was easy to see what the public missed. Guests failed to turn up at funerals and weddings, town movie theatres were deserted by the rural population, and all sorts of associations had to call off their meetings.

The newspaper can also supply "information," true or false, which allows its readers to escape from their daily preoccupations. At the time of one of Queen Elizabeth's visits to France, the *Sunday Times* published an amusing account of the "news" about the English royal family that had appeared in the French press during the course of previous years: The Queen, apparently, had been pregnant ninety-two times, had had 149 accidents and nine miscarriages, had been on the verge of abdication sixty-three times and close to rupture with Prince Philip seventy-three times!

News about the weather and the local band concert, and escape or entertainment news dilute the political impact of both newspapers and television, which, in France, give priority to diversion. The regional daily that reports an automobile accident in a local edition, but says nothing about a strike or a workman's accident in a local factory, has a further depoliticizing effect. The numerous weekly and monthly magazines which make up the "lonely hearts press" and publish innumerable photo-novels also distract people's attention from politics.

In France, as in other countries, the excuse for not focusing newspaper and TV attention on complex social, economic, and political phenomena is that the reader and the television viewer are not asking for it. It can, of course, be argued that they are not asking for serious views because they have not been educated to use the media. The French school system does not prepare future citizens to look to the media for basic information about what is going on in their society. An ill-informed public makes it difficult, if not impossible, for those candidates most staunchly opposed to demagoguery to state their case. The Giscard/Mitterrand debate was of a much higher quality than the famous Kennedy/Nixon debates, in which the opponents avoided serious discussion of any important problem. Even so, both French candidates shied away from debate on the energy crisis—not only because they would have had to say disagreeable things, but because they knew how little the immense majority of a population uneducated in economics could hope to understand the subject.

It must not be concluded that the French are not interested in politics. The massive participation in the presidential election, especially by comparison with the United States, suffices to prove the contrary. But French interest in politics rests for the most part on a very pessimistic view of things. For the Frenchman, politics means corruption. "Why are you cheering General de Gaulle?" a journalist asked an elderly lady during one of the president's tours in the provinces. "Because at least he doesn't engage in politics!" was her reply. This attitude partly explains the popularity of the general. Some newspapers perpetuate it by dwelling on the shabbiest and most despicable side of men and events. The pattern can be seen in the pages of two weeklies of radically different ideologies. *Minute,* with a circulation close to 250,000, projects anti-Arab racism and an unfailing right-wing anti-Gaullism. *Canard Enchaîné,* a "satiric weekly appearing Wednesdays," as the other dailies call it when quoting its news, has been a veritable political institution for more than half a century. Its normal circulation surpasses 400,000 and approached a million at the time of the wire-tapping in the new offices it was constructing—the scandal that precipitated the downfall of Minister of Interior Raymond Marcellin in March 1974.

However, in a certain sense the principal target of the *Canard* has been Chaban-Delmas, whose defeat in the presidential election was largely due to charges about his tax return, printed by the newspaper while he was prime minister. *Canard Enchaîné* is, much more than *Minute* and without having the latter's taste for defamation and fakery, a great exposer of scandals, many of which are very real. Sometimes its attacks have results, spectacular or otherwise. (In France the sanction against a compromised minister or civil servant is not usually public.) More often, though, they have virtually no repercussions, which both shocks and gratifies the reader, who is reinforced in his severe opinion of politicians and in his certainty of possessing a unique understanding of political reality.

Many of the scandals which have undermined the credibility of the Gaullists have been discovered by *Canard*, but this is not its most positive role. It is at its best when it attacks, in precise and commonplace cases, what could be called the permanent scandals: the daily fate of the weak at the hands of the strong, whether the strong be the administration, business, or the courts. But that role it shares with other newspapers.

Indeed, a very marked change has occurred in the way the French press presents "news items." As the public has become more conscious of the most shocking aspects of inequality and social justice, newspapers have given more space to this sort of news. The growth of the Left and the rallying of all the candidates to many views which were still considered "advanced" a few years ago must be explained by this evolution, which several newspapers have accelerated. The time of "blood on page one," of tales of crime to make the reader shudder has passed, at least for the most serious newspapers. Among these one must include *France-Soir*, which questions the structures of society much more than any other large circulation daily in London, New York, or Hamburg. *Figaro*, too, reports workmen's accidents and unequal justice for rich and poor, often without regard for the prejudices of its clientele.

Le Monde also offers a case in point. More and more, during the course of the sixties and seventies, this newspaper of international reputation (particularly because it devotes a quarter of its editorial space to international politics and foreign countries) features kinds of stories that seldom turn up in the *New York Times*, the *Times*, or the *Frankfurter Allgemeine*. These are minor items about obscure people—a school closed for lack of heat, an Algerian worker arrested—that fit into a mosaic of great social significance.

The Influence of the Media

The influence of the media is not easily measurable, and some of the evidence suggests that it is not very great. The Republicans would win every election in the United States if the press, which is largely republican, determined the vote; similarly, the "Red" suburbs of Paris ought to have stopped voting Communist long ago, because people there read *Parisien Libéré* and *France-Soir* rather than *Humanité*. The former does not even attempt to hide its "right-wing Gaullist" orientation, while the latter has been subtler in supporting the government. However, it is possible to imagine that *Parisien Libéré*, with its shock headlines and its call for ready indignation against all who threaten good order, favors the "petit bourgeois" tendencies of the working class, especially toward immigrant workers.

It is in its influence on attitudes that one must look for the impact of television. Except in unusual cases, such as the downfall of Chaban-Delmas, television hardly shakes opinion, but it unifies what could be called the cultural outlook of the French. The Communist party's change of style is not only due to the decisions of its leaders. Until the spread of television, they could maintain a sort of Communist subculture within the national political culture as it was transmitted by the schools. There was almost a language peculiar to the party, a special system of references, and a mythology transmitted by the party's own information circuit. But how could the voters be convinced that Soviet troops had saved Czechoslovakia from facism in 1968 when these voters had all seen on their screens the invasion of Prague and the tears of an entire people?

The rise of public opinion polls has raised the question whether polls dispossess journalists of their role as interpreters of opinion. Traditionally, the editorial writer and the reporter interpret, each in his way, the feelings of the readers and even of the population as a whole. Their articles help to fashion the image that citizens have of what most people think. But today this image is transmitted (and in part created) by polls.

By this, large newspapers lose in a large measure their representative quality and their role of spokesman for the electorate before the political and governing milieus. In the past, this phenomenon coincided with another, which also diminishes the influence of newspapers on these milieus: under the Third and Fourth republics, well-known journalists and important editors were in constant contact with politicians, who needed them in order to reach their publics. This sort of direct power has considerably diminished since 1958. Nevertheless, the struggles of the political milieu are still largely influenced by a part of the press which is rather easily defined. A large circulation newspaper such as *Parisien Libéré*, which is scarcely representative of its readers, is not part of this press, nor is the high-quality newspaper *La Croix*, since its sphere of influence is ignored by the political world. Certainly *Figaro* belongs to it, as do the three weekly magazines, *Express, Point,* and *Nouvel Observateur,* and especially *Le Monde*, which, in addition to the news and commentary of its editors, often publishes the positions of political leaders, and is, even for those who criticize it most vigorously, a sort of forum for political dialogue.

Other social groups are perhaps easier to define, but not to analyze in terms of their permeability to the influence of the mass media. The most active press organs are probably of a type that has not yet been discussed here: specialized weeklies and monthlies, each addressing a specific professional category, are being read more and more. One example: it is very possible that *Agri-Sept* does more to form the opinions of many farmers than the regional dailies they also read.

Perhaps the best example of a specialized audience (and of the difficulty of assessing the influence of the media) is provided by readers of the Catholic press. More than 90 percent of the French are baptized Catholics but far fewer are churchgoers or people claiming that their behavior is inspired by their faith. Traditionally, the organized Church, most of the Catholic newspapers, and the mass of the Catholic voters were on the conservative side. Since the fifties, the evolution towards the Left has been rather quick, with a sharp acceleration after the Vatican Council. In 1972, the general assembly of French bishops meeting at Lourdes approved a text, "For a Christian Practice of Politics," in which they indicated some "ethical guidelines" to be deduced from the Bible: "Respect for the poor, help for the weak, protection of foreigners, skepticism about wealth and condemnation of the rule of money"; and where they listed the emergency problems of political life: "Exploitation of foreign workers, plunder of the Third World, and the dehumanizing effects of technological society and a profit economy; the will to power of oligarchies and nations, the powerlessness of salaried workers as opposed to the privileged social classes. . . ."

When, on the eve of the presidential elections, the widely read weekly, *Vie catholique illustrée*, says in an editorial that it will not make a choice but only recall what the bishops have said, who is in fact asking the Catholic voter to take a stand on the socialist side— the newspaper or the bishops? But did not the bishops write their text because they were influenced by the leftist groups inside French Catholicism, among which are the left-oriented weeklies and monthlies?

Clearly the influence of the media is difficult to determine. Some interesting evidence is what Frenchmen themselves think about the relative role of the media, as furnished by a poll taken by SOFRES on 14 May, shortly before the second round of elections, and published by *Nouvel Observateur* on 21 May. To the question, "Are you following the electoral campaign?" 59 percent replied, "Yes, almost every day," 32 percent, "Yes, from time to time," and 9 percent,

"Not at all." The motives given for this interest were very diverse, and probably did not entirely correspond to real motivations. Another question was: What is the most efficient means for (1) choosing a candidate, (2) making a choice at the time of voting, (3) knowing what politicians are like, and (4) having arguments for debate? Posters, tracts and meetings were rejected (1 percent). Conversations were considered slightly useful for (3) (4 percent), but important for (4) (12 percent). But it was the mass media which prevailed, however unevenly. Newspapers scored from 18 percent (arguments) to 7 percent (view of politicians), with 12 percent and 13 percent for (1) and (2), while radio made respectively 11 percent, 10 percent, 6 percent, and 10 percent, and television outdid all the other news media with 64 percent, 61 percent, 74 percent, and 45 percent. The only voters reticent toward television were the Communists (38 percent, against 62 and 66 percent among the other tendencies), who had more confidence in newspapers, conversations, and meetings—which confirms the existence or the survival of the Communist subculture.

The Press and the Presidential Campaign

Most of the choices of the newspapers were unsurprising. It was clear from the beginning that *Humanité* would support Mitterrand and that only the French sports daily *Equipe* would refuse to choose. (On 16 May the paper published an excellent article giving the answers of Mitterrand and Giscard d'Estaing to twelve questions on sports, most of them with financial implications.) It could also have been predicted that *Canard Enchaîné* would help Mitterrand and refrain from directing its irony against the Left, even though it would stand ready to resume the role of critic should it win the election. (But this was not entirely sure. Once in its history, *Canard* supported a cabinet, that of Pierre Mendès-France in 1954.)

The Catholic press had, roughly speaking, three types of attitudes during the campaign. The small conservative weekly, *France catholique*, took a stand against Mitterrand, without saying very much about the problems that in other times or in other countries had seemed vital to the Church, such as the status of Catholic schools or the question of abortion. At the other end of the political spectrum, the weekly *Témoignage chrétien* was very firm in saying it was quite impossible to be a good Christian without being a Socialist. *La Croix*, the only Catholic daily, took neither attitude. It published contributions from all shades of opinion but remained very cautious about its own position, suggesting that its staff was divided. It tried to avoid any kind of bias in its editorials and analysis. When, just before the second ballot, Mitterrand published a letter to the teachers of the Catholic schools, *La Croix* printed it (the issue dated 17 May, which was published on the evening of 16 May) with the public reaction of Giscard d'Estaing, and the next day it published the highly critical comments of the national secretariat of the Catholic schools, but refrained from editorial comment. The best political debate appearing in a newspaper was probably that between Edgar Faure and Michel Rocard organized and published by *La Croix* (16 May) and, with the exception of *Le Monde* and *Figaro*, nowhere was there a better synopsis of the main stands of the candidates than in *La Croix* of 3 May, the five central themes being "institutions and civil rights," "economy and society," "family," "education," and "foreign policy."

As other chapters of this book show, the transfer of "Catholic" votes to the Left was one of the main reasons for Mitterrand's gains. How important those voters were to the whole Left was demonstrated by the three full pages which *Humanité* dedicated (from 18 April on) to the theme "Communistes et chrétiens," including interviews with priests and with a bishop.

One of the most interesting changes in French public life is that people are saying more and more openly how they will vote, whereas in the past the vote and personal income were the two pillars of French privacy. Many people were willing this time to let their names be published at the bottom of electoral appeals. Not only the usual intellectuals were mobilized, but also many people ready to use the social influence they might have in favor of one of the candidates. Manifestoes were published by the press, especially by *Le Monde*. This paper devoted much space to a rather unusual type of signatory: journalists. The headlines were, "281 Parisian journalists to vote for the candidate of the Left" (17 May), and "Nearly 500 journalists favor the leftist candidate and 500 economic writers call his program just, realistic, and plausible." Many of these journalists wrote for papers that had endorsed Giscard d'Estaing. In both issues, it was pointed out that because of *Le Monde's* rule against signing manifestoes, no *Le Monde* people were on the lists.

After the first ballot some newspapers found themselves in the difficult position of having to support a candidate they had violently criticized. The best examples are the *Parisien Libéré* and *Minute*. *Parisien* had supported Jacques Chaban-Delmas, not because he was a liberal, but because he was (or was presented by the paper as being) a faithful Gaullist with a sharp nationalist orientation. The support *Parisien* gave to Giscard d'Estaing after 5 May was cool, and was followed by a highly critical attitude after his victory. *Minute* had explained to its readers that there were two honorable candidates, Jean-Marie Le Pen and Jean Royer; the paper supported Royer because he seemed likely to win. After the first ballot, *Minute* felt compelled to fight the "Red danger" by reluctantly supporting the very man every issue had condemned during his years as minister of finance, Giscard d'Estaing.

On the whole, the level of political fighting in the press was quite honorable. One of the exceptions was the treatment in the press of the revelation that Guenter Guillaume, close collaborator of German Chancellor Brandt, was a spy. The front-page headlines of *Parisien Libéré* (8 May) were not very consistent, but they showed rather well what the paper hoped to achieve by giving so much space to the case: "Setback for European unity. Nobel prize winner's duplicity used by multi-national groups to check social democracy. Willy Brandt dropped by the Russians." *Aurore* wrote the same day: "Certainly an odd way to show the alliance between a social democracy full of good will and seeming candor and a communism, implacable in its methods and objectives. I understand the fear of certain socialist leaders that they will see the specter of Willy Brandt cross the Rhine and emerge suddenly from the mists of our own electoral campaign. . . ."

The level was good—but for a reader who would think that the best possible style is that of the *New York Times* (clear stand for one of the candidates in the editorials, complete, balanced, unemotional coverage of the campaigns of both candidates), the two most important Paris papers might have been less than satisfactory. For general information and comment, *Figaro* was rather good and complete, and it devoted much space to columns by people supporting opposite candidates. But very early it became obvious that the style of the paper's editor was less reserved. In an editorial of 29 April, he asserted that it would be murderous for France to vote for Mitterrand.

> With fluttering eyelids, his smile forced and his lyricism old hat, in spite of his gains from the moment where the mirage of power dazzled him, François Mitterrand is beginning to look more and more like what he never ceased to be: a chameleon—a little too cunning, an old hand at politics— always able to quickly change himself into a voluntary victim of forces released by his desire for power. . . . The shadow behind Mitterrand is not the shadow of Jean Jaures or of Leon Blum, but the mingled and sinister shadows of Georges Marchais and his master, Stalin.

Very soon the paper took a stand in favor of Giscard d'Estaing, but not in an entirely fair way. Whereas one of its columnists, Raymond Aron, could write a brilliant piece showing that Giscard was the best choice (three articles, "The Stakes," from 17 to 19 April), another writer, Jean Charlot, discovered that his article, rather favorable to Chaban-Delmas, would not be published; as a consequence he resigned as columnist. Before the second ballot, even Aron's analysis became rather one-sided, and it was only after Giscard's victory that he pointed out the probable weaknesses of Giscard's policies. This change in tune was ironically and acrimoniously analyzed and censured by the editorialist of Le Monde, Pierre Viansson-Ponté, in the 26-27 May issue of his paper.

But had Le Monde itself been really balanced during the campaign? The editorials in which its editor, Jacques Fauvet, had expressed his support for Mitterrand (3 and 17 May) were far more moderate in tone than those of Jean d'Ormesson. But most of the information and most of the commentaries published by the paper had been somewhat biased in favor of the left-wing candidates, especially as Le Monde is far more eager than the New York Times to offer explanations and interpretations as well as news. The persistent temptation is to "explain" by reference (implicit even more than explicit) to the values and preferences of the explainer.

After the battle, each paper commented in its own fashion, generally without passion. For most of them, the important fact was the election of Giscard d'Estaing. But the six-column headlines on the front page of Humanité of 20 May were:

The most important success yet obtained by the Popular Front
F. MITTERRAND NARROWLY MISSES
AN ABSOLUTE MAJORITY
The people's candidate wins 2 million votes
Giscard d'Estaing elected with 50.7 percent of the vote

Perhaps the relative success of the Left really was the most significant event in the long run. But ultimately the Communist paper was performing a traditional function: to give party followers the feeling of victory. The other papers, too, went on confirming their readers in the opinions they already held.

8

THE LANGUAGE OF TELEVISION CAMPAIGNING

Monica Charlot

The Candidates and Television

In the 1974 French presidential election the role of broadcasting was undoubtedly greater than in any previous French election. The number of broadcasts devoted to the campaign was greater than ever before, particularly on the two radio stations not controlled by the state, Europe 1 and Radio Luxembourg. Both of these stations launched a number of feature programs on the election. Europe 1 organized confrontations between candidates and between prominent members of the political organizations to which the candidates belonged, while Radio Luxembourg ran a series of "grand jury" programs, which interviewed each of the candidates in turn. The grand jury was made up of representatives of the candidates not being interviewed. These programs absorbed a great deal of peak broadcast time on both stations, and certainly aroused great interest. Even on the more subdued state radio and television networks, coverage of meetings and speeches was wider than had been the case during previous presidential elections.

In addition to all this, during the last fortnight of the first ballot campaign (between 19 April and 3 May), each candidate was allotted a certain amount of broadcast time on radio and television. These broadcasts are often referred to as "the official campaign." In France candidates may not purchase time on radio or television. Instead, each is given the same amount of free time. The system of complete equality of all candidates is strictly observed. Qualifying as a candidate presents no great difficulty; all that is needed is a petition signed by 100 elected officials—mayors, departmental councillors, or members of Parliament—out of a total of 40,000 such officeholders, and a small cash deposit (which is refunded unless the candidate receives less than 5 percent of the vote). It is not, therefore, surprising that there should have been thirteen candidates on the first ballot. If the rules remain as they are, there may well be more next time.

Each candidate was allocated sixty-five minutes of television time. Each was also given free radio time and a free mailing of his election address to every voter in the country. No wonder that this proved a temptation to minor political groups, pressure groups, and eccentric individuals. As a result, during the 1974 campaign there were over fourteen hours "official" campaigning on television alone.

Interest in the campaign was high, and this was reflected in an exceptional turnout for both ballots, but observers disagreed, as usual, about the role of the media. Some thought the candidates overexposed, and the voters consequently bored. Others thought there was more interest and viewing than ever before and that this was a fillip to democracy. In any case, television is now part of French culture. There are three French TV channels, two of which broadcast nationwide and all of which are in the hands of the state. The latter fact may explain why the broadcasts made by the candidates themselves, rather than any commentary or news features, are thought of as the essential part of the campaign. Commentary is not necessarily considered less interesting, but the voter is far from convinced that it is unbiased.

Interest in the official television campaign is increased by the fact that the amount of time given the candidates, plus the coverage given their speeches and meetings, prevents any candidate from simply plugging away at a single issue and still managing to seem a responsible statesman. For instance, René Dumont put himself up as the "ecology" candidate. The public may have found him interesting on the subject of the environment, but he was never really taken seriously as a candidate because his platform was not broad enough.

The style of the official campaign is direct, allowing no room for gimmicks or effects. Candidates cannot show films or conduct interviews in the street—or anywhere save in the studio. The amount of time a candidate may spend actually recording his broadcasts is severely limited, and although he may make more than one version of a broadcast, he may not piece together bits from successive recordings. He may only chose between recording A and recording B.

During the first ballot campaign there was no confrontation of candidates on television, for the neutrality principle would have meant that all thirteen candidates would have had to be present. Similarly, there was no voter participation in the television program, nothing similar to the phone-ins or television fórums of the 1974 election in Britain. French state television has not yet established real two-way communication with its audience.

Not until the second ballot was there a breakthrough. The presidential electoral system in France only permits the two candidates who come out on top of the first ballot to stand on the second. With only two candidates a TV debate was possible, and for the first time French presidential candidates debated each other on television. François Mitterrand and Valéry Giscard d'Estaing needed no prompting from the two journalists, Jacqueline Baudrier and Alain Duhamel, who moderated the debate. The candidates showed an extraordinary capacity to carry on their own monologues, to ask each other vicious questions that never received replies, and to talk past each other rather like characters in a Chekhov drama. No one pointed out the internal contradictions of either candidate's statements, but (hopefully) the viewers were not completely hypnotized. On the night when the debate took place (10 May), the pollsters, pundits, and psephologists waited with baited breath. Here was history in the making. Everyone expected the result of the broadcast to be a clear-cut victory for one candidate, and there was much evocation of the Kennedy-Nixon debates of 1960. However, the situation was fundamentally different. The number of undecided voters at this stage was small, especially since most voters had committed themselves for or against the Left on the first ballot. Also, the debate was not part of a series. But, if it did not immediately select the winner, the broadcast did generate great enthusiasm on both sides, and it was probably one of the elements that contributed to the unprecedented 87.89 percent turnout on 19 May.

Opinion Polls and the Official Campaign

Whatever the real impact of the official television campaign, one thing is certain: it was considered of paramount importance by the candidates themselves. They believed that this was the means by which they could reach the greatest number of voters and the opinion polls showed that, indeed, 66 percent of the electors did watch the telecasts.[1] Moreover, in this election even to convince a handful of voters was seen to be of major importance, for two reasons. First the unpredictability of non-Left voters was very great since three candidates from the ranks of the Gaullist majority had run in the first ballot (Jacques Chaban-Delmas, Valéry Giscard d'Estaing, and Jean Royer).

[1] SOFRES, 22 April 1974, published in *Figaro*.

Table 8-1

VOTER PREFERENCES FOR CHABAN AND GISCARD,
16 APRIL–3 MAY 1974

(percents)

Candidate	16 April	18 April	22 April	25 April	29 April	3 May
Chaban	25	23	23	18	18	15
Giscard	27	25	26	31	31	30

Source: *Institut Français d'Opinion Publique* (IFOP).

This, of course, had not been the case in the two preceding presidential elections, when the only majority candidate had been first Charles de Gaulle and then Georges Pompidou. Faced with this new situation how would the Gaullist electorate react? Which of the majority candidates would they favor? Would they recognize one as Pompidou's natural heir? Might some of them conceivably be won over by the Left?

This last possibility was all the more crucial because the gap between Left and Right had dwindled steadily in the course of the campaign and was now only marginal. The majority might be divided, but the Left was united, and it no longer seemed impossible for the left-wing candidate to obtain a majority.

The opinion polls on the impact of television certainly show that the public was ready to modify its opinions. If we take a look at the scores of the three major candidates on successive opinion polls we can see that as the campaign progressed Chaban-Delmas's support dwindled. There is little doubt that the television campaign played a major part in this. It was between 22 and 25 April that the biggest drop in Chaban's support occurred, and by then the official campaign was well under way. Even if the erosion of Chaban's electorate had begun before the TV campaign started, his television performances certainly served to accelerate it.

One of the major French polling organizations, *Institut Français d'Opinion Publique* (IFOP), has completed detailed studies for *Point* of the impact of the television appearances of Chaban-Delmas, Giscard d'Estaing, and Mitterrand, during the first two weeks of the official three-week campaign.[2] The poll shows clearly that the telecasts increased the prestige of Giscard and Mitterrand and sealed the fate of Chaban-Delmas. The public was asked whether the television

[2] IFOP, 24-25 April 1974, published in *Point*, 6 May 1974.

Table 8-2

IMPACT OF THE TELEVISION BROADCASTS ON PUBLIC OPINION OF CANDIDATES' FITNESS FOR THE PRESIDENCY[a]

(percent)

	Chaban	Giscard	Mitterrand
More capable	31	50	51
Less capable	32	13	13
Don't know	37	37	36
Total	100	100	100

[a] The question was: "Whatever your political options, does the candidate seem more or less capable of being a president of the Republic?"
Source: IFOP, published in *Point*, 6 May 1974.

broadcasts had changed their general opinion of the candidates' fitness to become president of the republic. Less than a third of Chaban's viewers, as against half of Giscard's and half of Mitterrand's, thought that the broadcasts had improved his image.

If one looks at the different "technical" qualities that are reviewed in the IFOP poll, selecting only those questions to which over two-thirds of the viewers replied, one finds that each time Chaban's image is less favorable than those of his rivals. The tone of voice used by Chaban was considered disagreeable by 39 percent of the viewers, over twice as many as thought the same of Mitterrand (16 percent)

Table 8-3

REACTION TO THE CANDIDATES' FIRST PERFORMANCES ON TELEVISION

Candidate	Percent Distribution of Positive Reactions[a]			
	Good voice	Extemporaneous delivery	Natural manner	Concrete discussion of issues
Chaban	35 [39]	35 [35]	35 [46]	35 [30]
Giscard	58 [14]	50 [22]	55 [25]	45 [21]
Mitterrand	58 [16]	46 [24]	51 [30]	47 [18]

[a] Negative reactions in brackets.
Source: Adapted from IFOP, published in *Point*, 6 May 1974.

Table 8-4

POSITIVE REACTIONS TO THE CANDIDATES AFTER
THEIR FIRST PERFORMANCES ON TELEVISION
(percents)

Candidate	More Pleasant	More Serious	More Sincere	Firmer
Chaban	19	29	16	36
Giscard	34	22	21	41
Mitterrand	42	37	29	43

Source: Adapted from IFOP, published in *Point*, 6 May 1974.

and nearly three times as many as for Giscard (14 percent). Mitterrand (47 percent) and Giscard (45 percent) were seen to be far more concrete in their speeches than Chaban (35 percent), while Chaban was seen as considerably more unnatural (46 percent, as against 30 percent for Mitterrand and 25 percent for Giscard). A third of the voters found him boring, while only a fifth were bored by his rivals.

When it comes to looking beyond the technical aspects of the one-man shows to the men behind the image, the public is much less sure of its opinions. Only between a fifth and half were willing to assess the pleasantness, sincerity, seriousness, or firmness of the candidates. But even so, the scales were again tipped against Chaban. If he was seen by almost a third of the viewers as firmer and more serious after his television performances, he was also judged less sincere and less pleasant. Reactions to both Mitterrand and Giscard were far more favorable. At each step, however, Mitterrand clearly outdistanced Giscard, probably because the image the public had of Giscard was already that of a serious, firm finance minister. Mitterrand's television appearances enabled him—the leader of an opposition often poorly treated by the French state radio and television—to project the image of a statesman.

Thus, television played a part in scotching Jacques Chaban-Delmas's hopes and in establishing Mitterrand's image, and it is therefore of interest to explore the manner in which the candidates used the TV time allotted to them, not only, nor even primarily, the content of their broadcasts, but the manner of presentation—the speed at which they spoke, the simplicity (or otherwise) of their discourse, and the very words they used.

The Manner of Presentation

Linguistics was once the exclusive preserve of the dictionary makers and grammarians, but in recent years the study of language has become more and more widespread. Little research if any, however, has been done in France on the manner in which politicians adapt their discourse to the audience they are addressing and to the medium they are using. This paper is an attempt to see how the candidates on the first ballot of the 1974 presidential election made use of one medium, television. Of course, the official campaign only represents a fraction of the total number of words poured out during the election. But it was the only part to reach a sizable number of voters. We have selected for analysis the candidates' television speeches, a corpus which is complete and was of major importance during the campaign. It would have been possible to analyze all the speeches of all the candidates, but it seemed to us that from the outset only four candidates had a chance of coming in first or second on the first ballot: Chaban-Delmas, Giscard d'Estaing, Mitterrand, and Jean Royer. As it turned out, Royer's estimated 10 percent of the vote did not grow, but dwindled rapidly. We have kept his speeches as part of our study for three reasons. First, the drop in Royer's support was by no means a foregone conclusion. Second, his inexperience with the media enables us to see the difference between a candidate surrounded by a team and able to use the facilities of a political party, and an outsider, playing a lone hand. And third, Chaban, Giscard, and Royer were all seeking to appeal to the same potential electorate.

The speeches have been studied exhaustively using a computer. The broadcasts were transcribed and then the texts were put onto magnetic tapes. A program enabled the computer to determine the total number of words emitted, the total number of *different* words emitted, and the number of times each word was pronounced. Frequency tables were then drawn up, and these indicated the elements which were numerically of the greatest interest.[3]

The speeches varied in length, but each candidate made six broadcasts during the first ballot campaign, two lasting eighteen minutes each, one lasting nine minutes, one lasting eight, one lasting seven, and one lasting five. Candidates were allowed to present their speeches as an interview by a journalist of their choice, or to share

[3] These frequency tables were drawn up by Honeywell-Bull—thanks to the Cleveland time-sharing system. A very rapid analysis of the candidates' language was presented by Monica Charlot and Isabelle Croizard on Radio Luxembourg in a program directed by Jacques Paoli, on the eve of the first ballot, 4 May 1974.

Table 8-5

TELEVISION BROADCASTS BY MAJOR CANDIDATES,
19 APRIL–3 MAY 1974

Candidate	Date	Time	Length (minutes)
Chaban	Friday, 19 April	2035	7
Giscard	Friday, 19 April	2035	7
Mitterrand	Saturday, 20 April	2035	7
Royer	Saturday, 20 April	2035	7
Chaban	Monday, 22 April	1305	18
Giscard	Monday, 22 April	2035	9
Royer	Tuesday, 23 April	1305	8
Mitterrand	Wednesday, 24 April	1305	8
Chaban	Wednesday, 24 April	2030	9
Giscard	Thursday, 25 April	1305	8
Mitterrand	Friday, 26 April	1305	18
Chaban	Friday, 26 April	2030	18
Giscard	Saturday, 27 April	1305	18
Royer	Saturday, 27 April	2030	18
Chaban	Monday, 29 April	1305	8
Royer	Monday, 29 April	2030	9
Giscard	Tuesday, 30 April	2030	18
Mitterrand	Tuesday, 30 April	2030	18
Royer	Thursday, 2 May	1305	18
Mitterrand	Thursday, 2 May	2030	9
Mitterrand	Friday, 3 May	2030	5
Chaban	Friday, 3 May	2030	5
Royer	Friday, 3 May	2030	5
Giscard	Friday, 3 May	2030	5

Source: Author.

their program with others of their political persuasion. Chaban-
Delmas invited André Malraux to appear on 24 April and Michel
Jobert to appear on 29 April. Giscard d'Estaing shared the screen
with Jean Lecanuet (the centrist leader) and Michel Poniatowski on
27 April, and with Christian Bonnet on 30 April, while Mitterrand
shared one eighteen-minute broadcast with Georges Marchais (the
Communist leader), Michel Fabre (the Radical), and Pierre Mauroy
(a Socialist leader) on 24 April. As a result, we have had to restrict

Table 8-6

CANDIDATES' PACE OF DELIVERY

Candidate	Average Number of Words Pronounced per Minute		Proportional Difference in Percentage Points
	First telecast	Last telecast	
Chaban	89.4	98.0	+9.6
Giscard	115.7	118.6	+3.1
Mitterrand	98.8	111.0	+12.3
Royer	105.1	92.0	−12.5

Source: Author.

our analysis to the first and last speeches of each candidate, the only occasions on which all four candidates gave one-man shows.

The art of public speaking, especially when the speaker cannot see the reactions of his audience, necessitates a vocabulary and a pace well attuned to one another, and qualities very different from those needed in writing. In fact, the best qualities of a literary work can easily become defects when it is read over the air. For instance, André Gide praised the wide vocabulary used by Victor Hugo—over 40,000 different words. If each word were simply to be pronounced once over the air the reading would take at least seven hours of continuous broadcasting!

Of the four major candidates, Chaban-Delmas used the slowest delivery in his first telecast, eighty-nine words a minute. In his first broadcast, Giscard spoke far more quickly, 115 words a minute. Giscard's text was nearly a third as long again as that of Chaban (exactly 29.4 percent). Mitterrand fell roughly between the two. He spoke faster than Chaban but slower than Giscard, with the result that Giscard's text was almost a fifth longer (exactly 17.1 percent).

By the end of the campaign there had been changes, though it is significant that Giscard d'Estaing, who certainly appeared the most at ease on television and is widely considered a master of the medium, varied his pace least. Royer slowed down considerably. The campaign had proved extremely difficult for him. His meetings had not only had more than their share of hecklers, but he had also become the target of the extreme Left, who had even used violence to prevent some of his meetings from taking place. So it was probably a weary,

Table 8-7

RICHNESS OF THE CANDIDATES' VOCABULARY

	First Speech			Last Speech		
Candidate	Number of words	Number of different words	Ratio of words per new word	Number of words	Number of different words	Ratio of words per new word
Chaban	626	289	2:1	490	259	1:8
Giscard	810	238	3:4	593	260	2:2
Mitterrand	692	314	2:2	555	255	2:1
Royer	736	325	2:2	460	225	2:0

Source: Author.

disheartened man who spoke to the public for the last time. Both Chaban-Delmas and Mitterrand stepped up their delivery considerably, possibly to cram as much as possible into the last appeal.

But speed alone is of little significance. It is its relation to the vocabulary used which is important. Giscard's language was more repetitive than that of his rivals. In his first speech, with only 238 different words or forms [4] for the 810 words pronounced, he used on the average less than 1 new word for every 3 pronounced, while for his rivals practically every other word was either a new word or a new form. In his last speech he was less repetitive, and only marginally more so than his competitors, using 1 new word for every 2.2 words, as against 1 for 2.1 for Mitterrand, 1 for 2.0 for Royer, and 1 for 1.8 for Chaban (who used the most varied vocabulary throughout). It would seem, therefore, that there is a fairly clear relation between speed and vocabulary. The higher the speed, the less rich the vocabulary; the lower the speed, the richer the vocabulary. Only for Royer, the candidate least used to television, does this rule not entirely hold true.

It is interesting to note that Mitterrand and Royer have the same score for their first speeches as that run up by Pompidou in his first television speech of the 1969 campaign and by Giscard for the second ballot of 1974.[5] But more striking still is the comparison of

---

[4] The computer has necessitated, at this first stage, the distinction of all different groups of letters. Thus a word used in the plural will not be counted with the singular form of the same word.

[5] We have had access to the frequency tables of some of Pompidou's speeches established by Cotteret and Gerstlé.

the repetitive element in the speeches of the 1974 election candidates and that of de Gaulle on the eve of the first ballot of 1965. Jean Marie Cotteret and René Moreau have shown in their interesting book on de Gaulle's vocabulary [6] that there is a remarkable stability in the relationship between the number of words de Gaulle used and the number of new words he used, whether the speech was made during an election or referendum or at the opening of a press conference. De Gaulle's vocabulary was varied and the speed at which he spoke was slow. He was a master of the art of using the pause to underline essential parts of his discourse. Once again the relationship of speed to the variety of words and word forms used is borne out. In any case, the number of words a candidate can use in the time allotted to him is very restricted, and, therefore, the choice of words assumes great importance. De Gaulle was well aware of this, and he played with words as no candidate did in the 1974 campaign. De Gaulle was always introducing archaic words, sending reporters to their dictionaries to find out the exact meaning of *"tohu-bohu"* ("hurly-burly") or *"quarteron"* ("handful"), or using words which smacked sufficiently of slang for the public to be taken by surprise, as when he applied *"le chien-lit"* ("the bed wetters") to the students in 1968 or when he used the phrase *"la hargne, la rogne et la grogne"* ("the peevish, the ill-tempered, and the grumblers"). Unfortunately, picturesque language and words to make headlines were absent from the 1974 campaign; the identifiable slogan was preferred to the sensational word.

The problem of knowing to what extent a text has been understood by the man-in-the-street has been studied more systematically in the United States than in France. As early as 1949 Rudolf Flesch worked out a readability score,[7] and in more recent years Robert Gunning has produced another index [8] also aimed at studying to what extent a text is easy or difficult to understand. Both these indices take as their primary unit the sentence, and this is, of course, perfectly justifiable. An author chooses where he puts periods, and the reader is influenced by the punctuation. For our purpose—the study of television broadcasts—it seemed more satisfactory to use another primary unit, because the sentence is not readily perceptible to the listener. This can easily be verified by asking two different typists

---

[6] Jean Marie Cotteret and René Moreau, *Le Vocabulaire du Général de Gaulle,* Fondation Nationale des Sciences Politiques, Travaux et recherches de science politique no. 3 (Paris: Armand Colin, 1969), 247 pages.

[7] Rudolf Flesch, *How to Test Readability* (New York: Harper and Row, 1949).

[8] Robert Gunning, *The Technique of Clear Writing* (New York: McGraw-Hill, 1968).

Table 8-8

GUNNING'S FOG INDEX SCORES FOR THE CANDIDATES

Candidate	A (number of words per unit)	B (percent of words of more than 3 syllables)	Total Score (A + B × 0.4)
Chaban	14.9	5.43	8.13
Giscard	14.2	4.93	7.65
Mitterrand	17.7	4.91	9.04
Royer	32	12.77	17.9

Source: Author.

to transcribe a broadcast. The number of sentences, the use of semicolons, et cetera, will be different for each. We have therefore considered as a primary unit any succession of significant words forming an autonomous whole. The punctuation of such a unit may be a period, a question mark, a semicolon, or, in some cases, simply a comma. For example, the first sentence in Chaban's first broadcast ("Would a peasant leave his field half-tilled, would a bricklayer leave his house half-built, would a worker leave his piece half-worked?" [9]) has been counted as three separate units.

Gunning's "fog index" is based on the fact that long sentences are more difficult to understand than short ones, and that the most common words in English have one, two, or three syllables. This is also true for French, and we can therefore apply Gunning's formula:

$$\text{Fog index} = \left(\begin{array}{c} \text{number of words} \\ \text{per sentence} \end{array} + \begin{array}{c} \text{percent of words of} \\ \text{more than 3 syllables} \end{array} \right) \times 0.4$$

The multiplication of 0.4 enables the index, as we shall see, to be correlated with reading grades in American schools. The higher the score the foggier the text; the lower the score the more easily accessible. This index shows Giscard as the most easily understood, followed by Chaban and then by Mitterrand, with Royer far behind. Gunning puts the danger line at thirteen. Above this level the script is only likely to be understood by high school graduates or university students. No mass-circulation magazine has this level of complexity. It is probable, according to this index, that Jean Royer's speeches went

---

[9] "Un agriculteur abandonnerait-il son champ à moitié labouré, un maçon abandonnerait-il sa maison à demi-construite, un ouvrier abandonnerait-il sa pièce à demi usinée?"

over the heads of most viewers.[10] Nine is the score for material accessible to those who have completed nine years of schooling, through the American first year of high school, which is the equivalent of the last year of compulsory schooling in France. The reading level is that of *Reader's Digest*—and of roughly 75 percent of the population. It is probable that prose with a score of less than nine is the result of a deliberate effort at simplification.

Words, Words, Words

The content of speeches during French election campaigns has tended to be analyzed in terms of themes rather than in terms of words and word pictures. This is an attempt to treat the problem from a different angle, to analyze what may be called the political vocabulary of the candidates. This should enable us to perceive the underlying ideology of the candidates.

If we begin by listing the twelve words—excluding proper names—most used by each of the candidates, we will have an overall perception of their programs. The pictures created by these words are fundamentally different, although it will be noticed that they all have a nationalist ring. But whereas Mitterrand stressed the world of work, insisting on collectivism (which he redefined), on the standard of living, on the family, and on the positive virtues of the Left, Chaban was more concerned with attacking the Right and with presenting his "new society," defending the institutions and calling for great efforts, and promoting unification and social peace. Giscard was the partisan of change, the competent finance minister dealing with prices, revenues, resources and employment, and insisting on security.

A first glance at their grammatical structure shows that the use of the first person singular is considerably more frequent in Giscard's speeches than in those of his rivals, despite the fact that he was not the only candidate to devote a whole broadcast to his autobiography. If we analyze the last speech of each candidate, the differences between them are particularly striking. Giscard used almost exclusively the first person singular—"I"—which accounts for 72.9 percent of all of his pronouns. Mitterrand used the first person plural—"we"—more than any other pronoun, for 32.2 percent, while Chaban favored the second person plural—"you"—for

---

[10] It is interesting to note that de Gaulle's speeches were complex. The Gunning fog index for his 3 December 1965 speech, on the eve of the second ballot, gives him a score of 12.3, calculated as follows: $(25.2+5.7) \times 0.4$—the reading level of the American magazine, *Harper's*.

239

Table 8-9
NOUNS MOST FREQUENTLY USED BY THE CANDIDATES[a]

Order of Frequency	Chaban	Giscard	Mitterrand
1	France	France	France
2	Société	Changement	Vie
3	Droite	République	Hommes
4	Institutions	Prix	Monde
5	Monde	Travail	Travail
6	Paix	Travailleurs	Gauche
7	Rassemblement	Majorité	Guerre
8	Effort	Revenus	Propriété
9	Etat	Securité	Confiance
10	Homme	Emploi	Famille
11	Pays	Ressources	Niveau
12	République	Société	Collectivisme

[a] Words referring to time sequences (days, years, months, et cetera) and to political functions or elections (president, election, problem, et cetera) have been omitted.
Source: Author.

45 percent. Giscard was personal, Mitterrand stressed the collective, and Chaban was the most directive and least inclusive.

Giscard was also the most direct and positive of the three. He uses, for instance, fewer negations than either Mitterrand or Chaban, a third fewer than either if we consider all the speeches. In Giscard's last speech there is not a single negative form, as against eleven for Chaban and nine for Mitterrand.

References to political parties and movements were particularly frequent in Chaban's speeches. Both he and Mitterrand spoke in terms of Left and Right, Mitterrand seventeen times, with an emphasis on the positive aspects of the Left, Chaban fourteen times, with the emphasis on the negative aspects of the Right that he claimed Giscard was resuscitating. Giscard, more reminiscent of de Gaulle in his approach, spent little time on such distinctions. His key word was "majority." Mitterrand spoke little of left-wing union and his Communist allies. Chaban attacked Communists and Socialists with some ferocity, and he alone mentioned the Communists in both his first and last broadcasts. Though Giscard spoke little of either, he was the only one to use the term "socialo-communism."

Table 8-10

CANDIDATES' REFERENCES TO POLITICAL PARTIES
AND MOVEMENTS

Words Used	Chaban	Giscard	Mitterrand
Left	5	2	12
Right	9	0	5
Center	1	2	0
Majority	1	14	6
Opposition	2	0	1
Union	0	1	1
"Rassemblement"[a]	8	0	2
Communist/Communism	6	3[b]	1
Socialist/Socialism	4	1	1
Gaullist/Gaullism	9	0	2
UDR	1	2	0
Republican Independent	0	2	0
Radicals	1	0	1
Centrists	0	2	0
Total	47	29	32

[a] Left in French because the English translation, "gathering," does not evoke the Gaullist reference to the *Rassemblement du Peuple Français* (RPF)—the first Gaullist party founded by de Gaulle in 1947.
[b] Of which one reference is to "socialo-Communist".
Source: Author.

When we turn to the candidates' attitudes towards Gaullism, the first surprise is that Giscard says not one word about it. The second is that Mitterrand, in his very first television broadcast, speaks of it as a thing of the past, but without condemning it: "Gaullism is a whole. As all balance sheets it has its assets and its liabilities. Above all it is a heritage without an heir." [11] Chaban, who made no mention of Gaullism in his first broadcast, referred to it increasingly as the days went by.

What exactly was Gaullism for Chaban? Primarily he presented it as a means of resistance: "National union against the major danger

---

[11] "Le gaullisme est un bloc; comme tout bilan il présente un actif, il présente un passif. Mais c'est un héritage qui n'a pas d'héritier." François Mitterrand, 20 April 1974.

Table 8-11

GAULLIST VOCABULARY OF THE CANDIDATES

Most Frequent Nouns in de Gaulle's Speeches	Chaban	Giscard	Mitterrand
France	32	45	30
Republic (République)	0	17	7
State (Etat)	6	5	6
World (Monde)	8	10	15
People (Peuple)	1	0	7
Nation (Nation)	4	0	0
Total	51	77	65

Source: Author.

of the times,"[12] whether the danger be the occupying Germans in 1940, the disintegration of the state in 1958, or today's class war. Gaullism prevents class warfare and presents a certain number of precise objectives. It offers institutional continuity and national independence together with social evolution and the aim of ending inequality and injustice. Clearly, as the campaign advanced, Chaban identified Gaullism with his "new society."

Of the three major candidates, Chaban was undoubtedly the Gaullist. But it is perhaps interesting to try to measure the latent Gaullism of the other candidates by comparing their uses of words. If we take the six nouns that de Gaulle used most frequently in his speeches and press conferences,[13] we find that Mitterrand and above all Giscard used a Gaullist vocabulary. In particular Giscard's references to France have a Gaullist ring ("I want to look into France's eyes"; "Independence and power for France"[14]).

Certain other words, though less frequent in de Gaulle's vocabulary, are readily identifiable as authentically Gaullist—destiny, effort, independence, and order—and in his use of them Chaban showed his filiation. He alone spoke of 5 May as a day on which the destiny of France would hang in the balance. Altogether, he used "effort"

[12] "Le rassemblement national contre le danger dominant du moment." Chaban-Delmas, 26 April 1974.

[13] We have used the index of Jean Marie Cotteret and René Moreau to select the nouns recurring most often, but we have eliminated the noun which came second after France—Algeria—for obvious reasons.

[14] "Je veux regarder la France au fond des yeux." "L'indépendence et la puissance pour la France." Giscard d'Estaing, 19 April 1974.

seven times and "independence" five. But, once again, Giscard's preoccupation with the independence of France (three references in all) and his consciousness of the necessity to strive—he used the word "effort" a total of five times—mark him as at least a partial heir to the Gaullist inheritance.

People, Places, and Events

One very striking trait in the speeches of all four candidates throughout the campaign was the very limited use they made of historical references. The past is singularly absent from all of their speeches. There are no references to Jaurès or to Blum, to Poincaré or to Clemenceau. The symbolic dates the French are so familiar with— 1789 and the French Revolution, 1871 and the Commune, 1936 and the Popular Front—are completely absent save for one remark of Mitterrand's ("Armament factories have been nationalized since 1936" [15]) and one remark of Chaban's, in which he claims that he carried out as prime minister reforms such as had not been seen "since 1945, since 1936." History for all our candidates begins with the Second World War.

All the other references to prewar years are purely personal. Giscard's date of birth is 1926 [16]; World War I merely brings two cousins, whose father had been killed, to swell the ranks of the Mitterrand family where there were already eight children.[17]

The distribution of references to events in the years between the wars and the contrast between the Fourth Republic and the Fifth Republic are striking. Giscard and Chaban clearly wanted, not unnaturally, to stress their links with the Fifth Republic; Mitterrand, as we shall see, was less eager to remind the public of his ministerial activities under the Fourth Republic, during which he was a minister in eleven different governments. Clearly, the Fourth Republic is less than revered by both Right and Left.

Looking at the war period more closely, if we measure not the number of precise dates but the number of units each candidate devoted to his own personal wartime activities, we find that Mitterrand devoted thirty-seven, Giscard nine, and Chaban only five. If we look at the number of times each candidate used the word "Resis-

---

[15] "Les fabrications d'armes sont nationalisées depuis 1936." Mitterrand, 2 May 1974.

[16] "Je suis né le 2 février 1926." Giscard d'Estaing, 27 April 1974.

[17] "Huit frères et soeurs et deux cousins germains dont le père avait été tué à la guerre de 14-18." Mitterrand, 24 April 1974.

Table 8-12
REFERENCES TO THE RECENT PAST

Candidate	War Years (1939–45)	Fourth Republic (1946–57)	Fifth Republic (1958–Present)
Chaban	3	1	12
Giscard	2	4	13
Mitterrand	12	1	2
Royer	0	0	2

Source: Author.

tance," we find Mitterrand mentioned it twice, Giscard once, and Chaban not at all.

We may conclude that Chaban very deliberately did not emphasize his part in the Resistance and the war, which is surprising in that the Resistance is the very source of Gaullism, and Chaban's part in it was by no means negligible. He was the only candidate who held the award of Companion of the Liberation, the highest Resistance honor, and one rarely granted except posthumously. Perhaps Chaban believed his record to be so well known that insistence on it would be in bad taste; perhaps he believed this chapter of the past no longer appealed to the younger generations; perhaps here as elsewhere he deliberately depersonalized his campaign in the hope of winning over left-wing voters. Be that as it may, the only references to this period in his own life were, "I was already a gaullist in 1940,"[18] and a short passage in which, after having said, "They all tell their life stories, I shan't tell you mine,"[19] he explained that he responded to de Gaulle's appeal on 18 June 1940 and "became a secret agent."[20] Moreover, whereas both Mitterrand and Giscard devoted their entire second broadcasts to autobiography, Chaban only evoked his war activities in his fourth broadcast. No doubt sincerely, but slightly melodramatically, he noted that as with all young men of the period "it was certainly not of my career that I was thinking but of my country."[21]

---

[18] "J'étais déjà gaulliste en 1940." Chaban-Delmas, 22 April 1974.

[19] "Tous racontent leur vie, moi je ne raconterai pas la mienne." Chaban-Delmas, 26 April 1974.

[20] "Je suis entré dans l'action secrète." Chaban-Delmas, 26 April 1974.

[21] "Ce n'était sûrement pas à ma carrière que je pensais, mais c'était bien à la patrie." Chaban-Delmas, 26 April 1974.

In contrast, Giscard d'Estaing and Mitterrand both treated their war experience in detail. If Mitterrand's account was longer than Giscard's, it was probably because he is the elder of the two and his experience of the war began earlier. In 1939, when Giscard was only thirteen, Mitterrand was wounded, taken prisoner, and sent to Germany. Giscard, a mere schoolboy, an underling in the Resistance, as he says, first carried newspapers then arms. Both portrayed themselves playing heroic roles, but suggested that what they did was no more than many others did. For instance, Giscard, speaking of his service in the First French Army in 1944, said, "I was lucky enough for it to be my tank that was the first to enter the town of Constance."[22] As for Mitterrand he told of his two unsuccessful attempts to escape from the prisoner-of-war camp and then came to the third: "Third time lucky. In short I won my freedom. . . ."[23]

Both insisted on the positive aspects of this period in their lives, underlining its fraternity in their different ways. For Mitterrand his "real friends, those I am always ready to see, are my prisoner-of-war friends."[24] For Giscard, parading on 14 July 1945, there was "an enthusiasm, a joie de vivre I shall always remember."[25]

The only candidate to speak of his activities under the Fourth Republic—without, however, making clear that it was the Fourth Republic—was Giscard, who said that he first became connected with government when he became a member of Edgar Faure's personal team. He also stressed that he was "the only candidate among those who stand a chance of being present on the second round of the presidential election who has only held a post in a government under the Fifth Republic."[26] This is playing on words indeed, though technically a member of a "cabinet ministériel" is not a member of the government.

Chaban merely mentioned that he had been a minister several times, without indicating when, nor under which republic. His only specific mention of the Fourth Republic was negative.[27] As for

---

[22] "J'ai eu la chance que ce soit mon char qui soit entré le premier dans la ville de Constance." Giscard d'Estaing, 22 April 1974.

[23] "Enfin la troisième fois a été la bonne. Bref j'ai conquis ma liberté." Mitterrand, 24 April 1974.

[24] "Mes solides amis, ceux que je revois à tout moment c'est mes anciens camarades de captivité." Mitterrand, 24 April 1974.

[25] "Un enthousiasme, une gaieté, dont je me souviendrai toujours." Giscard d'Estaing, 22 April 1974.

[26] "Je suis le seul des candidats qui aient une chance d'accéder au second tour de l'élection présidentielle qui n'ait exercé de fonctions gouvernementales que sous la Vᵉ République." Giscard d'Estaing, 22 April 1974.

[27] "On veut renforcer les pouvoirs des assemblées et on a vu où cela avait conduit la IVᵉ République." Chaban-Delmas, 22 April 1974.

Mitterrand, his only mention of his career during the postwar period before the advent of the Fifth Republic concerned de Gaulle's first postwar government, which was a sort of no-man's-land between the Third and Fourth Republics. "I was a member of the first government of liberated France, under the authority of General de Gaulle. I was provisional general secretary of prisoners of war and the deported." [28]

Mitterrand and Giscard both clearly indicated their attitudes to de Gaulle's rise to power in 1958. Mitterrand had "answered categorically 'no' to a certain type of regime, to a military coup." [29] Giscard declared, when it came to de Gaulle's investiture as prime minister, "I voted in favor on 1 June 1958." [30] Chaban's approbation was no less evident, though only implicit when he spoke of "the great movement which in 1958 enabled General de Gaulle to restore the state." [31]

Giscard and Chaban both dwelt on the Fifth Republic essentially in terms of their own careers and achievements within its span, as one would expect. The voters were reminded that in 1959 Giscard had become the Fifth Republic's youngest minister; that in 1966, when de Gaulle offered the post of finance minister to Michel Debré, Giscard declined the alternative post that was offered him; and that in 1969 he returned to the finance ministry, this time under Georges Pompidou. For his part, Chaban constantly recalled the 1969–1972 period when he was prime minister. He evoked his major achievements: continuous adult education, monthly salaries for workers, financial stability, reduction in strikes, and the relaxation of state control of radio and television. None of the candidates dwelt on 1968, though probably all of them would have agreed that it was a turning point in the history of contemporary France. Neither Giscard nor Mitterrand so much as mentioned it. As for Chaban, he merely used the reference to criticize the Left (May 1968, "when we already saw Mr. Mitterrand outflanked by the extreme Left" [32]) and to situate his own government, which began just a year *after* 1968.

---

[28] "J'ai fait partie du premier gouvernement de la France libérée sous l'autorité du Général de Gaulle, en tant que Secrétaire Général provisoire aux Prisonniers de Guerre et aux déportés." Mitterrand, 24 April 1974.

[29] "En 1958 j'avais pris position par un non catégorique à certaine forme de régime et au coup d'Etat militaire." Mitterrand, 24 April 1974.

[30] "J'ai voté cette investiture le premier juin 1958." Giscard d'Estaing, 22 April 1974.

[31] "Le rassemblement qui en 1958 avait permis au Général de Gaulle de relever l'Etat." Chaban-Delmas, 29 April 1974.

[32] "On avait déjà vu M. Mitterrand débordé par l'extrême gauche." Chaban-Delmas, 22 April 1974.

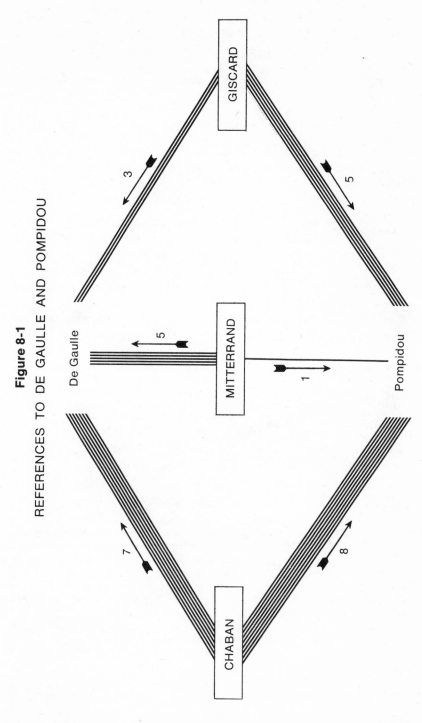

Figure 8-1
REFERENCES TO DE GAULLE AND POMPIDOU

Table 8-13
REFERENCES TO PERSONALITIES[a]

Candidate	Frenchmen	Foreign Statesmen
Chaban	8	0
Giscard	14	5
Mitterrand	13	0

[a] Excluding the candidates, de Gaulle, and Pompidou.
Source: Author.

References to the Fifth Republic were, in a sense, also made indirectly by mentioning one or another of the former presidents. Not surprisingly, Chaban-Delmas strove hardest to associate himself with the former Gaullist presidents, Pompidou and de Gaulle. Moreover, his references to his predecessors were more than factual. On several occasions he pointed to one or the other as a model to be followed. His conception of French institutions is modelled on that of de Gaulle, who had "shown that the most original characteristic of the Fifth Republic was to give the state a head."[33] The Europe he hoped for was also closely affiliated to that forged by de Gaulle, "a European Europe, as General de Gaulle used to say, that is, an independent Europe."[34]

Pompidou was no less a model than de Gaulle. Chaban indicated that the idea of monthly salaries for workers put into practice by his government was one of Pompidou's "key ideas."[35] A little later in the campaign he spoke of "President Pompidou, whose policies I for my part intend to follow."[36] In his last television appeal he urged the viewers to choose "the fraternal grouping round a certain conception of France, that of de Gaulle, that of Pompidou."[37] In Chaban's first two broadcasts, references to Pompidou outnumbered

[33] "Le Général de Gaulle avait . . . précisé que le caractère le plus original de la V{e} République c'était de donner une tête à l'Etat." Chaban-Delmas, 22 April 1974.

[34] "L'Europe européenne comme disait le Général de Gaulle, c'est-à-dire indépendante." Chaban-Delmas, 26 April 1974.

[35] "La mensualisation, idée clé de Georges Pompidou et qui a été réalisée sous mon gouvernement." Chaban-Delmas, 22 April 1974.

[36] "Président Pompidou dont pour ma part je veux poursuivre la politique." Chaban-Delmas, 29 April 1974.

[37] "Le rassemblement fraternel autour d'une certaine idée de la France, celle du Général de Gaulle, celle de Georges Pompidou." Chaban-Delmas, 3 May 1974.

references to de Gaulle, but as the campaign continued references to de Gaulle increased in a desperate attempt to recapture the traditional Gaullists he had not courted with enough fervor.

Giscard d'Estaing was more eager to stress the direct succession—Pompidou to Giscard—than to accentuate his Gaullism. His three references to de Gaulle all occurred in his second broadcast, early in the campaign. Of the three references two are statements of fact; de Gaulle gave him a post in his government, and de Gaulle formed a new government in which Giscard's post went to Michel Debré. The last reference is a somewhat ambiguous expression of his relations with de Gaulle: "It is true that I have had disagreements with General de Gaulle, but he has always had my esteem and been respected by me." [38] Giscard also slipped in a mention of the 170 private interviews de Gaulle granted him while Giscard was his finance minister. If a little of de Gaulle's prestige rubbed off on him, so much the better, but he in no way bound himself to de Gaulle's views and policies.

Similarly, references to Pompidou show that Giscard was, as it were, his natural heir. In his very first speech he reminded the electors that he had worked side-by-side with President Pompidou. In Giscard's second speech there were three references to Pompidou, the man whose finance minister he had been from 1969 until his death, the man he had accompanied abroad (first to the Azores and then to Iceland). In his third speech he clearly stated that to govern the country he needed all those who had supported Pompidou and those who had a new contribution to make. Having established his direct filiation, Giscard continued on his way with no further mention of his illustrious predecessors.

Mitterrand referred to Pompidou once only, in the first sentence of his first speech, when he noted that "after the passing away of President Georges Pompidou we all realized that a part of our history had come to an end." [39] De Gaulle is mentioned in two of Mitterrand's speeches. There were two such references in the second speech when Mitterrand traced his autobiography. (He was received by General de Gaulle in December 1943, and after the war was given a post in de Gaulle's first government, "a great experience," Mitterrand said.) In the broadcast devoted to a defense of nationalization

---

[38] "Il est vrai que j'ai eu certains différends avec le Général de Gaulle, mais je lui ai toujours conservé ma considération et mon respect." Giscard d'Estaing, 22 April 1974.

[39] "Après la disparition du Président Georges Pompidou nous avons tous compris qu'une période de notre histoire venait de s'achever." Mitterrand, 20 April 1974.

Mitterrand mentioned de Gaulle three times. It was he who had nationalized most of the banks; gas and electricity were also nationalized in 1945. For his part, Mitterrand "simply wanted to nationalize, as General de Gaulle wanted to, the commercial banks he regretted not having nationalized." [40] De Gaulle here was less a model than a guarantee.

The candidates' treatment of one another is no less varied than their treatment of their predecessors. As Figure 8–2 shows, Chaban-Delmas was most clearly on the defensive. Both the other candidates were seen by him as dangerous rivals. Mitterrand attacked little, because he knew that in the event of Giscard's coming in first he had some hope of capturing a part of Chaban's electorate and must therefore not alienate it. (On the second ballot he did indeed receive the votes of some 11 percent of Chaban's electorate.) His attack on Giscard was not particularly virulent either. On this first ballot it was more important for him to project a positive image of the Left than to attack.

Giscard saw Mitterrand as his most dangerous rival from the outset of the campaign. Even less than Mitterrand could he afford to alienate Chaban-Delmas's electorate. Moreover, his calm assurance that he and not Chaban would be facing Mitterrand on the second ballot no doubt contributed to the elimination of Chaban. Poise and self-confidence intensified the bandwagon effect.

Only Giscard mentioned foreign statesmen. Name dropping enabled him to envelop himself in an international aura. He mentioned foreign visits with Pompidou and receptions for Adenauer, Brandt, Brezhnev, and Nixon.

Chaban's references to Frenchmen were divided equally between majority and opposition personalities. Mitterrand referred twelve times to personalities of the Left and only once to a member of the majority (Marcel Dassault). Giscard's references divided thirteen to one in favor of the majority. Once again the strategies of Mitterrand and Giscard were close; both concentrated on the positive image.

With regard to the different age groups within the electorate, it is striking that, while Giscard was careful not to leave anyone out— he referred equally often to the old and the young and slightly more often to women than to men—Mitterrand ignored the latter, Chaban the former. So at first glance, Chaban's appeal was more virile, that of Mitterrand more protective. (He referred not only to women

---

[40] "Je veux simplement nationaliser comme voulait le faire le Général de Gaulle, ce qu'il a regretté de ne pas avoir fait, les banques d'affaires." Mitterrand, 2 May 1974.

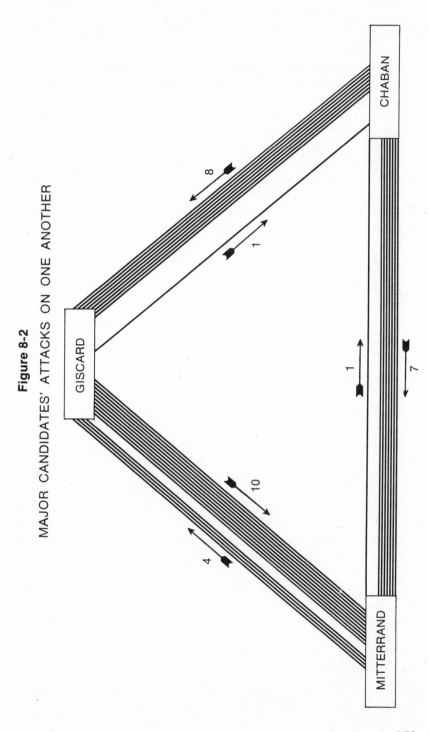

Figure 8-2

MAJOR CANDIDATES' ATTACKS ON ONE ANOTHER

generally but in particular to mothers, who are not mentioned at all by the other two candidates.)

References to places were roughly equally used by Mitterrand (twenty-three) and Giscard (twenty-five), and considerably less by Chaban (fourteen). One common denominator was the persistent attempt to underline the candidate's attachment to the provinces. Giscard underlined that his four grandparents were all buried in Auvergne, in the Puy de Dôme, in the canton of Saint-Amant-Tallende. Mitterrand noted that his father was from Berri and his mother from Saintonge, and that the greater part of his family lived in the provinces. He spoke of himself in lyrical terms as married to the Nièvre, and described Chateau-Chinon with emotion. Giscard noted the exact geographical composition of his constituency, bordering the Creuse and the Corrèze, and described it as typical of the average French constituency. Precise place names are warm and communicative, they smack of rural, eternal France—dear even to the townsfolk—and Chaban was doubtless unwise to use them little. He made a cold reference to Bordeaux as the fifth largest town of France and announced a tour of Brittany and Normandy, but evocative place names were absent from his discourse.

Conclusion

Through this somewhat summary attempt to dissect the language of the candidates, the words they used, and the references they made, pictures of very different men emerge. And, perhaps, over and above the programs they offered and the promises they made, this was the truly essential factor in influencing the decision the electors made.

Perhaps we can best illustrate the impression the three candidates made by putting into relief the formative elements in the life of each, at least as they presented them to us. The image that remains of Chaban, despite the rather sedate image his campaign consultants advised him to adopt, is that of a sportsman. At one stage he confessed with a certain pride, "I once wore the red, white, and blue shirt on the French [rugby] team," [41] and then went on to develop a long and complex comparison of government to a rugby match. His vision of society is one in which all play together, striving towards the goal—hard work, but rewarding.

Giscard's world is very different. Here intellectual excellence is the standard against which things are measured. He listed with

[41] "J'ai même porté le maillot tricolore dans l'équipe de France." Chaban-Delmas, 22 April 1974.

252

obvious satisfaction the grammar schools he had attended—including the prestigious Louis le Grand in Paris—and then proudly noted that after the war he had gained entrance to the famous Ecole Polytechnique (entrance to which is "by means of a highly competitive examination, as everyone knows" [42]) and later went to the National School of Administration. Giscard's world is one in which, if everyone has his place, competence alone will determine where it is.

The formative element, the cornerstone, in Mitterrand's world is family life. He notes with satisfaction that his parents were very happy together, and that the children—eight plus two cousins—formed a close-knit group. It is the family, he declared, that "has, I believe, given a sense of purpose to the rest of my life." [43] This gave him, no doubt, the warmth, the slightly old-fashioned lyricism, and the desire to protect that characterized his speeches.

The sportsman, the intellectual, the protector—perhaps it is not surprising that the French should first have rejected the sportsman, and in the last resort chosen the intellectual.

---

[42] "C'est un concours tout le monde le sait." Giscard d'Estaing, 22 April 1974.
[43] "Cela a dominé je crois le reste de ma vie." Mitterrand, 24 April 1974.

APPENDIX

A Summary of French Presidential Election Results 1965-74

Compiled by Richard M. Scammon

FRENCH PRESIDENTIAL ELECTION RESULTS, 1965-74, NATIONAL TOTALS

	Total Vote	Percent
1965		
First ballot		
Charles de Gaulle	10,828,523	44.6
François Mitterrand	7,694,003	31.7
Jean Lecanuet	3,777,119	15.6
Jean-Louis Tixier-Vignancour	1,260,208	5.2
Pierre Marcilhacy	415,018	1.7
Marcel Barbu	279,683	1.2
	24,254,554	100.0
Second ballot		
Charles de Gaulle	13,083,699	55.2
François Mitterrand	10,619,735	44.8
	23,703,434	100.0
1969		
First ballot		
Georges Pompidou	10,051,816	44.5
Alain Poher	5,268,651	23.3
Jacques Duclos	4,808,285	21.3
Gaston Defferre	1,133,222	5.0
Michel Rocard	816,471	3.6
Louis Ducatel	286,447	1.3
Alain Krivine	239,106	1.0
	22,603,998	100.0

255

	Total Vote	Percent
Second ballot		
Georges Pompidou	11,064,371	58.2
Alain Poher	7,943,118	41.8
	19,007,489	100.0
1974		
First ballot		
François Mitterrand	11,044,373	43.25
Valéry Giscard d'Estaing	8,326,774	32.60
Jacques Chaban-Delmas	3,857,728	15.11
Jean Royer	810,540	3.17
Arlette Laguiller	595,247	2.33
René Dumont	337,800	1.32
Jean-Marie Le Pen	190,921	.75
Emile Muller	176,279	.69
Alain Krivine	93,990	.37
Bertrand Renouvin	43,722	.17
Jean-Claude Sebag	42,007	.16
Guy Héraud	19,255	.08
	25,538,636	100.00
Second ballot		
Valéry Giscard d'Estaing	13,396,203	50.8
François Mitterrand	12,971,604	49.2
	26,367,807	100.0

PRESIDENTIAL ELECTION RESULTS, 1965, FIRST BALLOT, BY DEPARTMENT

Department	De Gaulle	Mitterrand	Lecanuet	Tixier-Vignancour	Other[a]	Total
Metropolitan France						
Ain	71,246 43.0[b]	50,379 30.4	30,416 18.4	8,317 5.0	5,197 3.1	165,555
Aisne	118,720 47.4	79,897 31.9	37,036 14.8	8,804 3.5	6,093 2.4	250,550
Allier	73,973 36.6	84,861 41.9	26,369 13.0	11,045 5.5	6,140 3.0	202,388
Alpes (Basses-)	17,738 35.0	19,990 39.5	6,782 13.4	4,573 9.0	1,571 3.1	50,654
Alpes (Hautes-)	19,328 42.8	14,638 32.4	7,347 16.3	2,289 5.1	1,590 3.5	45,192
Alpes-Maritimes	140,830 41.2	96,884 28.4	50,935 14.9	42,760 12.5	10,331 3.0	341,740
Ardèche	58,538 42.7	44,526 32.5	23,172 16.9	7,396 5.4	3,538 2.6	137,170

Department	De Gaulle	Mitterrand	Lecanuet	Tixier-Vignancour	Other[a]	Total
Ardennes	65,430 46.5	47,046 33.4	20,423 14.5	4,502 3.2	3,297 2.3	140,698
Ariège	26,206 34.3	38,316 50.1	5,861 7.7	4,465 5.8	1,595 2.1	76,443
Aube	56,530 43.4	45,400 34.8	20,667 15.9	4,724 3.6	2,957 2.3	130,278
Aude	44,123 30.0	73,485 50.0	15,874 10.8	10,028 6.8	3,483 2.4	146,993
Aveyron	63,337 40.3	43,974 28.0	37,745 24.0	6,864 4.4	5,156 3.3	157,076
Bouches-du-Rhône	215,475 35.7	237,573 39.3	58,070 9.6	75,206 12.5	17,517 2.9	603,841
Calvados	117,219 48.8	48,975 20.4	56,790 23.6	10,482 4.4	6,902 2.9	240,368
Cantal	42,169 49.1	21,829 25.4	15,808 18.4	3,642 4.2	2,523 2.9	85,971
Charente	72,440 42.1	53,840 31.3	16,622 9.7	8,409 4.9	20,727 12.0	172,038
Charente-Maritime	95,813 40.6	74,895 31.8	38,551 16.3	15,186 6.4	11,372 4.8	235,817

Cher	63,405 / 41.1	59,749 / 38.7	19,026 / 12.3	7,233 / 4.7	4,874 / 3.2	154,287
Corrèze	53,010 / 39.5	60,187 / 44.8	12,621 / 9.4	4,822 / 3.6	3,615 / 2.7	134,255
Corse	56,524 / 56.5	25,661 / 25.7	7,717 / 7.7	9,140 / 9.1	996 / 1.0	100,038
Côte-d'Or	76,536 / 39.9	62,076 / 32.3	37,804 / 19.7	9,921 / 5.2	5,713 / 3.0	192,050
Côtes-du-Nord	123,355 / 44.0	97,981 / 34.9	48,103 / 17.2	5,814 / 2.1	5,203 / 1.9	280,456
Creuse	35,211 / 41.6	35,718 / 42.2	8,453 / 10.0	3,268 / 3.9	2,049 / 2.4	84,699
Dordogne	85,780 / 40.1	83,771 / 39.1	25,223 / 11.8	12,826 / 6.0	6,461 / 3.0	214,061
Doubs	89,562 / 47.3	58,716 / 31.0	30,126 / 15.9	6,367 / 3.4	4,405 / 2.3	189,176
Drôme	63,808 / 39.5	56,367 / 34.9	23,813 / 14.8	10,613 / 6.6	6,810 / 4.2	161,411
Eure	81,262 / 43.9	54,035 / 29.2	37,640 / 20.3	7,119 / 3.8	5,100 / 2.8	185,156

Department	De Gaulle	Mitterrand	Lecanuet	Tixier-Vignancour	Other[a]	Total
Eure-et-Loir	67,747	43,751	25,987	6,277	4,418	148,180
	45.7	29.5	17.5	4.2	3.0	
Finistère	207,615	115,487	77,223	10,145	8,219	418,689
	49.6	27.6	18.4	2.4	2.0	
Gard	73,892	104,144	29,121	19,821	7,122	234,100
	31.6	44.5	12.4	8.5	3.0	
Garonne (Haute-)	115,419	129,579	38,856	28,476	8,850	321,180
	35.9	40.3	12.1	8.9	2.8	
Gers	25,177	41,337	16,311	8,078	2,622	93,525
	26.9	44.2	17.4	8.6	2.8	
Gironde	205,744	147,898	74,812	41,291	16,384	486,129
	42.3	30.4	15.4	8.5	3.4	
Hérault	84,882	114,145	33,721	30,810	8,115	271,673
	31.2	42.0	12.4	11.3	3.0	
Ille-et-Vilaine	168,730	67,156	65,763	11,623	9,634	322,906
	52.3	20.8	20.4	3.6	3.0	

Indre	49,265 37.5	50,271 38.3	20,372 15.5	7,235 5.5	4,260 3.2	131,403
Indre-et-Loire	86,900 42.1	61,224 29.7	37,409 18.1	13,715 6.6	7,229 3.5	206,477
Isère	133,193 37.5	132,869 37.4	54,101 15.2	22,270 6.3	13,038 3.7	355,471
Jura	50,294 42.7	37,787 32.1	22,498 19.1	3,821 3.2	3,259 2.8	117,659
Landes	67,832 45.0	51,731 34.4	19,697 13.1	8,138 5.4	3,189 2.1	150,587
Loir-et-Cher	57,029 41.5	43,176 31.4	25,335 18.4	7,438 5.4	4,347 3.2	137,325
Loire	130,557 38.6	103,668 30.7	75,250 22.3	16,887 5.0	11,526 3.4	337,888
Loire (Haute-)	45,533 40.3	25,614 22.7	29,870 26.5	8,292 7.3	3,558 3.2	112,867
Loire-Atlantique	184,556 44.5	105,779 25.5	96,328 23.2	17,272 4.2	11,189 2.7	415,124
Loiret	96,321 46.6	60,344 29.2	33,300 16.1	10,109 4.9	6,820 3.3	206,894

Department	De Gaulle	Mitterrand	Lecanuet	Tixier-Vignancour	Other[a]	Total
Lot	33,246 39.3	30,933 36.6	14,100 16.7	3,948 4.7	2,285 2.7	84,512
Lot-et-Garonne	46,654 31.4	57,734 38.8	24,127 16.2	15,154 10.2	5,048 3.4	148,717
Lozère	22,333 51.7	9,702 22.5	7,818 18.1	2,375 5.5	953 2.2	43,181
Maine-et-Loire	135,520 48.9	50,977 18.4	70,078 25.3	12,534 4.5	8,185 3.0	277,294
Manche	130,591 57.4	33,599 14.8	49,155 21.6	8,428 3.7	5,737 2.5	227,510
Marne	95,892 44.3	68,748 31.8	39,190 18.1	7,205 3.3	5,207 2.4	216,242
Marne (Haute-)	53,527 52.6	29,166 28.6	13,623 13.4	3,297 3.2	2,244 2.2	101,857
Mayenne	66,475 49.9	20,383 15.3	37,504 28.2	5,019 3.8	3,745 2.8	133,126

Department											Total
Meurthe-et-Moselle	154,800	48.7	95,848	30.2	50,141	15.8	9,961	3.1	6,800	2.1	317,550
Meuse	57,477	55.5	21,968	21.2	18,325	17.7	3,553	3.4	2,263	2.2	103,586
Morbihan	148,824	53.2	66,997	23.9	51,339	18.3	7,668	2.7	5,089	1.8	279,917
Moselle	259,048	63.2	76,613	18.7	56,575	13.8	9,723	2.4	7,836	1.9	409,795
Nièvre	42,554	32.3	69,188	52.5	13,588	10.3	3,982	3.0	2,500	1.9	131,812
Nord	552,584	48.1	409,462	35.6	124,794	10.9	36,910	3.2	26,076	2.3	1,149,826
Oise	119,008	48.5	73,994	30.1	33,526	13.7	11,377	4.6	7,590	3.1	245,495
Orne	73,803	51.1	26,121	18.1	34,145	23.6	6,057	4.2	4,341	3.0	144,467
Pas-de-Calais	295,281	44.8	264,052	40.0	65,954	10.0	20,296	3.1	14,205	2.2	659,788
Puy-de-Dôme	105,756	40.9	91,811	35.5	36,771	14.2	14,375	5.6	9,658	3.7	258,371

Department	De Gaulle	Mitterrand	Lecanuet	Tixier-Vignancour	Other[a]	Total
Pyrénées (Basses-)	118,496 46.0	60,489 23.5	48,946 19.0	23,226 9.0	6,185 2.4	257,342
Pyrénées (Hautes-)	41,356 36.4	47,033 41.4	14,249 12.5	8,081 7.1	2,898 2.6	113,617
Pyrénées-Orientales	45,163 34.8	53,010 40.8	15,379 11.8	13,456 10.4	2,906 2.2	129,914
Rhin (Bas-)	244,970 63.7	39,532 10.3	85,231 22.1	8,980 2.3	6,108 1.6	384,821
Rhin (Haut-)	169,895 59.1	38,651 13.4	66,788 23.2	7,056 2.5	5,053 1.8	287,443
Rhône	197,913 37.9	161,735 31.0	110,182 21.1	34,253 6.6	17,846 3.4	521,929
Saône (Haute-)	51,543 46.2	38,229 34.3	15,920 14.3	3,638 3.3	2,210 2.0	111,540
Saône-et-Loire	106,752 40.6	93,846 35.7	42,548 16.2	12,447 4.7	7,318 2.8	262,911

Sarthe	95,960 42.7	73,254 32.6	39,342 17.5	9,550 4.2	6,785 3.0	224,891
Savoie	53,185 41.4	42,795 33.3	22,296 17.4	5,964 4.6	4,133 3.2	128,373
Savoie (Haute-)	78,809 47.8	41,513 25.2	32,786 19.9	6,667 4.0	4,960 3.0	164,735
Seine	1,152,351 41.8	983,451 35.7	398,464 14.5	132,616 4.8	88,982 3.2	2,755,864
Seine-Maritime	217,420 41.2	178,890 33.9	101,889 19.3	17,012 3.2	12,931 2.4	528,142
Seine-et-Marne	126,260 45.7	84,691 30.7	43,412 15.7	13,031 4.7	8,765 3.2	276,159
Seine-et-Oise	515,091 41.8	441,356 35.8	173,366 14.1	60,525 4.9	43,144 3.5	1,233,482
Sèvres (Deux-)	71,695 42.7	45,786 27.3	37,917 22.6	7,344 4.4	5,266 3.1	168,008
Somme	121,271 46.1	93,382 35.5	32,240 12.2	10,191 3.9	6,247 2.4	263,331
Tarn	64,683 36.0	68,565 38.2	27,930 15.5	13,074 7.3	5,413 3.0	179,665

Department	De Gaulle	Mitterrand	Lecanuet	Tixier-Vignancour	Other[a]	Total
Tarn-et-Garonne	32,736 34.5	36,208 38.1	13,867 14.6	9,217 9.7	2,993 3.1	95,021
Territoire de Belfort	23,935 44.8	18,137 33.9	8,341 15.6	1,778 3.3	1,283 2.4	53,474
Var	101,018 39.3	84,899 33.1	27,334 10.6	36,096 14.1	7,501 2.9	256,848
Vaucluse	53,899 32.6	63,053 38.2	21,452 13.0	20,108 12.2	6,589 4.0	165,101
Vendée	112,640 51.5	37,960 17.4	52,448 24.0	9,985 4.6	5,557 2.5	218,590
Vienne	78,520 45.7	47,191 27.5	31,681 18.4	8,768 5.1	5,686 3.3	171,846
Vienne (Haute-)	74,573 39.5	87,191 46.2	13,959 7.4	7,093 3.8	6,097 3.2	188,913
Vosges	100,826 52.5	48,664 25.3	30,475 15.9	7,002 3.6	5,178 2.7	192,145

Yonne	144,080	3,991 2.8	7,425 5.2	23,261 16.1	45,256 31.4	64,147 44.5

	Total					
Yonne	144,080	3,991 2.8	7,425 5.2	23,261 16.1	45,256 31.4	64,147 44.5
Overseas						
Guadeloupe	79,296	290 .4	523 .7	502 .6	8,229 10.4	69,752 88.0
Guyane	8,908	102 1.1	199 2.2	124 1.4	2,449 27.5	6,034 67.7
Martinique	97,050	549 .6	393 .4	538 .6	8,873 9.1	86,697 89.3
Réunion (La)	118,065	1,477 1.3	1,751 1.5	1,206 1.0	5,806 4.9	107,825 91.3
Comores	109,861	69 .1	39 0	121 .1	658 .6	108,974 99.2
Côte française des Somalis	26,302	115 .4	194 .7	181 .7	303 1.2	25,509 97.0
Nouvelle- Calédonie et ressortissants français des Nouvelles- Hébrides	26,787	454 1.7	2,110 7.9	5,797 21.6	1,935 7.2	16,491 61.6

Department	De Gaulle	Mitterrand	Lecanuet	Tixier-Vignancour	Other[a]	Total
Polynésie française	15,574 62.4	6,894 27.6	879 3.5	804 3.2	791 3.2	24,942
Saint-Pierre et Miquelon	1,510 67.5	57 2.5	366 16.4	234 10.5	69 3.1	2,236
Wallis et Futuna	3,423 99.6	7 .2	1 0	3 .1	4 .1	3,438
Total	10,828,523 44.6	7,694,003 31.7	3,777,119 15.6	1,260,208 5.2	694,701 2.9	24,254,554

[a]Other vote includes: Pierre Marcilhacy, 415,018; Marcel Barbu, 279,683.
[b]Percent of total vote.

PRESIDENTIAL ELECTION RESULTS, 1965, SECOND BALLOT, BY DEPARTMENT

Department	De Gaulle	Mitterrand	Total
Metropolitan France			
Ain	90,898	72,066	162,964
	55.8	44.2	
Aisne	137,906	109,135	247,041
	55.8	44.2	
Allier	90,020	109,592	199,612
	45.1	54.9	
Alpes (Basses-)	22,037	28,152	50,189
	43.9	56.1	
Alpes (Hautes-)	24,639	21,021	45,660
	54.0	46.0	
Alpes-Maritimes	165,877	162,699	328,576
	50.5	49.5	
Ardèche	74,503	59,920	134,423
	55.4	44.6	
Ardennes	77,254	62,329	139,583
	55.3	44.7	
Ariège	29,290	48,828	78,118
	37.5	62.5	
Aube	69,112	58,062	127,174
	54.3	45.7	
Aude	52,034	96,225	148,259
	35.1	64.9	
Aveyron	86,478	66,905	153,383
	56.4	43.6	
Bouches-du-Rhône	256,917	334,226	591,143
	43.5	56.5	

Department	De Gaulle	Mitterrand	Total
Calvados	146,863 64.4	81,277 35.6	228,140
Cantal	53,236 62.4	32,041 37.6	85,277
Charente	89,493 53.1	78,970 46.9	168,463
Charente-Maritime	118,109 51.1	113,030 48.9	231,139
Cher	76,460 50.1	76,057 49.9	152,517
Corrèze	61,445 45.6	73,448 54.4	134,893
Corse	64,381 59.7	43,550 40.3	107,931
Côte-d'Or	97,806 53.1	86,460 46.9	184,266
Côtes-du-Nord	152,190 54.8	125,512 45.2	277,702
Creuse	41,535 47.5	45,859 52.5	87,394
Dordogne	100,108 46.9	113,186 53.1	213,294
Doubs	108,833 58.5	77,310 41.5	186,143
Drôme	79,986 50.7	77,721 49.3	157,707
Eure	99,835 55.8	78,975 44.2	178,810
Eure-et-Loir	82,473 57.2	61,688 42.8	144,161

Department	De Gaulle	Mitterrand	Total
Finistère	260,051 63.2	151,697 36.8	411,748
Gard	92,004 39.9	138,455 60.1	230,459
Garonne (Haute-)	135,429 42.7	181,861 57.3	317,290
Gers	32,428 34.8	60,875 65.2	93,303
Gironde	241,383 51.0	231,628 49.0	473,011
Hérault	105,805 39.9	159,238 60.1	265,043
Ille-et-Vilaine	212,296 67.6	101,651 32.4	313,947
Indre	60,631 46.7	69,208 53.3	129,839
Indre-et-Loire	106,807 53.3	93,633 46.7	200,440
Isère	169,174 48.5	179,413 51.5	348,587
Jura	65,060 55.7	51,835 44.3	116,895
Landes	78,727 53.4	68,826 46.6	147,553
Loir-et-Cher	71,334 53.1	62,892 46.9	134,226
Loire	174,933 53.8	150,042 46.2	324,975
Loire (Haute-)	65,462 60.4	42,856 39.6	108,318

Department	De Gaulle	Mitterrand	Total
Loire-Atlantique	244,625 60.7	158,133 39.3	402,758
Loiret	117,054 58.2	84,173 41.8	201,227
Lot	41,074 48.9	42,979 51.1	84,053
Lot-et-Garonne	59,437 40.6	87,074 59.4	146,511
Lozère	28,520 66.8	14,193 33.2	42,713
Maine-et-Loire	180,603 67.5	86,971 32.5	267,574
Manche	159,828 73.3	58,193 26.7	218,021
Marne	117,740 55.9	92,877 44.1	210,617
Marne (Haute-)	62,138 62.0	38,085 38.0	100,223
Mayenne	88,074 69.8	38,070 30.2	126,144
Meurthe-et-Moselle	181,858 58.7	128,010 41.3	309,868
Meuse	67,368 66.7	33,636 33.3	101,004
Morbihan	182,421 66.5	91,979 33.5	274,400
Moselle	290,843 71.8	114,314 28.2	405,157
Nièvre	51,398 39.0	80,474 61.0	131,872

Department	De Gaulle	Mitterrand	Total
Nord	633,162 55.5	507,482 44.5	1,140,644
Oise	136,985 57.0	103,248 43.0	240,233
Orne	92,963 67.2	45,404 32.8	138,367
Pas-de-Calais	334,443 50.9	322,832 49.1	657,275
Puy-de-Dôme	131,735 51.7	122,990 48.3	254,725
Pyrénées (Basses-)	147,627 59.3	101,185 40.7	248,812
Pyrénées (Hautes-)	49,805 44.4	62,453 55.6	112,258
Pyrénées-Orientales	54,914 42.5	74,355 57.5	129,269
Rhin (Bas-)	297,169 79.9	74,851 20.1	372,020
Rhin (Haut-)	205,802 74.0	72,296 26.0	278,098
Rhône	263,416 53.4	229,694 46.6	493,110
Saône (Haute-)	60,826 54.6	50,594 45.4	111,420
Saône-et-Loire	133,221 51.3	126,589 48.7	259,810
Sarthe	118,383 53.6	102,672 46.4	221,055
Savoie	68,436 53.9	58,468 46.1	126,904

Department	De Gaulle	Mitterrand	Total
Savoie (Haute-)	102,642	58,941	161,583
	63.5	36.5	
Seine	1,385,848	1,253,300	2,639,148
	52.5	47.5	
Seine-Maritime	263,685	247,507	511,192
	51.6	48.4	
Seine-et-Marne	149,593	117,943	267,536
	55.9	44.1	
Seine-et-Oise	616,617	573,149	1,189,766
	51.8	48.2	
Sèvres (Deux-)	95,790	68,268	164,058
	58.4	41.6	
Somme	140,125	120,065	260,190
	53.9	46.1	
Tarn	80,980	96,445	177,425
	45.6	54.4	
Tarn-et-Garonne	41,562	52,388	93,950
	44.2	55.8	
Territoire de Belfort	28,354	24,606	52,960
	53.5	46.5	
Var	119,531	132,451	251,982
	47.4	52.6	
Vaucluse	67,299	94,319	161,618
	41.6	58.4	
Vendée	150,834	61,147	211,981
	71.2	28.8	
Vienne	95,972	71,921	167,893
	57.2	42.8	
Vienne (Haute-)	84,291	105,539	189,830
	44.4	55.6	

Department	De Gaulle	Mitterrand	Total
Vosges	119,353	70,385	189,738
	62.9	37.1	
Yonne	77,941	62,983	140,924
	55.3	44.7	
Overseas			
Guadeloupe	74,174	12,170	86,344
	85.9	14.1	
Guyane	6,635	2,952	9,587
	69.2	30.8	
Martinique	89,798	10,311	100,109
	89.7	10.3	
Réunion (La)	97,831	19,311	117,142
	83.5	16.5	
Comores	108,838	601	109,439
	99.5	.5	
Côte française des Somalis	25,178	1,185	26,363
	95.5	4.5	
Nouvelle-Calédonie et ressortissants français des Nouvelles-Hébrides	17,088	8,339	25,427
	67.2	32.8	
Polynésie française	15,701	10,554	26,255
	59.8	40.2	
Saint-Pierre et Miquelon	1,496	313	1,809
	82.7	17.3	
Wallis et Futuna	3,433	14	3,447
	99.6	.4	
Total	13,083,699	10,619,735	23,703,434
	55.2	44.8	

PRESIDENTIAL ELECTION RESULTS, 1969, FIRST BALLOT, BY DEPARTMENT

Department	Pompidou	Poher	Duclos	Defferre	Rocard	Other[a]	Total
Metropolitan France							
Ain	67,929 46.4	38,197 26.1	26,274 18.0	5,820 4.0	4,858 3.3	3,252 2.2	146,330
Aisne	95,897 40.6	50,565 21.4	65,433 27.7	9,566 4.1	7,976 3.4	6,594 2.8	236,031
Allier	72,003 38.5	36,195 19.4	59,572 31.9	9,446 5.1	5,718 3.1	3,894 2.1	186,828
Alpes (Basses-)	19,002 38.6	10,841 22.0	12,151 24.7	3,886 7.9	1,886 3.8	1,426 2.9	49,192
Alpes (Hautes-)	18,778 43.7	9,973 23.2	9,849 22.9	1,643 3.8	1,525 3.5	1,209 2.8	42,977
Alpes-Maritimes	125,270 39.1	94,352 29.4	74,424 23.2	10,610 3.3	7,837 2.4	8,251 2.6	320,744
Ardèche	58,441 45.5	30,170 23.5	27,386 21.3	5,741 4.5	4,004 3.1	2,676 2.1	128,418

Department							
Ardennes	54,514 / 42.5	27,150 / 21.2	31,579 / 24.6	6,453 / 5.0	4,721 / 3.7	3,765 / 2.9	128,182
Ariège	26,732 / 37.6	17,344 / 24.4	18,086 / 25.4	5,079 / 7.1	2,278 / 3.2	1,645 / 2.3	71,164
Aube	53,182 / 43.9	29,237 / 24.1	26,066 / 21.5	6,527 / 5.4	3,171 / 2.6	2,931 / 2.4	121,114
Aude	51,538 / 36.9	33,587 / 24.1	34,988 / 25.1	11,948 / 8.6	4,670 / 3.3	2,810 / 2.0	139,541
Aveyron	82,735 / 55.5	34,470 / 23.1	18,617 / 12.5	5,878 / 3.9	4,308 / 2.9	3,007 / 2.0	149,015
Bouches-du-Rhône	194,989 / 34.8	104,092 / 18.6	172,595 / 30.8	61,156 / 10.9	16,466 / 2.9	11,396 / 2.0	560,694
Calvados	110,643 / 48.2	60,677 / 26.4	35,566 / 15.5	8,020 / 3.5	8,748 / 3.8	5,860 / 2.6	229,514
Cantal	58,645 / 69.8	7,477 / 8.9	11,777 / 14.0	3,053 / 3.6	1,944 / 2.3	1,138 / 1.4	84,034
Charente	66,520 / 42.3	38,348 / 24.4	37,085 / 23.6	6,654 / 4.2	4,920 / 3.1	3,732 / 2.4	157,259
Charente-Maritime	92,239 / 42.2	60,781 / 27.8	42,531 / 19.4	9,337 / 4.3	8,208 / 3.8	5,731 / 2.6	218,827

Department	Pompidou	Poher	Duclos	Defferre	Rocard	Other[a]	Total
Cher	57,767 40.0	33,177 23.0	41,789 28.9	4,633 3.2	3,670 2.5	3,471 2.4	144,507
Corrèze	56,695 43.9	20,273 15.7	40,979 31.7	5,628 4.4	3,441 2.7	2,181 1.7	129,197
Corse	59,076 53.5	26,978 24.4	17,735 16.0	4,770 4.3	1,231 1.1	726 .7	110,516
Côte-d'Or	81,946 45.7	49,447 27.5	28,365 15.8	8,569 4.8	7,020 3.9	4,141 2.3	179,488
Côtes-du-Nord	113,520 43.0	59,523 22.6	62,584 23.7	10,059 3.8	12,557 4.8	5,507 2.1	263,750
Creuse	31,884 41.2	13,207 17.1	23,919 30.9	4,898 6.3	1,893 2.4	1,524 2.0	77,325
Dordogne	80,312 39.8	50,562 25.0	52,222 25.9	9,233 4.6	5,467 2.7	4,189 2.1	201,985
Doubs	86,203 48.9	39,401 22.3	27,997 15.9	9,571 5.4	8,629 4.9	4,514 2.6	176,315
Drôme	60,083 39.5	40,342 26.5	33,115 21.8	8,125 5.3	6,114 4.0	4,230 2.8	152,009

Eure	75,442 42.7	45,441 25.7	32,680 18.5	12,342 7.0	6,243 3.5	4,566 2.6	176,714
Eure-et-Loir	64,069 45.0	36,143 25.4	26,247 18.4	7,811 5.5	4,871 3.4	3,357 2.4	142,498
Finistère	210,366 53.4	74,276 18.9	67,141 17.1	16,547 4.2	18,273 4.6	7,069 1.8	393,672
Gard	81,998 37.9	44,334 20.5	65,483 30.3	11,427 5.3	7,941 3.7	4,981 2.3	216,164
Garonne (Haute-)	120,898 39.7	82,845 27.2	59,561 19.5	20,482 6.7	13,737 4.5	7,312 2.4	304,835
Gers	29,715 34.7	28,600 33.4	15,868 18.5	5,508 6.4	3,809 4.4	2,101 2.5	85,601
Gironde	183,559 40.8	129,110 28.7	81,698 18.1	30,145 6.7	16,541 3.7	9,096 2.0	450,149
Hérault	100,779 39.5	59,022 23.2	65,430 25.7	15,891 6.2	8,281 3.2	5,477 2.1	254,880
Ille-et-Vilaine	162,518 52.5	81,948 26.5	36,813 11.9	11,838 3.8	10,112 3.3	6,149 2.0	309,378
Indre	44,465 36.5	34,206 28.1	33,116 27.2	4,468 3.7	2,838 2.3	2,839 2.3	121,932

Department	Pompidou	Poher	Duclos	Defferre	Rocard	Other[a]	Total
Indre-et-Loire	79,717 41.3	58,511 30.3	33,865 17.5	9,271 4.8	6,934 3.6	4,806 2.5	193,104
Isère	122,478 39.3	75,247 24.2	73,649 23.7	17,136 5.5	14,742 4.7	8,111 2.6	311,363
Jura	47,598 44.2	29,505 27.4	18,997 17.6	4,201 3.9	4,165 3.9	3,193 3.0	107,659
Landes	66,508 45.9	34,789 24.0	27,249 18.8	9,335 6.4	3,968 2.7	2,893 2.0	144,742
Loir-et-Cher	48,999 38.2	40,902 31.9	25,704 20.0	5,823 4.5	4,003 3.1	2,884 2.2	128,315
Loire	135,191 44.0	76,698 24.9	61,909 20.1	12,890 4.2	13,145 4.3	7,708 2.5	307,541
Loire (Haute-)	54,025 52.8	25,028 24.5	12,789 12.5	5,026 4.9	3,171 3.1	2,276 2.2	102,315
Loire-Atlantique	199,390 49.5	105,801 26.3	50,932 12.7	18,036 4.5	20,678 5.1	7,676 1.9	402,513
Loiret	92,414 46.6	49,185 24.8	35,764 18.0	9,223 4.7	6,902 3.5	4,787 2.4	198,275

Lot	39,144 47.6	21,999 26.7	14,804 18.0	2,686 3.3	2,267 2.8	1,363 1.7	82,263
Lot-et-Garonne	51,573 36.7	39,549 28.1	35,837 25.5	5,814 4.1	4,449 3.2	3,458 2.5	140,680
Lozère	25,508 63.1	6,699 16.6	4,963 12.3	1,308 3.2	1,125 2.8	794 2.0	40,397
Maine-et-Loire	143,690 54.1	66,718 25.1	28,733 10.8	10,193 3.8	10,915 4.1	5,560 2.1	265,809
Manche	117,403 56.6	54,417 26.3	16,610 8.0	7,769 3.7	6,931 3.3	4,157 2.0	207,287
Marne	91,069 44.1	46,044 22.3	46,581 22.6	10,252 5.0	7,566 3.7	4,939 2.4	206,451
Marne (Haute-)	44,922 47.5	24,117 25.5	15,870 16.8	3,463 3.7	3,818 4.0	2,460 2.6	94,650
Mayenne	67,431 53.8	35,902 28.7	11,291 9.0	4,463 3.6	3,534 2.8	2,656 2.1	125,277
Meurthe-et-Moselle	126,763 43.9	72,624 25.2	60,034 20.8	10,885 3.8	11,729 4.1	6,702 2.3	288,737
Meuse	46,643 49.7	24,720 26.3	13,470 14.3	3,052 3.3	2,881 3.1	3,119 3.3	93,885

Department	Pompidou	Poher	Duclos	Defferre	Rocard	Other[a]	Total
Morbihan	146,901 54.9	59,586 22.3	40,349 15.1	9,263 3.5	6,971 2.6	4,604 1.7	267,674
Moselle	189,268 50.9	95,833 25.8	53,279 14.3	10,433 2.8	13,071 3.5	10,275 2.8	372,159
Nièvre	42,384 35.5	32,429 27.1	30,962 25.9	7,754 6.5	3,437 2.9	2,569 2.1	119,535
Nord	463,255 42.6	186,376 17.1	292,022 26.9	79,019 7.3	36,527 3.4	29,855 2.7	1,087,054
Oise	99,479 42.4	51,991 22.1	57,034 24.3	10,306 4.4	9,287 4.0	6,712 2.9	234,809
Orne	61,860 46.4	44,185 33.2	15,017 11.3	4,706 3.5	4,273 3.2	3,142 2.4	133,183
Pas-de-Calais	247,358 39.2	114,590 18.2	179,256 28.4	47,141 7.5	20,119 3.2	22,477 3.6	630,941
Puy-de-Dôme	108,421 44.5	46,204 19.0	54,853 22.5	17,763 7.3	10,404 4.3	5,725 2.4	243,370
Pyrénées (Basses-)	122,615 50.5	60,174 24.8	33,189 13.7	13,122 5.4	8,352 3.4	5,117 2.1	242,569

Pyrénées (Hautes-)	41,837 39.5	27,340 25.8	26,335 24.9	4,556 4.3	3,754 3.5	2,128 2.0	105,950
Pyrénées-Orientales	47,453 38.5	28,951 23.5	34,887 28.3	5,379 4.4	3,744 3.0	2,780 2.3	123,194
Rhin (Bas-)	203,416 59.8	93,997 27.6	20,659 6.1	10,039 2.9	6,303 1.9	5,917 1.7	340,331
Rhin (Haut-)	147,200 57.4	71,985 28.1	17,098 6.8	8,803 3.4	6,018 2.3	5,229 2.0	256,333
Rhône	225,742 42.9	139,284 26.5	103,892 19.7	22,418 4.3	23,596 4.5	11,391 2.2	526,323
Saône (Haute-)	46,419 44.5	30,657 29.4	16,331 15.7	4,381 4.2	4,071 3.9	2,451 2.3	104,310
Saône-et-Loire	104,896 42.9	60,338 24.7	56,397 23.1	10,263 4.2	7,260 3.0	5,115 2.1	244,269
Sarthe	86,760 41.2	56,730 26.9	45,388 21.6	9,745 4.6	7,409 3.5	4,575 2.2	210,607
Savoie	53,604 44.1	30,582 25.2	24,448 20.1	4,797 3.9	5,076 4.2	2,966 2.4	121,473
Savoie (Haute-)	72,891 47.1	43,179 27.9	23,164 15.0	6,202 4.0	5,362 3.5	3,985 2.6	154,783
Paris	495,647 45.2	258,607 23.6	203,989 18.6	65,216 6.0	46,908 4.3	25,431 2.3	1,095,798

Department	Pompidou	Poher	Duclos	Defferre	Rocard	Other[a]	Total
Seine-Maritime	205,912 41.4	104,162 21.0	132,556 26.7	22,095 4.4	19,858 4.0	12,292 2.5	496,875
Seine-et-Marne	118,151 44.3	60,524 22.7	61,506 23.1	9,789 3.7	9,520 3.6	7,150 2.7	266,640
Yvelines	159,666 43.6	80,631 22.0	80,796 22.1	18,206 5.0	18,110 4.9	8,685 2.4	366,094
Sèvres (Deux-)	77,029 49.0	45,508 29.0	17,392 11.1	7,528 4.8	6,186 3.9	3,408 2.2	157,051
Somme	100,497 40.0	51,308 20.4	72,738 28.9	10,956 4.4	8,322 3.3	7,492 3.0	251,313
Tarn	77,305 44.9	42,793 24.9	31,503 18.3	11,169 6.5	5,621 3.3	3,713 2.2	172,104
Tarn-et-Garonne	38,198 42.7	25,819 28.9	15,368 17.2	4,835 5.4	3,025 3.4	2,151 2.4	89,396
Var	98,265 40.6	57,998 24.0	59,708 24.7	13,766 5.7	6,817 2.8	5,493 2.3	242,047
Vaucluse	54,425 34.6	43,680 27.7	38,698 24.6	10,521 6.7	5,628 3.6	4,545 2.9	157,497
Vendée	125,389 59.7	47,380 22.6	18,865 9.0	7,627 3.6	6,102 2.9	4,606 2.2	209,969

Vienne	70,344 / 44.0	44,702 / 27.9	30,114 / 18.8	5,943 / 3.7	5,368 / 3.4	3,577 / 2.2	160,048
Vienne (Haute-)	66,486 / 38.1	26,981 / 15.5	58,677 / 33.6	13,497 / 7.7	5,341 / 3.1	3,428 / 2.0	174,410
Vosges	85,630 / 48.3	44,133 / 24.9	29,236 / 16.5	7,292 / 4.1	6,019 / 3.4	4,848 / 2.7	177,158
Yonne	60,632 / 44.9	34,627 / 25.6	26,906 / 19.9	5,615 / 4.2	4,058 / 3.0	3,223 / 2.4	135,061
Territoire de Belfort	21,614 / 44.7	11,360 / 23.5	8,976 / 18.5	3,015 / 6.2	2,240 / 4.6	1,187 / 2.5	48,392
Essonne	114,515 / 39.6	61,625 / 21.3	78,205 / 27.0	13,163 / 4.5	14,667 / 5.1	7,230 / 2.5	289,405
Hauts-de-Seine	264,394 / 41.6	127,499 / 20.1	163,188 / 25.7	33,850 / 5.3	31,411 / 4.9	14,841 / 2.3	635,183
Seine-Saint-Denis	169,296 / 34.0	84,970 / 17.0	192,512 / 38.6	19,875 / 4.0	20,578 / 4.1	11,136 / 2.2	498,367
Val-de-Marne	182,007 / 38.5	93,558 / 19.8	43,743 / 30.4	21,525 / 4.6	21,418 / 4.5	10,638 / 2.2	472,889
Val-d'Oise	113,318 / 39.3	58,111 / 20.2	84,531 / 29.3	12,572 / 4.4	12,991 / 4.5	6,558 / 2.3	288,081

Department	Pompidou	Poher	Duclos	Defferre	Rocard	Other[a]	Total
Overseas							
Guadeloupe	26,064 60.8	3,643 8.5	11,219 26.2	1,304 3.0	192 .4	444 1.0	42,866
Guyane	5,249 69.6	1,723 22.8	201 2.7	188 2.5	78 1.0	108 1.4	7,547
Martinique	50,143 74.1	4,825 7.1	10,926 16.1	852 1.3	296 .4	652 1.0	67,694
Réunion (La)	79,504 82.2	7,218 7.5	5,448 5.6	1,614 1.7	994 1.0	1,988 2.1	96,766
Comores	73,396 79.8	17,062 18.5	205 .2	820 .9	199 .2	325 .4	92,007
Territoire français des Afars et des Issas	26,833 76.8	7,565 21.7	87 .2	130 .4	118 .3	197 .6	34,930
Nouvelle-Calédonie et Nouvelles-Hébrides	13,441 52.5	10,781 42.1	375 1.5	338 1.3	259 1.0	415 1.6	25,609
Polynésie française	11,844 44.5	13,693 51.4	241 .9	202 .8	254 1.0	407 1.5	26,641

Saint-Pierre et Miquelon	1,585 76.4	326 15.7	39 1.9	23 1.1	25 1.2	76 3.7	2,074
Wallis et Futuna	2,460 77.4	682 21.5	5 .2	18 .6	5 .2	7 .2	3,177
Total	10,051,816 44.5	5,268,651 23.3	4,808,285 21.3	1,133,222 5.0	816,471 3.6	525,553 2.3	22,603,998

[a]Other vote includes: L. Ducatel 286,447; A. Krivine 239,106.

PRESIDENT ELECTION RESULTS, 1969, SECOND BALLOT, BY DEPARTMENT

Department	Pompidou	Poher	Total
Metropolitan France			
Ain	75,666	53,270	128,936
	58.7	41.3	
Aisne	106,414	86,864	193,278
	55.1	44.9	
Allier	80,773	58,830	139,603
	57.9	42.1	
Alpes (Basses-)	22,365	20,937	43,302
	51.6	48.4	
Alpes (Hautes-)	21,710	16,596	38,306
	56.7	43.3	
Alpes-Maritimes	138,523	129,702	268,225
	51.6	48.4	
Ardèche	65,203	46,604	111,807
	58.3	41.7	
Ardennes	60,933	45,127	106,060
	57.5	42.5	
Ariège	31,757	31,456	63,213
	50.2	49.8	
Aube	58,491	47,241	105,732
	55.3	44.7	
Aude	59,064	61,964	121,028
	48.8	51.2	
Aveyron	91,377	49,109	140,486
	65.0	35.0	
Bouches-du-Rhône	223,654	199,094	422,748
	52.9	47.1	

Department	Pompidou	Poher	Total
Calvados	119,310 58.9	83,086 41.1	202,396
Cantal	64,511 82.9	13,283 17.1	77,794
Charente	75,226 54.9	61,716 45.1	136,942
Charente-Maritime	102,949 52.7	92,348 47.3	195,297
Cher	63,605 56.3	49,427 43.7	113,032
Corrèze	64,920 64.4	35,846 35.6	100,766
Corse	68,553 63.9	38,757 36.1	107,310
Côte-d'Or	88,399 54.7	73,201 45.3	161,600
Côtes-du-Nord	127,925 57.8	93,477 42.2	221,402
Creuse	36,910 58.8	25,868 41.2	62,778
Dordogne	92,100 52.7	82,671 47.3	174,771
Doubs	95,635 61.5	59,787 38.5	155,422
Drôme	68,129 50.6	66,381 49.4	134,510
Eure	81,498 53.0	72,135 47.0	153,633
Eure-et-Loir	69,313 55.7	55,058 44.3	124,371

Department	Pompidou	Poher	Total
Finistère	230,814 67.2	112,770 32.8	343,584
Gard	92,281 55.9	72,778 44.1	165,059
Garonne (Haute-)	136,790 49.8	137,645 50.2	274,435
Gers	35,022 43.1	46,192 56.9	81,214
Gironde	203,222 50.5	199,143 49.5	402,365
Hérault	113,365 53.4	98,961 46.6	212,326
Ille-et-Vilaine	175,415 62.4	105,681 37.6	281,096
Indre	50,862 49.3	52,255 50.7	103,117
Indre-et-Loire	86,682 50.7	84,223 49.3	170,905
Isère	138,362 53.1	122,160 46.9	260,522
Jura	54,391 54.5	45,430 45.5	99,821
Landes	74,700 57.6	54,911 42.4	129,611
Loir-et-Cher	54,631 48.1	59,017 51.9	113,648
Loire	152,158 59.4	103,990 40.6	256,148
Loire (Haute-)	62,022 63.1	36,299 36.9	98,321

Department	Pompidou	Poher	Total
Loire-Atlantique	213,436 60.3	140,409 39.7	353,845
Loiret	99,415 58.0	71,930 42.0	171,345
Lot	44,887 58.8	31,505 41.2	76,392
Lot-et-Garonne	59,356 47.9	64,656 52.1	124,012
Lozère	27,817 72.6	10,481 27.4	38,298
Maine-et-Loire	151,860 63.7	86,668 36.3	238,528
Manche	126,858 64.5	69,897 35.5	196,755
Marne	98,525 58.9	68,869 41.1	167,394
Marne (Haute-)	49,479 59.0	34,329 41.0	83,808
Mayenne	72,714 62.6	43,440 37.4	116,154
Meurthe-et-Moselle	135,757 58.1	97,706 41.9	233,463
Meuse	49,877 59.5	33,910 40.5	83,787
Morbihan	158,126 66.9	78,312 33.1	236,438
Moselle	202,958 60.6	132,139 39.4	335,097
Nièvre	48,061 45.5	57,530 54.5	105,591

Department	Pompidou	Poher	Total
Nord	504,448 59.7	341,156 40.3	845,604
Oise	107,086 56.7	81,818 43.3	188,904
Orne	68,427 54.9	56,251 45.1	124,678
Pas-de-Calais	273,985 55.7	217,512 44.3	491,497
Puy-de-Dôme	121,627 60.1	80,719 39.9	202,346
Pyrénées (Basses-)	136,804 60.0	91,064 40.0	227,868
Pyrénées (Hautes-)	48,597 52.9	43,214 47.1	91,811
Pyrénées-Orientales	55,543 52.6	50,136 47.4	105,679
Rhin (Bas-)	215,581 65.9	111,423 34.1	327,004
Rhin (Haut-)	161,240 65.5	84,846 34.5	246,086
Rhône	246,226 57.2	184,307 42.8	430,533
Saône (Haute-)	51,593 53.2	45,430 46.8	97,023
Saône-et-Loire	116,571 56.6	89,493 43.4	206,064
Sarthe	94,858 54.1	80,492 45.9	175,350
Savoie	59,141 56.3	45,876 43.7	105,017

Department	Pompidou	Poher	Total
Savoie (Haute-)	81,360 57.4	60,276 42.6	141,636
Paris	524,388 58.4	373,744 41.6	898,132
Seine-Maritime	220,051 57.9	159,803 42.1	379,854
Seine-et-Marne	126,103 58.7	88,703 41.3	214,806
Yvelines	170,404 59.1	118,023 40.9	288,427
Sèvres (Deux-)	83,637 56.6	64,118 43.4	147,755
Somme	110,987 54.9	91,152 45.1	202,139
Tarn	87,051 54.9	71,602 45.1	158,653
Tarn-et-Garonne	43,418 51.6	40,806 48.4	84,224
Var	110,587 55.2	89,927 44.8	200,514
Vaucluse	62,595 44.4	78,497 55.6	141,092
Vendée	134,565 67.8	63,843 32.2	198,408
Vienne	78,013 54.7	64,588 45.3	142,601
Vienne (Haute-)	77,159 59.3	53,001 40.7	130,160
Vosges	94,010 58.8	65,793 41.2	159,803

Department			Total
Yonne	66,431	52,077	118,508
	56.1	43.9	
Territoire de Belfort	24,088	18,428	42,516
	56.7	43.3	
Essonne	121,661	91,556	213,217
	57.1	42.9	
Hauts-de-Seine	277,612	186,862	464,474
	59.8	40.2	
Seine-Saint-Denis	171,383	117,073	288,456
	59.4	40.6	
Val-de-Marne	187,320	130,421	317,741
	59.0	41.0	
Val-d'Oise	118,877	83,587	202,464
	58.7	41.3	

Overseas
Guadeloupe	40,716	8,956	49,672
	82.0	18.0	
Guyane	5,666	2,034	7,700
	73.6	26.4	
Martinique	67,321	6,649	73,970
	91.0	9.0	
Réunion (La)	98,746	12,295	111,041
	88.9	11.1	
Comores	101,208	9,812	111,020
	91.2	8.8	
Territoire français des Afars et des Issas	30,935	5,560	36,495
	84.8	15.2	
Nouvelle-Calédonie et Nouvelles-Hébrides	14,570	12,089	26,659
	54.7	45.3	

Department	Pompidou	Poher	Total
Polynésie française	12,947 48.2	13,927 51.8	26,874
Saint-Pierre et Miquelon	1,714 82.6	362 17.4	2,076
Wallis et Futuna	2,365 76.0	746 24.0	3,111
Total	11,064,371 58.2	7,943,118 41.8	19,007,489

PRESIDENTIAL ELECTION RESULTS, 1974, FIRST BALLOT, BY DEPARTMENT

Department	Mitterrand	Giscard d'Estaing	Chaban-Delmas	Royer	Laguiller	Other[a]	Total
Metropolitan France							
Ain	68,990	67,653	22,551	4,491	4,603	5,765	174,053
	39.6	38.9	13.0	2.6	2.6	3.3	
Aisne	127,522	71,613	39,922	6,710	8,392	8,989	263,148
	48.5	27.2	15.2	2.6	3.2	3.4	
Allier	99,487	67,529	19,738	4,964	5,818	5,641	203,177
	49.0	33.2	9.7	2.4	2.9	2.8	
Alpes-de-Haute Provence	28,262	17,601	7,767	1,112	1,611	2,446	58,799
	48.1	29.9	13.2	1.9	2.7	4.2	
Alpes (Hautes-)	21,950	16,530	8,521	1,272	1,414	1,970	51,657
	42.5	32.0	16.5	2.5	2.7	3.8	
Alpes-Maritimes	169,029	151,753	41,899	7,987	4,171	13,852	388,691
	43.5	39.0	10.8	2.1	1.1	3.6	
Ardèche	60,245	46,817	24,235	3,895	3,765	4,139	143,096
	42.1	32.7	16.9	2.7	2.6	2.9	

Ardennes	68,283	44,680	17,102	3,916	3,750	4,649	142,380
	48.0	31.4	12.0	2.8	2.6	3.3	
Ariège	45,149	14,618	13,673	1,287	2,494	2,361	79,582
	56.7	18.4	17.2	1.6	3.1	3.0	
Aube	58,536	46,375	19,083	4,470	3,435	4,245	136,144
	43.0	34.1	14.0	3.3	2.5	3.1	
Aude	86,453	32,363	23,907	2,484	3,526	4,902	153,635
	56.3	21.1	15.6	1.6	2.3	3.2	
Aveyron	60,709	65,075	19,257	6,264	4,814	3,842	159,961
	38.0	40.7	12.0	3.9	3.0	2.4	
Bouches-du-Rhône	341,419	195,924	71,304	10,476	11,052	25,472	655,647
	52.1	29.9	10.9	1.6	1.7	3.9	
Calvados	102,871	99,850	38,994	9,824	6,498	9,882	267,919
	38.4	37.3	14.6	3.7	2.4	3.7	
Cantal	29,864	42,227	11,007	2,077	3,657	1,973	90,805
	32.9	46.5	12.1	2.3	4.0	2.2	
Charente	78,122	39,658	42,687	5,240	5,440	4,812	175,959
	44.4	22.5	24.3	3.0	3.1	2.7	
Charente-Maritime	104,743	63,994	58,688	8,414	6,686	7,969	250,494
	41.8	25.6	23.4	3.4	2.7	3.2	

Department	Mitterrand	Giscard d'Estaing	Chaban-Delmas	Royer	Laguiller	Other[a]	Total
Cher	72,588 45.0	50,375 31.2	21,323 13.2	7,209 4.5	5,326 3.3	4,663 2.9	161,484
Corrèze	70,585 49.7	39,583 27.9	22,079 15.6	2,456 1.7	4,190 3.0	3,021 2.1	141,914
Corse	53,832 44.6	29,560 24.5	33,587 27.8	883 .7	650 .5	2,287 1.9	120,799
Côte-d'Or	89,229 43.1	74,453 36.0	26,172 12.7	5,598 2.7	4,494 2.2	6,968 3.4	206,914
Côtes-du-Nord	133,505 45.2	105,157 35.6	35,143 11.9	6,450 2.2	7,492 2.5	7,749 2.6	295,496
Creuse	42,797 49.8	25,285 29.4	10,165 11.8	2,078 2.4	3,618 4.2	1,936 2.3	85,879
Dordogne	107,082 47.7	44,140 19.7	56,496 25.2	4,638 2.1	6,333 2.8	5,916 2.6	224,605
Doubs	85,728 41.9	77,405 37.8	22,308 10.9	6,012 2.9	5,929 2.9	7,465 3.6	204,847

Drôme	81,167 45.8	53,237 30.1	26,473 14.9	4,820 2.7	4,799 2.7	6,662 3.8	177,158
Eure	87,846 42.6	69,367 33.7	30,443 14.8	5,492 2.7	5,585 2.7	7,393 3.6	206,126
Eure-et-Loir	68,084 41.0	58,286 35.1	22,276 13.4	6,699 4.0	4,718 2.8	5,874 3.5	165,937
Finistère	160,978 37.1	179,913 41.5	59,426 13.7	11,378 2.6	9,532 2.2	12,783 3.0	434,010
Gard	127,269 50.7	72,911 29.0	31,316 12.5	5,198 2.1	5,342 2.1	9,143 3.6	251,179
Garonne (Haute-)	178,133 49.9	102,395 28.7	49,146 13.8	5,709 1.6	8,815 2.5	12,794 3.6	356,992
Gers	49,561 50.8	22,546 23.1	17,575 18.0	2,019 2.1	2,954 3.0	2,934 3.0	97,589
Gironde	215,799 42.4	74,032 14.5	183,367 36.0	10,257 2.0	10,306 2.0	15,462 3.0	509,223
Hérault	149,392 49.8	87,704 29.2	38,664 12.9	8,082 2.7	4,903 1.6	11,561 3.9	300,306
Ille-et-Vilaine	115,790 33.3	151,470 43.5	50,558 14.5	12,029 3.5	8,295 2.4	10,043 2.9	348,185

Department	Mitterrand	Giscard d'Estaing	Chaban-Delmas	Royer	Laguiller	Other[a]	Total
Indre	59,185 43.6	37,579 27.7	18,575 13.7	12,221 9.0	4,824 3.6	3,532 2.6	135,916
Indre-et-Loire	78,934 35.1	44,733 19.9	16,853 7.5	76,055 33.8	3,576 1.6	4,816 2.1	224,967
Isère	174,815 47.1	114,401 30.9	47,823 12.9	8,950 2.4	9,938 2.7	14,920 4.0	370,847
Jura	52,762 42.7	43,747 35.4	13,776 11.2	4,401 3.6	4,205 3.4	4,691 3.8	123,582
Landes	72,406 44.7	30,348 18.7	48,349 29.8	3,505 2.2	3,499 2.2	4,018 2.5	162,125
Loir-et-Cher	59,669 40.5	46,044 31.3	18,583 12.6	14,714 10.0	4,243 2.9	4,093 2.8	147,346
Loire	141,065 41.5	123,542 36.3	43,643 12.8	11,945 3.5	8,828 2.6	11,253 3.3	340,276
Loire (Haute-)	39,090 34.5	49,531 43.7	13,930 12.3	4,288 3.8	3,511 3.1	2,975 2.6	113,325

Loire-Atlantique	166,341	37.0	172,096	38.3	68,627	15.3	19,571	4.4	9,361	2.1	13,705	3.1	449,701
Loiret	88,590	38.2	83,444	35.9	32,787	14.1	12,622	5.4	6,616	2.9	8,165	3.5	232,224
Lot	41,568	47.1	24,268	27.5	15,283	17.3	1,979	2.2	2,917	3.3	2,304	2.6	88,319
Lot-et-Garonne	74,260	47.1	35,271	22.4	34,880	22.1	3,271	2.1	4,497	2.9	5,441	3.5	157,620
Lozère	13,470	31.6	20,010	46.9	5,607	13.2	1,366	3.2	1,206	2.8	986	2.3	42,645
Maine-et-Loire	92,566	30.8	120,999	40.2	41,963	14.0	29,703	9.9	7,238	2.4	8,279	2.8	300,748
Manche	70,242	29.9	102,667	43.7	37,773	16.1	12,283	5.2	5,366	2.3	6,809	2.9	235,140
Marne	102,688	43.2	82,112	34.6	32,055	13.5	5,759	2.4	5,672	2.4	9,402	4.0	237,688
Marne (Haute-)	43,810	41.9	35,521	34.0	15,571	14.9	3,088	3.0	3,078	2.9	3,524	3.4	104,592
Mayenne	39,621	28.7	61,910	44.8	21,383	15.5	8,474	6.1	3,273	2.4	3,637	2.6	138,298

Department	Mitterrand	Giscard d'Estaing	Chaban-Delmas	Royer	Laguiller	Other[a]	Total
Meurthe-et-Moselle	152,796 46.5	120,340 36.7	32,061 9.8	7,492 2.3	5,417 1.7	10,283 3.1	328,389
Meuse	43,762 41.8	39,324 37.6	12,214 11.7	3,570 3.4	2,521 2.4	3,342 3.2	104,733
Morbihan	98,912 33.7	134,887 46.0	36,743 12.5	7,927 2.7	6,611 2.3	8,236 2.8	293,316
Moselle	186,298 42.4	169,503 38.6	51,900 11.8	9,133 2.1	8,097 1.8	14,178 3.2	439,109
Nièvre	76,087 57.0	35,220 26.4	12,825 9.6	3,457 2.6	2,703 2.0	3,138 2.4	133,430
Nord	571,071 48.1	342,317 28.8	182,377 15.4	25,277 2.1	29,566 2.5	37,555 3.2	1,188,163
Oise	124,824 45.4	80,752 29.4	41,688 15.2	8,902 3.2	8,019 2.9	10,750 3.9	274,935
Orne	49,306 33.1	57,294 38.5	25,239 17.0	7,941 5.3	4,244 2.9	4,816 3.2	148,840

Pas-de-Calais	360,463 51.6	177,112 25.4	106,194 15.2	14,559 2.1	20,438 2.9	19,514 2.8	698,280
Puy-de-Dôme	119,630 42.5	126,833 45.1	12,288 4.4	5,203 1.9	9,971 3.5	7,559 2.7	281,484
Pyrénées-Atlantiques	101,538 37.1	76,725 28.0	73,798 27.0	7,010 2.6	5,919 2.2	8,611 3.2	273,601
Pyrénées (Hautes-)	60,653 50.7	28,757 24.0	21,392 17.9	2,280 1.9	3,116 2.6	3,551 3.0	119,749
Pyrénées-Orientales	75,485 51.3	42,226 28.7	18,678 12.7	2,698 1.8	2,488 1.7	5,560 3.8	147,135
Rhin (Bas-)	122,929 31.0	173,020 43.7	59,523 15.0	7,954 2.0	6,097 1.5	26,572 6.7	396,095
Rhin (Haut-)	85,877 29.2	118,911 40.4	48,331 16.4	5,097 1.7	4,877 1.7	31,531 10.7	294,624
Rhône	249,411 42.0	233,995 39.4	60,071 10.1	16,247 2.7	12,076 2.0	21,947 3.7	593,747
Saône (Haute-)	52,525 45.0	41,328 35.4	13,461 11.5	2,939 2.5	3,020 2.6	3,400 2.9	116,673
Saône-et-Loire	127,001 45.6	93,123 33.4	37,070 13.3	7,261 2.6	6,698 2.4	7,586 2.7	278,739

Department	Mitterrand	Giscard d'Estaing	Chaban-Delmas	Royer	Laguiller	Other[a]	Total
Sarthe	100,748 41.4	75,709 31.1	37,471 15.4	15,779 6.5	6,429 2.6	7,078 2.9	243,214
Savoie	63,230 43.6	44,772 30.9	23,333 16.1	4,167 2.9	4,107 2.8	5,514 3.8	145,123
Savoie (Haute-)	68,405 35.9	78,177 41.0	25,357 13.3	6,491 3.4	4,297 2.3	7,840 4.1	190,567
Paris	388,322 37.3	411,229 39.5	143,378 13.8	32,784 3.2	16,275 1.6	47,953 4.6	1,039,941
Seine-Maritime	264,711 47.2	182,580 32.5	68,230 12.2	11,876 2.1	13,977 2.5	19,640 3.5	561,014
Seine-et-Marne	141,060 42.8	106,126 32.2	48,803 14.8	10,796 3.3	8,476 2.6	14,122 4.3	329,383
Yvelines	184,386 40.6	167,173 36.8	58,928 13.0	13,629 3.0	8,945 2.0	20,714 4.6	453,775
Sèvres (Deux-)	61,009 35.0	60,730 34.8	29,756 17.1	12,973 7.4	5,498 3.2	4,590 2.6	174,556

	C1		C2		C3		C4		C5		C6		Total
Somme	133,035	47.3	75,923	27.0	44,290	15.7	6,601	2.4	8,437	3.0	13,026	4.6	281,312
Tarn	83,063	44.3	55,059	29.4	33,590	17.9	4,390	2.3	5,674	3.0	5,818	3.1	187,594
Tarn-et-Garonne	44,827	44.8	26,025	26.0	20,308	20.3	2,179	2.2	3,118	3.1	3,537	3.5	99,994
Var	137,896	46.1	103,323	34.6	36,840	12.3	5,621	1.9	4,034	1.4	11,156	3.7	298,870
Vaucluse	89,469	48.1	55,551	29.8	24,743	13.3	3,848	2.1	4,611	2.5	7,988	4.3	186,210
Vendée	66,631	27.8	100,859	42.0	45,019	18.8	14,566	6.1	6,343	2.6	6,528	2.7	239,946
Vienne	72,876	40.0	52,332	28.7	32,869	18.0	13,944	7.6	5,428	3.0	4,959	2.7	182,408
Vienne (Haute-)	105,315	53.5	47,333	24.1	28,661	14.6	4,212	2.1	6,175	3.1	5,052	2.6	196,748
Vosges	80,260	40.1	75,278	37.6	25,317	12.6	5,801	2.9	6,257	3.1	7,337	3.7	200,250
Yonne	64,683	41.7	55,428	35.7	20,474	13.2	5,331	3.4	3,623	2.3	5,642	3.6	155,181

Department	Mitterrand	Giscard d'Estaing	Chaban-Delmas	Royer	Laguiller	Other[a]	Total
Territoire de Belfort	27,089	17,348	7,901	1,073	1,504	2,078	56,993
	47.5	30.4	13.9	1.9	2.6	3.7	
Essonne	176,308	115,382	48,080	10,479	8,437	17,377	376,063
	46.9	30.7	12.8	2.8	2.2	4.6	
Hauts-de-Seine	284,868	227,642	85,173	17,060	11,700	29,432	655,875
	43.4	34.7	13.0	2.6	1.8	4.5	
Seine-Saint-Denis	291,365	131,525	61,918	12,162	12,131	20,846	529,947
	55.0	24.8	11.7	2.3	2.3	3.9	
Val-de-Marne	256,470	157,370	63,221	13,748	9,926	22,467	523,202
	49.0	30.1	12.1	2.6	1.9	4.3	
Val-d'Oise	166,727	109,013	42,383	8,343	7,804	14,944	349,214
	47.7	31.2	12.1	2.4	2.2	4.3	
Overseas							
Guadeloupe	25,800	7,971	15,046	138	648	752	50,355
	51.2	15.8	29.9	.3	1.3	1.5	
Guyane	3,626	1,480	3,119	50	109	145	8,529
	42.5	17.4	36.6	.6	1.3	1.7	

	Col1	%	Col3	%	Col5	%	Col7	%	Col9	%	Col11	%	Total
Martinique	29,523	34.9	11,698	13.8	40,642	48.1	279	.3	931	1.1	1,496	1.8	84,569
Réunion (La)	55,674	47.8	20,634	17.7	34,170	29.3	686	.6	971	.8	4,377	3.8	116,512
Comores	27,513	24.6	9,995	8.9	73,253	65.4	121	.1	295	.3	840	.8	112,017
Territoire français des Afars et des Issas	6,082	17.7	3,110	9.1	24,306	70.7	106	.3	120	.4	635	1.9	34,359
Nouvelle-Calédonie et Nouvelles-Hébrides	14,521	42.5	8,524	25.0	9,575	28.0	139	.4	436	1.3	951	2.8	34,146
Polynésie française	17,651	50.3	7,382	21.0	8,900	25.3	126	.4	241	.7	824	2.4	35,124
Saint-Pierre et Miquelon	530	21.5	938	38.0	803	32.5	7	.3	154	6.2	38	1.5	2,470
Wallis et Futuna	51	1.7	1,186	39.8	1,705	57.1	3	.1	3	.1	36	1.2	2,984
Total	11,044,373	43.3	8,326,774	32.6	3,857,728	15.1	810,540	3.2	595,247	2.3	903,974	3.5	25,538,636

[a]Other vote includes: R. Dumont, 337,800; Jean-Marie Le Pen, 190,921; E. Muller, 176,279; A. Krivine, 93,990; Bertrand Renouvin, 43,722; J. Claude Sebag, 42,007; G. Héraud, 19,255.

PRESIDENTIAL ELECTION RESULTS, 1974, SECOND BALLOT, BY DEPARTMENT

Department	Giscard d'Estaing	Mitterrand	Total
Metropolitan France			
Ain	100,137	82,283	182,420
	54.9	45.1	
Aisne	120,197	150,749	270,946
	44.4	55.6	
Allier	96,210	115,102	211,312
	45.5	54.5	
Alpes-de-Haute Provence	28,672	33,013	61,685
	46.5	53.5	
Alpes (Hautes-)	28,135	26,167	54,302
	51.8	48.2	
Alpes-Maritimes	215,292	185,968	401,260
	53.7	46.3	
Ardèche	78,134	71,065	149,199
	52.4	47.6	
Ardennes	68,717	79,243	147,960
	46.4	53.6	
Ariège	30,740	53,561	84,301
	36.5	63.5	
Aube	71,800	68,913	140,713
	51.0	49.0	
Aude	61,032	99,263	160,295
	38.1	61.9	
Aveyron	94,646	72,530	167,176
	56.6	43.4	
Bouches-du-Rhône	299,327	386,541	685,868
	43.6	56.4	

Department	Giscard d'Estaing	Mitterrand	Total
Calvados	151,585 55.6	121,137 44.4	272,722
Cantal	58,761 61.5	36,786 38.5	95,547
Charente	83,119 46.0	97,596 54.0	180,715
Charente-Maritime	130,933 50.4	128,831 49.6	259,764
Cher	79,989 48.0	86,709 52.0	166,698
Corrèze	65,269 44.4	81,617 55.6	146,886
Corse	72,676 53.2	63,937 46.8	136,613
Côte-d'Or	110,346 51.6	103,520 48.4	213,866
Côtes-du-Nord	152,089 49.8	153,455 50.2	305,544
Creuse	40,326 44.0	51,259 56.0	91,585
Dordogne	102,754 44.5	128,249 55.5	231,003
Doubs	111,305 52.5	100,686 47.5	211,991
Drôme	88,836 48.2	95,647 51.8	184,483
Eure	107,626 51.0	103,505 49.0	211,131

Department	Giscard d'Estaing	Mitterrand	Total
Eure-et-Loir	88,694 52.2	81,326 47.8	170,020
Finistère	262,320 58.4	186,833 41.6	449,153
Gard	115,539 44.0	147,059 56.0	262,598
Garonne (Haute-)	160,695 43.6	207,524 56.4	368,219
Gers	43,336 42.2	59,265 57.8	102,601
Gironde	232,082 45.4	278,836 54.6	510,918
Hérault	141,753 45.2	171,710 54.8	313,463
Ille-et-Vilaine	220,934 61.8	136,705 38.2	357,639
Indre	67,807 47.9	73,652 52.1	141,459
Indre-et-Loire	120,877 53.1	106,832 46.9	227,709
Isère	180,023 46.7	205,624 53.3	385,647
Jura	66,085 51.0	63,506 49.0	129,591
Landes	77,747 46.7	88,694 53.3	166,441
Loir-et-Cher	78,059 51.4	73,772 48.6	151,831

Department	Giscard d'Estaing	Mitterrand	Total
Loire	184,268 52.1	169,144 47.9	353,412
Loire (Haute-)	71,657 59.7	48,380 40.3	120,037
Loire-Atlantique	262,282 57.0	198,083 43.0	460,365
Loiret	131,346 55.3	106,061 44.7	237,407
Lot	42,557 46.1	49,784 53.9	92,341
Lot-et-Garonne	73,009 45.0	89,272 55.0	162,281
Lozère	29,105 64.3	16,148 35.7	45,253
Maine-et-Loire	194,384 63.2	113,011 36.8	307,395
Manche	157,792 65.4	83,407 34.6	241,199
Marne	124,234 50.9	119,830 49.1	244,064
Marne (Haute-)	57,004 52.3	51,980 47.7	108,984
Mayenne	94,541 67.0	46,599 33.0	141,140
Meurthe-et-Moselle	167,479 49.5	170,992 50.5	338,471
Meuse	58,301 54.1	49,461 45.9	107,762

Department	Giscard d'Estaing	Mitterrand	Total
Morbihan	187,531 62.2	114,070 37.8	301,601
Moselle	244,450 54.0	208,416 46.0	452,866
Nièvre	53,585 38.7	85,028 61.3	138,613
Nord	558,957 45.9	659,363 54.1	1,218,320
Oise	133,596 47.4	148,106 52.6	281,702
Orne	92,675 60.6	60,231 39.4	152,906
Pas-de-Calais	301,473 42.1	414,634 57.9	716,107
Puy-de-Dôme	152,916 52.2	140,103 47.8	293,019
Pyrénées-Atlantiques	159,395 56.2	124,228 43.8	283,623
Pyrénées (Hautes-)	54,057 43.2	71,134 56.8	125,191
Pyrénées-Orientales	67,082 43.3	87,664 56.7	154,746
Rhin (Bas-)	274,918 67.0	135,228 33.0	410,146
Rhin (Haut-)	198,921 65.8	103,533 34.2	302,454
Rhône	321,781 52.7	288,710 47.3	610,491

Department	Giscard d'Estaing	Mitterrand	Total
Saône (Haute-)	61,306 50.2	60,866 49.8	122,172
Saône-et-Loire	142,225 49.0	147,821 51.0	290,046
Sarthe	128,269 51.4	121,294 48.6	249,563
Savoie	76,621 50.6	74,685 49.4	151,306
Savoie (Haute-)	118,242 59.4	80,829 40.6	199,071
Paris	604,389 56.9	457,429 43.1	1,061,818
Seine-Maritime	267,086 46.6	306,427 53.4	573,513
Seine-et-Marne	170,834 50.7	166,109 49.3	336,943
Yvelines	246,002 53.1	216,889 46.9	462,891
Sèvres (Deux-)	104,132 57.7	76,263 42.3	180,395
Somme	131,292 45.7	156,201 54.3	287,493
Tarn	94,424 48.9	98,774 51.1	193,198
Tarn-et-Garonne	49,699 48.0	53,763 52.0	103,462
Var	152,950 49.4	156,535 50.6	309,485

Department	Giscard d'Estaing	Mitterrand	Total
Vaucluse	88,176 45.9	103,796 54.1	191,972
Vendée	164,149 66.9	81,070 33.1	245,219
Vienne	97,402 51.9	90,287 48.1	187,689
Vienne (Haute-)	81,563 40.0	122,311 60.0	203,874
Vosges	112,579 54.3	94,842 45.7	207,421
Yonne	84,694 52.7	75,868 47.3	160,562
Territoire de Belfort	27,558 46.6	31,601 53.4	59,159
Essonne	177,664 46.5	204,803 53.5	382,467
Hauts-de-Seine	336,640 50.4	330,659 49.6	667,299
Seine-Saint-Denis	206,954 38.4	331,839 61.6	538,793
Val-de-Marne	239,465 44.9	293,396 55.1	532,861
Val-d'Oise	163,791 46.0	191,980 54.0	355,771
Overseas Guadeloupe	34,386 43.6	44,456 56.4	78,842
Guyane	5,410 53.1	4,785 46.9	10,195

Department	Giscard d'Estaing	Mitterrand	Total
Martinique	55,120 57.1	41,441 42.9	96,561
Réunion (La)	66,685 49.6	67,643 50.4	134,328
Comores	83,772 74.3	28,983 25.7	112,755
Territoire français des Afars et des Issas	26,977 77.1	8,003 22.9	34,980
Nouvelle-Calédonie et Nouvelles-Hébrides	18,913 50.3	18,711 49.7	37,624
Polynésie française	18,094 48.6	19,161 51.4	37,255
Saint-Pierre et Miquelon	1,971 74.9	659 25.1	2,630
Wallis et Futuna	2,869 94.9	155 5.1	3,024
Total	13,396,203 50.8	12,971,604 49.2	26,367,807

CONTRIBUTORS

J. Blondel is a Frenchman who has continuously taught in Britain, except for periods at Yale and Ottawa in Canada. He is now professor of government at the University of Essex, where he was the founding chairman of the department. He has also helped to create the European Consortium for Political Research, of which he has been the executive director from its beginnings in 1970. His publications include "Voters, Parties, and Leaders," "Public Administration in France," "An Introduction to Comparative Government," "Comparing Political Systems," "The Government of France," and "Comparative Legislatures."

Jean Charlot is professor of political science at the Institut d'etudes politiques, Paris, from which he graduated in 1956, and general secretary of the Association française de science politique. Editorialist in *Figaro*, he commented on the 1974 presidential election for French television and radio and has written several books on political parties and on Gaullism, among which is *The Gaullist Phenomenon*.

Monica Charlot, agrégée and Doctorat d'Etat, holds a chair in British political institutions at the Sorbonne. She also directs the Institut des Pays Anglophones. She has written several books on election campaigning in France and Britain, in addition to numerous articles and contributions to collective works. She commented on the language of the candidates in the presidential election of 1974 on Radio-Télé Luxembourg.

Alfred Grosser is a professor at the Institut d'etudes politiques, director of the graduate program of the Fondation Nationale des Sciences Politiques, Paris, and a political columnist for *Le Monde* and *Ouest-France*. He has taught at the Bologna Center of Johns Hopkins

317

University and at Stanford University and was vice-president of the International Political Science Association, 1970–1973. His recent books include *Gegen den Strom, La Politique en France, L'Explication politique, Germany in Our Time,* and *Au nom de quoi?*

SERGE HURTIG is secretary-general of the Fondation Nationale des Sciences Politiques and professor of political science at the Institut d'etudes politiques, Paris. From 1961 to 1967 he was secretary-general of the International Political Science Association.

ALAIN LANCELOT is director of studies and research at the Fondation Nationale des Sciences Politiques and professor at the Institut d'etudes politiques, Paris. He has been regularly studying French elections for fifteen years, and is secretary-general of the French Political Science Association, coeditor of the *Revue française de Science politique,* and scientific adviser to SOFRES, the public opinion survey institute. He is the author of *Les attitudes politiques, L'abstentionisme électoral en France,* and many books and articles on French political history and sociology.

MARIE-THERESE LANCELOT is research assistant at the Fondation Nationale des Sciences Politiques and secretary-general of the post-graduate program on survey techniques and market research of the Institut d'etudes politiques, Paris. She is author and coauthor of several books and articles dealing with French elections and politics, including: *Atlas des circonscriptions électorals en France depuis 1875, L'organisation armée secrète,* and *Atlas des élections françaises de 1968 et 1969.*

ROY PIERCE is professor of political science at the University of Michigan, where he also served as director of the Center for Western European Studies. He is the author of *Contemporary French Political Thought* and *French Politics and Political Institutions.* He is currently working on a study of political representation in France.

RICHARD M. SCAMMON, the coauthor of *This U.S.A.* and *The Real Majority,* is director of the Elections Research Center in Washington, D. C. He has edited the biennial statistical series, *America Votes,* since 1956.

INDEX